UNDER THE BIG SKY

JACKSON J. BENSON

Under the Big Sky

A Biography of A. B. Guthrie Jr.

UNIVERSITY OF NEBRASKA PRESS | LINCOLN & LONDON

Library of Congress Cataloging-
in-Publication Data

Benson, Jackson J.
Under the big sky : a biography of
A. B. Guthrie Jr. / Jackson J. Benson.
p. cm.
Includes bibliographical references
and index.
ISBN 978-0-8032-2286-1 (cl.: alk. paper)
1. Guthrie, A. B. (Alfred Bertram), 1901–
1991. 2. Guthrie, A. B. (Alfred Bertram),
1901–1991—Homes and haunts—Montana. 3. Authors, American—20th century—Biography. 4. Western stories—
Authorship. 5. West (U.S.)—In literature.
6. West (U.S.)—Civilization—20th century.
I. Title.
PS3513.U855Z53 2009
813'.52–dc22
[B]
2008047137

For Katrina and Kevin
and
Belinda and Brian

CONTENTS

List of Illustrations ix

Acknowledgments. xi

1. "By George, I'm Free!". 1

2. A Smart Aleck and a Wise Guy. .17

3. Alone in a Small and Self-Contained City. 32

4. Marriage, Family, and Separation 49

5. The First Novel and Plans for the Big One 65

6. The Big Break—the Nieman Fellowship. 83

7. *The Big Sky* Triumph and Tracking *The Way West* 100

8. To Hollywood and *Shane* and the Move to Montana 119

9. Bucking the Myth: *These Thousand Hills*. 137

10. Down in the Dumps—Drink and Divorce 155

11. Living with Janie and Courting Carol 171

12. The Old Man and the Young Woman Wed. 188

13. *Arfive*, and Speaking to the Young—Earth Day 205

14. The Twin Lakes Imbroglio and Building the "Barn" 226

15. "What Happened to Boone?" 247

16. *Fair Land, Fair Land*: The End of the Trail 268

Afterword: Fishing the Pishkun .287

Notes and Documentation. 295

Index 315

ILLUSTRATIONS

Following p. 48
Fishing trip on the Teton River
Bud at 9 years old
Bud's parents
Bud with Al Dolby
Bud at the sawmill in the mountains west of Choteau
Bud on fire patrol
Harriet Larson
Harriet, Helen, and Bud
Bert and Bud
Harriet, Bert, Harriet's mother and father, and Helen
Bud and his brother, Chick
Bert, Helen, and Bud

Following p. 136
Ted Morrison, Kay Morrison, Robert Frost
Bud and Bernard DeVoto
Autograph party for *The Big Sky*
Bud in the house at Great Falls
Bud with George Jackson
Bill Lederer, Bud, and Bernard DeVoto
Bud with daughter, Helen

Circle 8 Ranch

Still from *Shane*

Bert, Harriet, and Bud

Fritz Gannon, Shirley Gannon, Bud, and Randall Swanberg

Following p. 246

Bud and sister, Jane

Bud's niece Peggy, and sister, Jane

Bud at Twin Lakes, 1969

Herb and Amy Luthin, Bud, and Carol

Twin Lakes, 1979

Dr. Tom Clark and Bud

Bud and Carol at Twin Lakes, 1969

Jim and Lois Welch

Richard Hugo

Bud, ca. 1984

Bud and Miles Gaede, 1988

Carol, Bud, and a Forest Service filmmaker

ACKNOWLEDGMENTS

I am greatly in debt to all the members of A. B. Guthrie's family—their help made this biography possible. My thanks to Helen Guthrie Miller, Alfred Bertram Guthrie III, Peggy Bloom, Amy Sakariassen, and Bill Luthin. Most of all, my thanks to Carol, Guthrie's wife, who overcame a number of reservations about my project and ended up talking to me for several days about her husband and their experiences together.

I am also grateful to the many Guthrie friends who gave of their time to talk to me. I have listed and thanked many of them individually as sources in my chapter-by-chapter documentation at the end of this book. A special thanks to Ripley Hugo, who allowed me to use her husband's poem dedicated to Guthrie.

I want to express my gratitude to those who have written about Guthrie and whose work has served as a foundation for mine. Of all of these, the most important has been the work of Charles Hood. Professor Hood wrote a Master's thesis, a biography of Guthrie, in 1969, and he interviewed a number of relatives and friends who are now long deceased. He has very generously permitted me to quote extensively from those interviews, and I owe him much. I should also mention my debt to the work of Thomas W. Ford, William W. Bevis, and David Peterson.

I am also in debt to several libraries for their valuable assistance:

the Beinecke Rare Book and Manuscript Library at Yale University, which has most of Guthrie's letters; the K. Ross Toole Archives at the Maureen and Mike Mansfield Library, University of Montana, Missoula; and the Margaret I. King Library at the University of Kentucky.

I owe much to Diana Duke, for her research assistance, and to Fiona Becker, who transcribed my interviews.

Permission to quote from the letters, publications, and unpublished manuscripts of A. B. Guthrie Jr. has been granted by Herbert William Luthin Jr. Permission to quote from a letter from Wallace Stegner has been granted by Page Stegner; for a letter from Bernard DeVoto, Mark DeVoto; for the letters of Charles Guthrie, Carol Jan Guthrie Brown; for the letters of Theodore Morrison, Anne Morrison Smyth; for the letters of Professor Thomas Clark, Loretta Clark; for the letters of Harriet Larson Guthrie and of Helen Guthrie Miller, Helen Guthrie Miller; for the letters of Jane Guthrie Haugen, Peggy Haugen Bloom.

All of the photos, except where indicated otherwise, were provided by Amy Luthin Sakariassen (Guthrie's stepdaughter), and permission for all the family-provided photos is given by Herbert William Luthin Jr. (Guthrie's stepson). Amy also provided most of the captions. I am grateful to them both.

UNDER THE BIG SKY

CHAPTER ONE

"By George, I'm Free!"

lfred Bertram Guthrie Jr. was a hell of a writer, but he
could be an ornery cuss. Bud, as he was called, could be
dogmatic, insistent, opinionated, and contrary. At the
same time, however, he was a gentleman in the old-fashioned
sense of the word—gallant, fair-minded, generous, and kind. Some
people hated him for his unabashed political and environmentalist opinions, while others loved him for the man he was. He had
a firm social conscience and was determined in his writing to reflect what he saw as the historical truth. But he was not a stern
man—he could be funny, a prankster, and a person who loved a
good time, drinking, socializing, and telling stories. People liked
to be around him.

There is no doubt that his novel *The Big Sky* was his greatest
achievement. He has said that his attraction to the subject of the
mountain man came out of his attachment to the history of the
West and a desire to tell the truth about a character that was too

often treated heroically. He wanted to balance the scales, presenting both the character's unworthy and his worthy traits. He was at his core a realist. In trying to achieve this balance, get at the historical truth, and represent that truth in fiction, Guthrie joins a whole list of writers about the West who have tried to refute Western myth, to tell it as it was. These writers include Wallace Stegner, Ivan Doig, Fredrick Manfred, Vardis Fisher, Willa Cather, William Kittredge, Norman Maclean, James Welch, Mari Sandoz, Frank Waters—the list goes on and includes almost every Western writer we consider "literary" versus what Guthrie called the purveyors of the "gun and gallop" story.

Guthrie joins these other writers in another way: like them, he writes nostalgically of a West lost, lost to exploitation, development, and population growth. What Walter Van Tilburg Clark called the essential characteristic of the West, its open spaces, would seem either gone or in the process of going. Like these other writers, Guthrie was in love with the land he came to know intimately, and much of his fiction is touched by a regret for a lost love.

His childhood is the story of how he came to become so attached to the plains, benches, and mountains of Montana, an attachment that marked him so deeply that it became the generator of his character and the motive for his writing. He was born on January 13, 1901, in Bedford, Indiana—another among the many prominent Western writers born in the East or Midwest. Six months after his birth his family moved to Choteau, Montana, which, although he didn't always live there after he grew up, became his place, the center of his writing universe.

Choteau is in the central northwest of Montana, on the windswept, short-grass plains some thirty miles from the Eastern Front of the Rocky Mountains, which rise up steeply from the flatland without much in the way of foothills. The historian Joseph Kinsey

Howard talks about the appearance of these mountains as "a flat gray-blue silhouette . . . gigantic paper cutouts against the sky." As much a historian as fiction writer, Bud has said about the area he called home that "the nation got its first real knowledge of the region from the Lewis and Clark expedition of 1804–1806. The news the captains brought back alerted the fur dealers of St. Louis and the east, and it was a very few years before keelboats plied the upper Missouri, bringing trappers who scattered to the beavered streams."

Located on the Teton River, Choteau started in the early fur-trading days in the 1830s and 1840s as a trading outpost and then an Indian agency. Later it became a settlement, and at the turn of the century, a village with several hundred people. When the Guthries moved there in 1901, it had one church, four saloons, two general stores, and an elementary and high school.

To the north of Choteau is a large Blackfeet Reservation, which originally extended to include the town's present location. At that time, the town was the reservation headquarters, called Old Agency. The trading post was named after the general manager of the American Fur Company of St. Louis, Pierre Chouteau Jr. (the misspelling of the town was allowed to stand in order to distinguish it from nearby Chouteau County). In more recent years, the town has become the Teton County seat. Surrounding Choteau are the sheep and cattle ranches that supported and still support it. Farther out, going west up Teton Canyon Road, we can now enter what has become the Lewis and Clark National Forest; beyond that we encounter the vast Bob Marshall Wilderness area.

Bud's father had a friend, an attorney in Choteau, who helped him secure a position as the first principal of Teton County Free High School. The elder Guthrie had graduated from the University of Indiana, Bloomington, and had taught for several years in that state, but he looked toward the West, hoping for a challenge and a more open environment. His wife was also a college graduate, earning her degree from Earlam College, a Quaker school in Richmond, Indiana.

On their way to Choteau, the Guthries, with a small girl in tow and a baby in arms, got off a narrow-gauge railroad coach at the small station in Collins, some thirty miles from their destination. Speculating about their arrival, Bud has said that what they encountered must have been a shock: "They had never seen blanket Indians before, never beheld the rude makeshifts of early settlement, never had to reckon with what must have struck them as a body of rough and unreckoning men."

They traveled that last thirty miles by stagecoach and entered, in Choteau, what certainly seemed to them the frontier. To the town, Guthrie's parents must have seemed strange. As the son has pointed out, they were different for being college graduates and for loving books and caring about ideas. For some time after they arrived, although they made friends, the mother and father depended almost exclusively on each other for intellectual stimulation.

Nevertheless, the father luxuriated in his new environment. He told Bud about his first morning in Choteau. He had gotten up early and gone outside. He looked around him and saw that to the south rose two lonely buttes, westward stood the great blue lift of the Rockies, benches climbed out of the Teton River valley, and then to the east they leveled into flatlands that seemed to run on forever.

> Overhead—you could almost say on all sides, too—was the sky—deeper, bluer, bigger than he had ever known.
>
> He breathed the air. He looked. He heard the ring of silence. He felt somehow afloat in space. A shudder shook

him, the shudder of delight. He stretched his arms wide and said aloud, "By George, I'm free!"

"It is a feeling," his son said reflecting on this, "that surely everyone must have who has stood under the great sky and looked and lost his eye in the distance, and has listened and heard the silence sing."

Though the Guthries were closer to Unitarian than Fundamentalist in belief, the only church in town they could affiliate with was Methodist—that foe of fun, as Bud has described it. While the Guthries tended to equate drink with sin, the social centers of the town were the saloons, where the stockmen gathered to discuss cattle, sheep, and grass. Many of them thought of teaching as a sissy occupation. But the elder Guthrie was no sissy. He was one tough customer.

Shortly after the Guthries arrived in town, he was challenged. A man named McDermott, sitting on his horse, mocked him, and the senior Guthrie pulled him off his horse. As George Coffey recalls, Guthrie then invited the man to have it out, but the invitation was not accepted. Bud later used the incident as the basis for a short story, "First Principal." On another occasion, as Bud recollects, his father walked up to a man pointing a pistol first at a friend and then at him and disarmed him. But what was most remembered about him was his skill as a teacher and his scholarly bent. Although bookish, he was a strict disciplinarian and brooked no disturbance in his classrooms, and even though he was not a big man, he dealt with the big farm boys with a firm hand.

Underlining his bookishness, Mrs. Carl B. Field recalls that the senior Guthrie read a dictionary while presiding over study hall periods. Bud recalled his father's abilities as a teacher: "Latin, English, mathematics, history, the science of that time—he could teach them all and teach them well. Subjects came to life under his tutelage. Interests broadened. His advice gave depth and directions to more lives than I can say." George Coffey, who was in the 1905 graduating class, the senior Guthrie's second class, remembered that "he was a very fine instructor. . . . More than one student has come home to say Mr. Guthrie was a better instructor than he ever got in college." He received a number of offers to go elsewhere, but was never tempted to leave Choteau. His son felt that his father was afraid to go: "Outside the local, outside the physical, he had little confidence and, unsure of himself, stood solid and sullen against wider opportunity."

Nevertheless, the he was a remarkable man and had a great influence on his son's interests and the course of his life. Bud's brother, Charles, or "Chick," has written a remembrance of the relationship of son and father:

> Bud always was a great reader, with great ability to concentrate. Noise never seemed to distract him. His father must be given a great deal of credit for rousing Bud's interest in the West and its history. He had quite a library of western Americana and Bud took full advantage of it. *The Lewis and Clark Journals,* Chittenden's *American Fur Trade of the Far West,* Francis Parkman's *Oregon Trail* were grist for his mill. Also the old *Youth's Companion* and the *American Boy,* magazines which ran stories by James Willard Schultz, who was married to a Blackfeet squaw and who lived with or near the Blackfeet for many years.
>
> Dad and Bud did considerable hunting and fishing together, they took walks through the fields, studied birds and plants. The whole family enjoyed camping in the mountains and dad would spin yarns at the campfire, some real and many apocryphal.

Bud himself testified that he never had his father as a teacher; he recalled, "The stimulus and guidance that I got from him I got at home. I'm grateful for it. But for his interest in literature, but for his profound attachment to nature and the West, which took me into books and carried me afield to buffalo wallows, birds' nests, landmarks and sites of old excitement and made his loves my own, I doubt I would be writing now." He first learned from his father about the notable mountain men, such as Jedediah Smith, Tom Fitzpatrick, and Liver Eating Johnson. His father's tales about the adventures of these men were the main stimulus toward his voracious reading about the mountain men, even as a youngster.

Of all the books in his father's library of western lore, the one that seems to have made the strongest impression was Chittenden's *American Fur Trade of the Far West*. First published in 1902, Bud read it early in his life, later took notes on it, and then went back to it frequently in preparation for *The Big Sky*. Francis Parkman's *Oregon Trail* led father and son to go over a good part of the Oregon Trail, which, in turn, is related to the genesis of *The Way West* (he would go over the trail again twice later in life, once with Bernard DeVoto). Then father and son went to the scene of the Marias Massacre, which Bud used effectively, and sadly, to end *Fair Land, Fair Land*.

Bud had fond memories of his father reading aloud on long winter evenings, not just to the family but also to what friends the children (Bud, Chick, and Janie) had made:

"They would gather after supper and lie with us on the floor of the living room, where the Cole's Hot Blast maintained a sometimes spasmodic warmth, and from his seat in the Morris chair my father would reach for his book." Guthrie added that his father had a fine sense of theater, an elastic baritone voice, and an ability to assume dialects: "When he spoke for Uncle Remus, he *was*

Uncle Remus." And, of course, the children gathered around on the floor always begged for just one more. Telling stories and making up stories was part of Bud's childhood.

But the relationship was not entirely positive. Writing in his autobiography, Bud said about his father, "He loved us, this I know, but devils dwelt in him, inexplicable and uncontainable. He was a man of vast impatience, of dark and instant angers. Stupidity, the unforeseen, chance variations and interruptions of plans and routines, God knows what—these fired his blood."

Bud's son remembered his father telling him about a time when his grandfather was coming home from a trip to inspect the school in Bynum. One of his duties was to visit all the county schools at least once a year. On his return trip, driving his Model-T, it was nearly dark when he got three flat tires, one after another. In those days, for each flat, you had to jack up the car, take off the wheel, pry off the tire with a tire iron, take out the tube and patch it, and then put it all back and pump up the tire. When he was through, his anger far surpassed the normal irritation. He was so furious when he got home that everyone in the family faded away into the background or hid, afraid to be anywhere near him.

Mr. Guthrie's temper and stern temperament became legendary in the community. George Coffey recalled him as "a different kind of man from normal. He was Victorian, with a good sense of humor; but when he wasn't joking he was a very stern man."

His sternness would seem to have come out of a Victorian Puritanism. That and his quick temper, which was often aroused by trespasses against his Puritan consciousness, are both illustrated in a story that Bud told in his autobiography and in a piece of short fiction, "Ebbie." It is a sad and shocking tale of how his father, trying to teach his bird dog not to wander, blinded her in one eye when he "dusted her with birdshot." Then, when the dog, called

Jimps in real life, came into heat and male dogs hung around the house, his father became acutely embarrassed. Bud writes, "In his mind, I'm sure, there was an association here with evil. Sex on his doorstep!" One night Jimps escaped through the screened-in back porch and mated in the garden. In a fury, Bud's father grabbed his son's baseball bat, rushed out, and clubbed the dog on the head. The blow burst out the dog's one seeing eye, so that the father determined she would have to be shot, which he did reluctantly, "the demon in him overcome too late."

George Jackson, a lifelong friend of Bud's, remembered the incident and has said that "Buddy was quite a while getting over that. . . . Yep, he was quite a while getting over that." Mr. Guthrie's temper could be as quick as a lash, or as son Charles has said, "That aroused, he had all the good will of a rattlesnake." But as George Jackson has noted, his temper was "quick to mend"—still, that didn't necessarily make a situation better.

Relations between father and son, therefore, were complicated, as were Bud's emotional reactions to his father, whom he loved dearly but at times felt strongly he did not. In his autobiography, written long after his father's death, he wrote, "Whatever hate I had for him I loved is gone. I feel sorrow; and when I cast back to him without casting farther, I see his smile and feel his hand kind on my shoulder and hear his cheerful voice; and we have a chaw of licorice and catch a trout or find an arrowhead and speculate about the men who lived before us." However, Bud never really got over the religious fundamentalism in which he was raised and, he felt, indoctrinated. As he reached maturity, he rebelled strongly against it, drinking, smoking, and then, as a newspaperman, gambling (although he was considered by early friends to be "prim" in his relations with women). And fundamentalism seemed to be constantly in his mind as he wrote his novels, and it is invariably pictured as destructive. It begins, really, with his second novel in the series, *The Way West*, where, as Charles E. Hood put it, "Curtis Mack, a member of the Oregon-bound wagon train, recalls with bitterness the church back home "that had left its scars on him." . . . But Mack is victimized by his wife's puritanical upbringing as well as his own . . . [her] lingering sexual guilt makes her frigid."

The resulting frustration leads to a general anger that prompts Mack to wantonly kill an Indian and leads to a hunger that causes him to seduce a young woman, setting off a series of disastrous events. The expression of anti-fundamentalism we see here becomes stronger with each succeeding novel. Personal experience had given Guthrie insight into the Puritan mind and at the same time fueled the emotional reaction that kept the theme on his mind.

On the other hand, his father was not simply a fundamentalist. That strain in his character, as strong as it might have been, was balanced by another strain, his intellectualism. And whereas Bud reacted against the one, he embraced, with encouragement from his father, the other. The senior Guthrie's affinity for liberal thinkers would seem to contradict his Methodist Puritanism.

"I was reading Thoreau and John Burroughs during college, partly because my father liked them," Guthrie remembers. This conflict was never resolved in Guthrie's mind. "My father had the habits of fundamentalist, the observation of Sunday and all that. He was a liberal in philosophy and absolutist in behavior." By the time Guthrie was in college, his father was reading, and apparently appreciating, Darwin's theory.

Guthrie's mother, born Jenny June Thomas, was a different matter entirely. Her understanding love was crucial in providing an emotional anchor for Bud throughout his years of off-and-on conflict with his father and helped moderate his later rebellion. Whereas the father was a strict disciplinarian, intolerant of violations of his fundamentalist code, and impatient, Bud's mother was just about the opposite—tolerant, patient, and fun loving. Her tolerance, based on love and kindness, was almost beyond belief. As stern as her husband might have been, it was she who was clearly in charge of the home.

Chick, Bud's younger brother, has written a remembrance of their mother, in which he described her as a poor housekeeper. She tried, but she didn't want to be constantly fussing around—straightening rugs, rearranging chairs, and putting books and magazines where they belonged and thereby making everyone uncomfortable. He added, "She might have blamed her sons and their pals for the rumpled house. It was headquarters for the gang and the gang tracked in mud and brought disorder. In bad weather we played hide-and-seek inside, also ping-pong [on the dining room table] and marbles. Mom's supervision invariably was low-key and her patience practically unlimited. Being a scold was too high a price for a slick house."

Chick goes on to recall that his mother would wonder why she couldn't budget her time better and get more housework done. But the answer was plain even to her children—she didn't demand enough order from those who brought disorder. There were too many pillow fights and wrestling matches. She even let the kids play "basketball" in the dining room. They were restricted to four players and had to stay away from the china cabinet. They used a bean-bag and threw it up to catch on a hook that was screwed into the doorframe between the dining and living rooms. They had success, a "basket," when the beanbag stuck on the hook (later they used the cylinders from an old Edison phonograph). She admitted to Chick that she shouldn't have allowed the game, but she was glad she did. She laughed, "You boys had fun and I had fun watching you." Chick concluded, "She made the house too popular. George

Jackson was there daily. So was Frankie Monroe, a quarter-breed Indian boy who lived across the street. Ted MacDonald came. Also Jack Rose, Clark Coffey and Fatty Cowgill. They were all fond of Mom. She joked with them, listened to them, advised them, and gave them lemonade, bread, peanut butter and affection."

Although she was slow to anger, a major infraction of the rules of behavior would set her off. Chick recalled that when he and Bud pushed Frankie Monroe out of the hayloft and he sprained his ankle, punishment from his mom came swiftly and emphatically. Proper conduct was important to her, and she insisted on good manners. She wouldn't put up with rudeness, and as Chick notes, if you told a playmate to shut up, you wouldn't want to do so in earshot of his mother.

Mrs. Guthrie had fame among the neighbors and family friends as an excellent cook, although she was consistently modest about her cooking. Sitting down at the table for supper, she would regret that the meat was tough, the mashed potatoes dry, and the biscuits overdone. None of this was true, as evidenced by the many requests by family and guests for more meat, potatoes, and biscuits. She did all of her cooking on a wood stove, a Great Majestic, and she had to be alert, check the heat frequently, and then adjust the damper or feed more wood or coal when needed. There were no dials to set or buttons to push to regulate anything. If the heat was restored too late, a cake could collapse or a dinner be long delayed.

Chick recalled that Sunday was especially challenging for his mother:

On the day of rest housewives hurried home from church to slave in the kitchen. A big dinner was as mandatory as prayer. It meant chicken or roast, mashed potatoes and a gallon of gravy. It meant creamed peas and corn pudding, cranberry jelly or spiced peaches and, of course, pie or cake and ice cream. No pre-cooked ham or rolls, no frozen vegetables, no packaged potatoes or mixes. Not even running water. Just Mom and the Great Majestic doing their thing the hard way.

Dad would be in the living room with the guests. These might be widows or spinsters—or rootless and grizzled men. Mom was ever ready to share the family bounty with the homeless and deprived.

Bud has said that he is both amazed and oppressed as he thinks back on his mother's day-to-day situation. For water, they had a hand pump; for a toilet, they had an outhouse, and on frigid nights, chamber pots and slop jars. For light, they used coal-oil lamps (for those of us used to electric lights, these can be almost impossible to read by). And for washing, his mother had a tub and a board. For hot water, they had teakettles, buckets, and the reservoir on the kitchen range. For heat, there was the cooking range and a coal stove in the sitting room. They had no ice in the summer, and heat made it hard to tell the difference between butter and batter. Everyone in the family bathed in a circular washtub, taking turns in the same warm water.

Bud's memories of his mother's daily occupations differ somewhat from his brother's. Chick remembered a rumpled household and a mother who tried hard but didn't succeed. Bud recalled a mother constantly occupied: "Washing. Ironing. Dusting. Pushing broom or Bissell sweeper. Cooking. Pumping. Dumping swill. Sewing. Mending. In season canning wild and brought-in fruits. . . . Toting coal and firewood when we forgot or skimped our chores. By night and morning straining milk and putting it away to cool and then to skim. Churning. Making cottage cheese. Filling lamps. Trimming wicks. Polishing smoked chimneys. Putting down sauerkraut. Putting up mincemeat. Tending a baby in arms or carrying one in a womb. And all the time finding time for us who were older and for our friends." Bud's recital here not only details the rather hectic life of his mother but gives us a sense of the texture of life in small town, rural Montana in the early nineteenth century.

The mother's burdens, referred to above, involved not only multiple and ongoing household tasks but almost constant pregnancy from 1898 to 1913 (mother and father were married in 1896). Nine children were born, but only three survived—A. B. Junior, or Bud, born 1901; Charles, or Chick, born 1903; and Margaret Jane, or Janie; born 1913. His mother's many pregnancies and the many tragic infant deaths that resulted became another cause for Bud's resentment, although he never spoke of it to his father. In his autobiography, Bud wrote, "Twenty years and more after her death, I think of my mother as constant lovingkindness, and as constant, largely inward anxiety, for mortality ran so high among her children that people said privately we came of weak blood."

Whatever the reasons for the deaths might have been, Bud, when he was old enough to understand, resented his father's keeping his mother pregnant so much of the time—particularly when one death followed another. Both he and Chick recalled what seemed to be a central fact of their childhood; as Chick has said, "Too many deaths, too many funerals." Bud wrote in his autobiography, "My memory is full of funerals, of the cold, still parlor, of the cold coffin and the cold, still body lying in it." Bud thought this sad procession came from his father's lack of self-control, and to put it bluntly, he thought his father was oversexed and, in his relations with his wife, selfish. He never expressed these feelings to his father because talk of sex in the home was forbidden. He speculated long after his father's death: "Sometimes I wonder if he didn't fear sex because he had too much appetite for it, too much for a man committed to monogamy."

However, other aspects of nature were, for his father, subjects to be studied. With the aid of field guides, he came to know all the native birds and plants, and he became an excellent fisherman. He tied his own flies, Professors and Royal Coachmen, and could cast them exactly where he wanted, without cracking the line or slapping the water. He knew the waters, the favorite holding places of the native cutthroat trout, and what the fish would be feeding on in that season and stage of the river. What was odd, though, was he would be wearing—nearly always—a suit, white shirt, and bowtie, even though he would take off his jacket and sometimes roll up his sleeves and put on a fishing vest. He was a formal man in an informal, rough environment.

He passed on his knowledge of the outdoors and his hunting and fishing skills to his children. And they, in turn, spent what time they could get—after school, between chores, and during the summer—in the mountain forests, in the fields, and on the streams. Bud has reflected on this aspect of his childhood, writing: "I'm glad I grew up where I did, in the town of Choteau, in Teton County. I fished the streams, hunted the thickets, hunted the ponds, swam in Spring Creek in water so cold we always built a bonfire to gather 'round, blue-chilled and gasping after a few strokes. In June I gathered serviceberries, in September chokecherries. Nature was my teacher, and I loved the lessons."

Being so close to nature in childhood had long-term effects on his character and attitudes. One was an aversion to cities, places of stone and steel and crowds of people. That aversion began when he was a youngster visiting Great Falls, not really a city but a town of only twenty thousand. He worried that each of the people he encountered "instead of being green like [himself], was surely seasoned and disdainful." He added, "I feared that by some word or deed I'd betray my total ignorance." When he was twelve, Bud went with his mother and baby brother John to California, where they hoped that the baby would recover his health (he didn't). He wrote to Nancy, a classmate in Choteau, from Berkeley: "I am expecting a nice long letter from you, because you can write about a decent town, and I can only write a note about a crazy city." (This was 1913.) Throughout his life he never felt at ease in a city, however large or small it might be.

Another effect of his early exposure to nature was his commitment to environmentalism, a gradual commitment that grew more intense with every passing year. Looking back over the benefits of his Choteau childhood in nature, he wrote in his late eighties, only a few years before his death, "I would save these riches for the youngsters who come along in all the years ahead. I want them to enjoy what I did. I want the places to remain rewarding for them. That's one of the reasons I am an environmentalist."

CHAPTER TWO

A Smart Aleck and a Wise Guy

While growing up, Bud Guthrie received no allowance—none of the youngsters in grade school had even heard of such a thing. He did have chores, chopping wood, carrying it into the box, carrying coal to the coal shuttles, and cleaning out the ashes in the stoves. If he needed money, he would add to these chores by occasionally working for others. He could team up with a partner to use a cross-cut to saw up logs brought down from the mountains by those who were in those days called "breeds," part white, part Indian. For a load of cut wood, the two boys would get three dollars. A day picking potatoes would earn a boy a dollar, and three washed-out beer bottles would fetch a nickel at the backdoor of a saloon.

But all was not work. Even when school was in session, Bud had his choice of recreation after three o'clock and on weekends. When he was twelve, his father trusted him with his old shotgun, and although he was a good student, Bud could hardly wait for the final bell so he could run home, grab his gun and shells, and take off for the backcountry. He said, looking back, that "joy of hunting was beyond accounting," and recalled, "I loved to bring birds down, to take quick aim at mallards, pintails, teal and prairie chickens on the wing and feel the twelve-gauge bounce against my battered shoulder." Later in life his feelings had changed: "No longer do I like to kill or see things killed. When slaughter justifies itself by simple economics, I yield, although reluctantly. . . . The watcher lives to see watched things again."

The game of choice was baseball, which was something that Bud participated in from the middle of grade school through high school, first in pickup sandlot games and then with the town team. Chick can remember his father, during Sunday baseball, sitting on a shed to watch the game and yelling out to his son, "Give 'em hell!" The boys were blessed with plenty of open space for play— no bulldozers, no jackhammers, no construction trucks. But they did have wandering cows. The consequence, of course, was that they had to watch where they stepped, even on the dead run. The ball could also be a problem. You could pay as much as a quarter or, for used ones, as little as a nickel. The problem with the used ones was that after just a few times at bat, they went lopsided, and after a couple of innings, they became a tattered mess.

On Bud's team was a boy named Jack, who was a blithe spirit and who said whatever came into his head. During a game, Jack made disparaging remarks about Bud's baseball ability after he had struck out. Bud grabbed the ball and went after Jack, who had started running. The ball caught him on the back of the head and he went down, out cold. The ball was knocked lopsided. Although he was not a big boy, Bud was a tough kid and a scamp. Chick remembers one evening after his father had read aloud "The Hound of the Baskervilles"; Chick was sitting out in the outhouse, what they called the "biffy." Bud came up from behind and through the small opening, made wolf noises, growling and salivating, and scared the hell out of him.

Chick summed up his grade school experience with a line he used often: "I pretty near got sump'n right." But he expected his brother's grades to be right at the top and was sick at heart when they weren't. Bud was "a far greater hell raiser . . . but also smarter and more was expected of him. A smart aleck and a wise guy" who gave Chick "a bad time." While Bud was reading the history of the American fur trade and the *Lewis and Clark Journals*, Chick recalls that he was reading *Baseball Magazine* and *American Boy*.

The family had not only a library of books, western history, natural history, and some classic novels, but also had music, first with an Edison phonograph and later a Victrola. The father played the tuba in the town band, which practiced in the school gym. When he was in high school, Chick played the drums and played in a dance band on a substitute basis. (Bud would become incensed when Chick was bumped off the band in favor of Bill Coffey— Coffey had a bass drum, and Chick did not). And Bud and Jane took piano lessons until it was discovered that they had little talent for it.

Six years after he took over as principal of the high school, the senior Guthrie quit and bought the local paper, *The Choteau Acantha*, which he owned for six years. A couple of years after his father sold it, Bud, at age fourteen, got a steady summer job as printer's devil at the paper. His compensation for a six-day week was only the experience. It was an apprenticeship that, at the back of his mind, he hoped would lead to writing. But first he learned the printer's trade—to handset type, to make up and lock up a newspaper page, to feed the presses, and to operate the linotype. As he went on through high school, he summarized his activities—it was clear that here was a young man who not only had a driving ambition, but also a great deal of energy:" I built the early-morning fires at home, milked the cow, hurried as reporter to the Great Northern station for local items on arrivals and departures, rushed to the shop and kindled heaters there, and appeared in time for class, smelling of cow and kerosene, and divided Caesar's Gaul. From school I went back to the shop and worked till six o'clock and sometimes came back after supper. I worked on Saturdays, too, and, if need be, on Sundays. I made as much as fifteen dollars a week, though seldom during hunting seasons." His father approved. He thought that a man should know a trade, just in case "higher callings somehow didn't call." Guthrie reflected, "I don't know how I did so much, except that I was young, or how I kept my grades up, except I was absorbent."

In his own career, the father had also worked very hard and many long hours, but did not earn much as principal of the high school and full-time teacher. And as much as he loved his job, he worried for years about his ability to support his family. That was what led him to quit and buy the newspaper—that, and his love of print and publication. But this, too, failed to provide much of a living, and he went on, successively, to land-and-loan company representative (it wasn't his job, but he did provide, for free, appraisals of property for sale), county treasurer, and bank cashier for the Stockman's State Bank; finally, he went back to being principal of Teton High School. The most he ever earned as an educator was $3,300 a year. He served this term from 1926 until his retirement in 1940.

Bud said later that he never really realized his parents' struggle to provide. His father put the three children through college in part by borrowing on his insurance. As a desperate measure, he raised for sale a breeding stock of a few purebred sheep on his thirteen acres of land, a strategy that never panned out. After his father's death, Bud found that he had mortgaged the house for the $300 to install a water system. Bud commented, "Well, in her later years Mother was delivered from the hand pump and the outhouse."

By the time he got to his junior year, Bud was fed up with high school. He may have been a good student, but the required attendance, the constant burden of homework—homework that sometimes seemed nonsensical, and his feeling that some of his teachers were stupid had pushed him into resentment. He resented not only having to go to high school but his parents' expectations and what he thought was their pressure for him to do well and go on to college. When his father became aware of his son's resentment, he did not react with anger as his son had expected, but told him that he could quit school if he wanted. He told him he could get a job as a printer, or, since he knew a lot about ranch work, maybe they could get together enough money to give him a small start with a ranch. Bud didn't want to be a printer or a rancher; he wanted, even as early as midway through high school, to be a writer. He hurried back to his books. Although he didn't realize it at the time, his father had tricked him.

Bud and his parents decided he should go on to the University of Washington at Seattle. His leaving was difficult for all. In the car, on the way to Dutton, Montana, to catch the train to Seattle, his mother sang, "God Will Take Care of You" over and over. At the station he hugged and kissed his mother, and he and his father awkwardly shook hands, not looking at each other for fear of breaking down.

When he got to Seattle, he found "the city was too big" for him. He recalled, "So was the university. I was always alien there, a country boy unused to crowds, unaccustomed to procedures and too shy to inquire." He found he hated the climate—days almost without end of rain and drizzle, whose sky was unlike the "wide, deep and azure sky, seldom gray" of Montana. By the middle of the school year, he was determined not to stay in Seattle beyond June but to tough it out until then.

In March he wrote his father. In his letter he reveals that his father has been doing some writing, and Bud tells him he is glad that he is sending some of his "literary efforts" to him for review. As far as his own work is concerned, he confesses with some embarrassment that he has sent one of his stories to *Cosmopolitan*: "Don't get angry or laugh but bear with me. Of course it will not be accepted, but I was very curious and got Jim to type it for me. I will send it to you as soon as it gets back. Really, though, I am a little ashamed of what I have written. Something tells me it's very, very, poor, almost ludicrous. I wish I could get over that feeling." He closes by telling his father that he is okay with his only complaint—a longing for the coming of June. Then, "Tell mother I still remember her—a marvelous feat of memory because I have not heard of or from her for so long" (3/24/20)

The following year he transferred to the University of Montana at Missoula, where he would spend the next three years and graduate with his degree in journalism. That major seemed a good choice for someone who wanted to write. Looking back he thought that his father's experience as a country newspaper editor may also have been a factor. Bud was lucky in his selection in that the dean of the school was Arthur L. Stone. Stone had set up a structure that had a few required courses in the theory and practice of putting out a newspaper but that emphasized the need for a broad background in literature, history, ethics, and political science.

Bud was a lot happier at Missoula. Most of the other students were also from small towns and had country roots, and some, like Bud, had spent summers working on ranches. There was none of the pressure here to pretend to sophistication. His grades were excellent and his social life active. He even joined a fraternity, albeit somewhat hesitantly, and became its president. A more important function for him, however, was to help keep up the house grade point average because the fraternity's prize members were football players.

There was another important aspect of his life at this time and for many years to come. Since his sophomore year, Bud saw with fresh eyes a girl he had known since she was a toddler, Harriet Larson, who would become the woman he would marry. She was now fifteen, and he felt a bit embarrassed "robbing the cradle," as they said in those days, since he was in college and she was just beginning high school. Nevertheless, she was beautiful and charming, and he pursued her unremittingly for nine years before marrying her, courting her by letter and telephone, sending candy and other gifts. It was a difficult courtship because after graduation he was away from Montana most of the time, and his absence led Harriet to consider proposals from several other young men. She was a social creature who loved to go to dances and parties, and one of her favorite pastimes was shopping. She was, in short, a rather typical young woman of her time—although she was intelligent, she was neither an intellectual nor much of a reader. How she would get along with an intellectual, scholarly husband who would work long hours, first as a newspaperman and then as a fiction writer, would seem problematic.

College was for Guthrie a life-changing experience:

> I had been a believer and, through unexamined family background, a conservative, and I emerged from college an agnostic and a liberal [elsewhere he claims that "rebel" might be a more accurate label]. I suppose reading was the first cause, though my reading was spotty, partly because of

lack of continuity in English courses, partly because I had no program of my own and chose books hit or miss. *Main Street*, just out, unsettled yet delighted me, and I thought Sinclair Lewis great. Henry Mencken gave me exultant pause, though at first I sided with his adversary, Stuart Pratt Sherman. Hardy awakened me to universal tragedy, for years I walked in his dark shadow and to some extent still do. The naturalist John Burroughs, in prose an echo of Walt Whitman, was a comfort. I had to be told by a professor that one reason for my liking him was that his language was so spare; but I liked nature, too, and, forsaking Methodism, half-embraced a pantheistic faith and found defense against despair in declarations like "The longer I live the more my mind dwells on the beauty and wonder of the world." Thackeray, Voltaire, Anatole France, H. G. Wells, Theodore Dreiser—these and others played some part in my shaping. From Swinburne and his now-seen as too-facile lines, I got a pleasant melancholy and couldn't comprehend then what Father found in Frost.

The professor that told him why he liked Burroughs was H. G. Merriam, who had Guthrie for three quarters of creative writing during his senior year. Merriam remembered the incident: "I had asked members of my creative writing class to bring in a short piece they thought was particularly good. Bud came in with a writing by Burroughs. I asked him to count the number of adjectives and adverbs in it, and he couldn't find many. That struck him with quite an impact. Years later at a writing conference he said he had always remembered and appreciated that advice." The excerpt that Guthrie had selected to read was from the preface of *Summit of the Years*.

During his senior year, Guthrie published two poems and two short stories in the English department's literary magazine, *The Frontier*, and was for a period one of the editors. Professor Merriam did not think of Guthrie as a particularly outstanding student. He remembered that "in class he was writing mostly verse. He wrote his prose in journalism and his verse in the English department." He added, "Poetry writing is very, very good for prose." Guthrie was to write poetry for almost his entire life. It might be said that it was his first love, despite the fact that he published very little of it over the years and found fame and fortune with his prose fiction.

For the most part, Professor Merriam was not impressed with Guthrie. Looking back, he said, "I never thought that Bud would develop the way he did." However, he recalled one characteristic that made Guthrie different from the other students: he wouldn't accept criticism unless he agreed with it. Merriam said, "Bud was the sort of person who did not accept criticism until he himself understood the criticism and could see how his writing would improve if he followed it. He would rebel against your criticism until he understood it completely, then he would work out his problems until he got it right."

In this, as in his rejection of fundamentalism, or what he called "primitivism," he was a rebel, but his rebellion did not entirely free him from the pressures of his early indoctrination. He felt that this incipient pressure was responsible for a neurosis that manifested itself rather suddenly in his senior year of college. Merriam detected this neurosis as it manifested in class: "It wasn't a stuttering, exactly. I don't know what the block was, if it was emotional or physical. But he was not a fluent speaker." Guthrie himself recalled, "Called on to read or speak before a crowd or class or a company of even three or four, I got terrified, became hysterical. My face worked and my knees shook. My voice trembled and gave out . . . [I] wound up at a point at which I disliked to enter a store to buy a pair of socks unless I knew the clerk well." He attributed this fear to the need for a complete self-effacement that arose from his deep-seated sense of guilt as an inferior, "a sinner born in sin." It was a problem that he was eventually partially able to overcome, but it stayed with him to some extent, he felt, for the rest of his life.

In the spring of 1923, Guthrie graduated with honors from the University of Montana. He wanted to get a job on a newspaper, but not right away and not in Montana. The weeklies and even the daily papers in his own state were so small that they really offered no opportunity for advancement. He wanted to stay around Choteau for the summer after graduation—his girl was there; his friends, such as George Jackson, were there; and his family—mother, father, Chick, and Janie were there, too. So for the summer he went to work with a haying crew on a ranch near town.

He had had enough of schooling and was determined to see something of the world. His opportunity soon came. His former classmate at the University of Washington, Al Dalby, had come to Choteau to be the editor of the *Acantha*, and the Guthries invited him to stay at their home. Ten years older than Bud, Al was a big, amiable man with a face like that of prizefighter too long in the ring. Al also had a restlessness in him, and he and Bud decided to go that fall to Mexico, where Dalby's brother had a wheat and rice ranch. There would be work for them there if they wanted to stay on for a while.

The trip to Mexico was a series of disasters. Al had purchased a Model T Ford for a hundred and fifty dollars. He thought he had gotten a bargain but was soon disabused of that notion. They hadn't even gotten out of Montana before the brakes went out, then the reverse, and finally the clutch. Unfortunately, on their

way to Jerome, Arizona, where Al's uncle lived, mechanical break-
downs happened one after another, to the point that they began to
wonder whether their meager funds would hold out. In the heat of
their difficulties, Bud and Al began to quarrel and for a day didn't
even talk to each other. Finally, everything went out—brakes, reverse, clutch, and emergency brake—on the long switchback down
to Jerome. In a panic, Al, after yelling "Whoa!" to no avail, had
to run off the road into a boulder to stop the car. Once again they
had the Model T repaired and then, weary of their auto problems,
sold it in Nogales and took the train into Mexico.

At the station in Cajeme, Sonora, they were met by Al's brother,
who drove them to his ranch. The two men stayed there for five
months, working odd jobs and then harvesting rice. Since the wheat
could not be harvested for some time, Bud and Al left for Los Angeles to find newspaper jobs. But this was 1924, and they found
the state in a severe recession; newspapermen with long experience were driving laundry trucks. They lived off of the generosity
of old friends who were themselves hard up, and then moved on
to Fresno. No jobs there, so they went on to Oakland.

In Oakland, Bud first got a job at Western Electric in Emeryville,
near Oakland, through an employment agency. The company had a
cost-plus contract with another company and so hired many more
workers than they needed; Bud found himself pretending to look
busy and then sneaking off to take naps in a neglected pile of gun-
nysacks in a corner of the warehouse. Tired of pretense and in no
need of further sleep, he left to go to work in another warehouse
for a chain grocery store (probably Safeway). He earned twenty-
five dollars a week, but had to work up to fourteen hours a day
moving constantly over unforgiving concrete floors that caused
his legs to knot up. So he was happy when he was offered a job by
the U.S. Forest Service in the Choteau area taking an agricultural

census, and he was delighted to take the train back to Montana. The fare took all his money, so he subsisted for two days on three candy bars.

The job was only temporary, but Guthrie put his heart into it. He had to make his way all around the countryside and up into the hills, so he bought a used car. But in the winter, there were places where the car could not maneuver, and so he also rented a horse, a young, rather skittish gray mare. Winter came early that year. Guthrie recalled, "In weather thirty degrees and more below zero we made out, thanks to that fool filly's stamina and the heavy underwear, the heavy shirt and pants and chaps and mackinaw and mitts and ear-flapped cap and overshoes that kept me just above the freezing point." The ranchers, for the most part, were kind and generous, insisting on putting him up for the night and feeding him without pay. But some were suspicious, not of Bud but of what he was doing—suspicious perhaps of the government's motives.

He had many tales of his adventures in the boondocks. Among them was the visit he made to a manifestly poor ranch where he found a mother with three dirty children, and the house itself unfurnished except for a chair made by her husband out of a box. At noon she took a moldy piece of meat off of a shelf, and while cutting it up, asked him if he wouldn't stay and eat with them. At another ranch he took dinner with a family that could offer only radishes and bread and butter. All in all, it was, he said, "Hard times in Montana. Lonely people. No radios for most folk and little mail. Every thought known in wife's or husband's head and so no need to say it."

When his census work was done, he headed for Attica, New York, where an uncle and cousin owned a feed company, which mixed rations for cows, horses, and chickens. As he looked back, he said, "My position, if not my wage, was elevated by my relatives. I wrote direct-mail advertising, visiting small New York and Pennsylvania towns in the unfamiliar role of salesman and at times managed the retail store in Attica that the firm kept open as an adjunct." At one point he was promoted to assistant sales manager, but having no salesmen to manage, he wondered what the title meant. Although he wrote to Harriet that his heart wasn't in the job—that he didn't have a salesman's "crust"—he also wrote in retrospect that he had enjoyed his days in Attica. It was the people, kind and openhearted, who made the difference.

During this period of his life, however, Guthrie was in limbo. He may have enjoyed his job more than he was willing to admit to the folks back home in Choteau, but it was not one that he wanted to settle on. It was not one that he could use as a basis for getting married—that would come only with a job that he could feel might be a start toward a newspaper career.

While he was working in the East, he and Harriet Larson, called "Scoop" by friends and family, exchanged letters almost every day. (She was named "Scoop" by her father, Tom Larson, after a character in a cartoon strip, "Scoop and the Boss.") From 1924 to 1925 she was a high school senior in Choteau and looked forward to marrying Bud in the fall, after graduation. (At the same time she was worried about getting the consent of her parents, who expected her to go on to college.) In March of 1925 Scoop wrote to Bud, "About the ring, Bud, I shouldn't have told you I would like to have one because I know you want to save every nickel you can and I want you to too, and it can never be done buying rings etc. With the money you would spend for a ring I would much rather have you spend for something more useful for our home, and there will no doubt be lots of things that we will need."

All of her letters included intense protestations of love and frequent expressions of loneliness. On April 22, 1925 she wrote to Bud, "In your letter last evening you doubted whether I love you as much now as I did. I wish you wouldn't doubt my word. If I didn't love you even *more* than I did, I wouldn't say so. Perhaps you doubt it because I suggested the change in our plans for this fall. I love you more than I thought it was ever possible to love anyone and no one will ever know how desperately lonesome I get for you."

Scoop talks in her letters about doing her chores around the house—ironing, cleaning, and occasionally cooking for her father or her whole family. She was also concerned about improving herself so that she could be a suitable wife for Bud: "My interests I know have always been rather common but knowing you are interested in the best and highest things in life, I have tried to make myself interested in better things. I think I have improved. I like to read good books and a lot of things disgust me now which I used to think were all right and would indulge in occasionally" (6/26/25). Whatever these things were that disgusted her is not clear, but several months later, Bud wrote her asking her to please not smoke and telling her that he wanted her to "remain slender, and young, and full of teeth" (1/24/26). No more gorging on candy, he pleaded. Yet a month later he sent her a box of candy.

What was amazing was that Scoop's expressions of devotion lasted for years while Bud was mostly absent from Montana, trying to establish himself so he could support a family. She wrote frequently during that time, telling him on one occasion, "When I don't write for a couple of days it worries me and I'm not at peace until I do get one written" (6/26/25). Her devotion, strangely enough, lasted through a series of other boyfriends and even an engagement to someone else. In the fall of 1925 she went off to the University of Washington, but midyear decided, as Bud had decided, to transfer to the University of Montana. It was probably her acquiescence to her parents' desire for her to go to college that led her to postpone her plans for a wedding until the summer of 1926. She told Bud she could hardly wait—she wanted a family, a large family.

In the spring of 1926, the feed mill in Attica burned down and would not be rebuilt; Bud was out of a job, wondering where he was going to go and how in the world he would get there. He had very little money. But he did have another uncle, Dr. Mike Guthrie, in Lexington, Kentucky, who had been working on the editor of the *Lexington Leader*, Harry Jovanovie, to get Bud hired as a cub reporter. Mr. Jovanovie gave in and said he would try him out. But how to get there? Bud went to the bank. Without collateral or a cosigner, he was able to get a loan of three hundred dollars from the cashier, a kindness provided by a man with whom he had had several conversations about books and who, on that basis, trusted him.

CHAPTER THREE

Alone in a Small and Self-Contained City

With only the small salary of a cub reporter, Bud realized in 1926 that there was no way he could get married that fall. But he did have a job on a daily, and the prospect that he would have the opportunity to move up at the paper. And he would be writing for a living at last. Not only that, but in June he wrote to Scoop that he was starting on a novel. She replied, "It was quite a surprise to me. I didn't doubt your ability in the least, but I hardly expected you to tackle one so soon" (6/10/26).

When Bud arrived in Lexington, he had a suit too warm for the climate, a pair of shoes he had to fix every day with cardboard to cover holes in the soles, and an old portable typewriter. He looked for a room to rent that he could afford on his twenty-dollar-a-week salary. After inquiring at the YMCA, he had a list of several possibilities. Looking back on it, Bud felt that the luckiest thing that happened to him in those early days in Lexington was finding a room at the home of Mrs. Mary Elizabeth Keating, whom he came to call "Mary Lizzie."

Encountering her for the first time, he stereotyped her as old, overweight, and rather dull and was determined to avoid her as much as possible and then move out as soon as he could to more intellectually stimulating surroundings. But he soon changed his mind, finding her to be warm, intelligent, and funny and an extraordinary source of information about Kentucky's past, and who was who in its stratified, caste-ridden society. For twelve dollars a week, he had a rather shabby room, but also breakfast and dinner—not to mention a close friendship that developed with a remarkable woman.

As Bud described her in his autobiography, she was clearly a kindred spirit: "She was a lady of quality, a too-generous spirit, a woman of outrage assuredly but one of high morals also and of a quick and deep and diverting mind. If she liked to drink, it was never to numb her felt obligations. When she used improper expressions, as she often did, the words came in revolt against pretense and primness and over-pitched piety."

Lexington was a small and self-contained city, a center for growing and marketing tobacco and breeding and racing horses. The landscape of the surrounding Bluegrass Country did not appeal to Guthrie—everything looked too manicured and orderly—white painted fences and rows of planted trees. He preferred his beauty "grim . . . out of control" as in Montana. But in time he found the people generally were friendly and hospitable, despite their addiction to tradition and their class consciousness. But the city was also a city of gossip, practical jokers, and odd and sometimes outrageous characters, and all of these Bud learned to enjoy. He was perfectly happy to join the jokers and to savor the gossip.

Bud's first weeks on the *Leader* were tough. Without previous newspaper experience (aside from part-time work on the *Acantha* years earlier), he was the greenest of the green and an outlander to boot. In the beginning the other reporters at the paper gave him the cold shoulder, but he was so busy learning the ropes that he was hardly aware of it. But gradually there was a thaw. A young man, Dan Bowmar, who had spent some time in Montana, renounced the conspiracy and became a friend, as did Joe Jordan, who eventually became one of Bud's closest friends. Joe said that they had given Bud a frosty reception not because of his lack of credentials but because he "looked impossibly pious." Yes, admitted Bud in looking back, this was probably true, he might have looked like that, but he questioned it as the group's motive.

By the summer of 1927, Bud had saved enough money to take the train to Choteau and spend two weeks with his family and some time with Scoopie. She was disturbed to see him thinner than he had ever been as an adult and told him that she was worried about his health. They talked once again about marriage, but Scoop told him that she had decided that she couldn't marry until after her graduation from the university. He was disappointed because he thought that even with his meager salary they could somehow scrape by, particularly if they waited until the following summer.

The next summer, Bud again returned to Choteau for a vacation. Before he arrived, Harriet, still at school, had announced her engagement to someone else—to Ken, the son of a wealthy family. Devastated, Bud tried to talk her out of it, but she was firm in her resolve. It is clear from her letters that she still loved Bud, or at least she said so repeatedly, but it is not at all clear why she became engaged to someone else. Was she trying to punish him, make him jealous, urge him to action? Or was she just tired of her situation with Bud and fond enough of Ken that she wanted to come to some resolution? Maybe she was just in a state of emotional confusion. After Bud returned to Kentucky, she wrote to him:

> Doubt may temporarily be banished from my mind but never permanently. I never seem to know anything for sure but I might have married you this time if I hadn't put my foot in so deep just before I came home from school by announcing my engagement and all that goes with that sort of thing. . . . Above all I'm going to try to be sane and follow my most natural inclinations, and I really believe, Buddy, that they turn in your direction. . . . I love you so much, sweetheart, and you are much better company for me than Kenny—my spirits always take a big rise the minute I'm in your presence.

In a postscript she added, "Please be pretty good, and don't get matrimonially inclined when you're drunk" (8/3/28).

In several other letters that summer, she declares her love for Bud and compares Ken unfavorably to him. But her frequent protestations of love for Bud did not cheer him up. In those early days in Kentucky, when he was feeling a stranger in a strange city, her engagement was another blow to his morale. He recalled coming home from work on the bus and then walking several blocks to Mary Lizzie's house at 211 Rand Avenue, all the time "feeling low in mind." Not only did he feel unwelcome in town, but, he remembered, "The girl I had wanted so long to marry on nothing had gotten engaged to a miller, to a son and grandson of millers of wealth. A notice had appeared in the *Choteau Acantha*."

Sensing his mood, Mary Lizzie would, as she so often did, fix something special for him for supper. He calculated that the cost of the food she prepared for him certainly must exceed what he paid her for board. As he tried to divert himself by reading a magazine before supper, he would hear her calling from the kitchen, "Buddy. Oh, Buddy," and he knew that she was about to open a bottle of homemade wine. Warm and always encouraging, she kept him going.

Still, in August of 1928 Scoop wrote to Bud, "I have never been able to keep from comparing your love and his." And a week later she wrote again, scolding him for going out and drinking and losing money on the races. Writing nearly every day when Bud left for the East, then only once a week when he got to Kentucky, Scoop was now writing only once a month or so.

He remained in doubt about Scoop's intentions. In the fall of 1928 she wrote that she was still undecided, but she added, "I do know that as long as I am so much in love with you it would be unfair to all of us if I were to marry Kenny" (9/28/28). In doubt and downcast, he was still working on the novel (which remained untitled and unfinished) that he had started the year before. He was on the police beat, covering the courthouse and city hall for the paper, which meant long hours, but he still managed to struggle with his fiction in the evening. And it was a struggle. He found that he had a great deal of trouble developing plot and mentioned that in a letter to his father. His father, in turn, asked him if he had made an outline in advance; it might help him organize his material. On the other hand, he wrote, "My notion is that you might do better in analytic writing of some sort in which inventiveness in the matter of plot might not be so necessary." His father added that he was glad that Bud had decided to have a further try at writing poetry (3/3/29).

Doubt continued as Scoop wrote on August 2, 1929, that it would be better if Bud didn't come back to Choteau that summer—Kenny was there and would be staying a month or more. She apparently didn't think about his desire to see his parents. During this period he did get some good news—he was made city editor and editorial writer for the *Leader*. Writing editorials for the paper was a balancing act that sometimes led him to write against his inclinations, if not his principles.

He had become aware of a dichotomy, cultural and political, in Lexington. On the one hand, there was the Puritan sentiment, as Guthrie called it, and on the other, the liberal. The paper opposed pari-mutuel betting, and that meant that the Jockey Club and those associated with it didn't like the paper at all. The church people, many of them fundamentalists, thought that the *Leader* was right, and the editor himself was a fundamentalist. But as Guthrie has noted, since there were a lot more church people than horsemen, the paper had a good circulation. Despite the editor's narrowness of vision, Bud liked him, but the editor pushed him in a more Puritan direction than he was comfortable with.

The following January, Bud told Scoop that he been assigned to go down to Frankfort, the state capital, to cover the biennial meeting of the legislature. This would be his third year at the legislature. Once again he looked forward to it as a pleasant change from the work that chained him to the city desk. He wrote to Scoop,

> The handkerchiefs you sent me are mighty pretty and tasteful, and the fact that you held a thought for me helped me get through a Christmas at which I was depressed and sorrowful. I haven't been gay for a long time—perhaps from reading too much Hardy—and after spending Christmas morning at Dr. Guthrie's [his uncle] I went out in the afternoon determined to get tight. Even that retreat from brooding didn't provide any real asylum and I came home early, almost entirely sober, and wondering what your plans were. . . .

My delay in answering your last letter was not due to lack of interest nor indisposition, but to the fact that I hardly knew, nor know, what to say. How much longer are we to continue in our present relationship—when can you be sure of your decision and when you make it will it, as I often think with something like terror, be unfavorable to me—should I attempt a tour de force or wait for time and natural inclination to volunteer their answer?—these are all questions that distress me, at times, or, more accurately, when I let myself think about them, acutely. (1/1/30)

After another two weeks that summer in Choteau, Bud took his little sister, Janie, back to Lexington to live with him at Mary Lizzie's. Janie was happy to get away from parental pressures. Early that fall Scoop applied to fill a vacancy at the Teton grammar school. At the university she had not graduated but had gotten her teaching credential. Unfortunately, she had stiff competition (the effects of the Depression had already set in) and was turned down for lack of experience. All during the fall she looked forward to making a trip to the East after Christmas, where she would shop, visit relatives, and then stop by to see Bud for a couple of days.

She arrived in Lexington in June of 1931. But rather than taking the train back to Montana, she married Bud on the twenty-fifth at Mary Lizzie's home. He wrote later, "But for Mary Lizzie she might not have married me then. "Harriet Larson," Mary Lizzie kept telling her while I was at work, "if I had a daughter, you'd never have the chance to marry Bud Guthrie." Harriet liked her and came, too, to love her, as I knew she would. Once a week, nearly always, after we'd found our own quarters, we went to see her; and always on feast days she was our guest."

It was a dramatic turn of events. Perhaps Harriet Larson's visit with her father in Helena (her father was now in the legislature) earlier in the year cleared the way for her to accept Bud. Both her parents had, from the beginning, been somewhat dubious about him and his suitability for her. But Tom Larson, an old-time cattleman, would in time become one of Guthrie's closest friends and drinking buddies, providing valuable information about the evolution of Montana. Both sets of parents were relieved at the resolution of a tension that had been building in both families. Bud was thirty when he got married, and his parents had almost given up hope for grandchildren.

After getting the news, Bud's mother wrote first to Harriet and then to her son:

> We are mighty proud and happy to have you in the family. I'm sure you are going to seem like one of my very own.
>
> I'm hoping I shall prove as good a mother to you as Mother Guthrie has to me. In all the years I've been in the family, she has made not the least difference in her treatment of me and her own girls. If I can even approach her, I shan't be so bad.

> Dear Buddie—
>
> We are very happy in your happiness. If you make as fine a husband as you have a son I'm sure Harriet will find you very satisfactory and take growing pride in you. You will be able to do your best work now that your mind is not harassed by fears of losing Scoop. Having her to spur you on to success is just the incentive you need to make great things possible for you. (7/5/31)

Then a few days later, Bud's father wrote to tell his son that he was sending a check to help cover the cost of a trip by car to

Montana to see them. He apologized for having to cut the alfalfa before he and Chick got home because he knew that they were looking forward to pitching it while he looked on. However, he could dig up some odd jobs for them should time drag while they were there. It may be that "Papa Larson can rustle a little work out at the ranch, something in the way of herding bucks, sacking wool, or other chores suitable for newly-weds" (7/9/31).

In the meantime, Bud was looking for a house for him and Scoop to rent, and he found a small one at 205 Wabash Drive in Lexington. The following year, on November 4, secure in their new home decorated by Scoop, their first child was born, Alfred Bertram III. During his early years, he was called "Nonny," and back in Montana, as soon as he could walk and could be taken to the Larson ranch, he became entranced with animals. His grandfather, Tom, became his best friend, and his parents could hardly get him to come home to Choteau, some ten miles away, when he was old enough to go to visit Tom on the ranch on his own. The boy was fond not only of horses, cattle, and sheep, at one point he became attracted to snakes, and Bud recalled that they eventually had seventeen of them crawling all over the place. Their first snake was called "Thunkhouser," named (probably by Bud) after a professor at the university who had become notorious by declaring that his most abiding regret was that he had tried nearly everything but had never had the opportunity to sample human flesh.

The professor was not the only Lexingtonian who could be labeled a character. Another, who had taken the name "Sweet Evening Breeze" (James Headon), would descend on a lift from the Woodlawn Auditorium ceiling, blowing kisses to the audience at big events. The lift would stop part way down, and he would, in Bud's words, dance "the Passion Dance of the Bongo Bango." Another character would dress immaculately in a three-piece suit and stand on a street corner downtown, greeting every passerby with "Good Morning! Isn't it a nice day!" Even though innocuous and not really bothering anybody, he was banned from Main Street by the police.

Two more characters were policemen that Bud got to know working on his beat. Doug McClark was "a very thoughtful and witty Irishman who later got to be chief of police. He was a great character. Fun and his wit was coming every minute." Another of the great Lexington characters was Dudley B. Veal, who after many years as a city detective was elected as county jailer. Not well educated, he still held strong opinions and had a colorful way of expressing them. Bud recalled, "We used to bait Dud, not in ridicule but in the hope of getting him going. 'Dud,' we asked him once, 'how do you know the world is round?' Dud considered. . . . Out of his long knowledge as an agent of the law, the answer came: 'Because every no-good son of a bitch that ever left Lexington always came back.'" Dudley B. Veal, who was virtually illiterate, "was on the detective force, they said he was awfully good because he could think just exactly like a low grade criminal. He was a character."

Colorful characters came frequently into Bud's newspaper life. When he became editor, his desk faced the door and he became the gatekeeper of the newsroom. It was the Depression, and people came in every day hoping for a handout of money or free publicity. Among the panhandlers was a young man who posed as the prizefighter Sammy Mandell but whose lack of muscularity testified to his inability to push even a thumbtack, and a sculptor who claimed to have learned his art in studios abroad. He was broke, so they chipped in for him but later found they had been taken in—he had been schooled in the penitentiary. Bud recalled those days as "the heydays of impostors, pretenders and bums, and of kids and crazy adults crazy for lines in the paper."

But there were characters and hijinks in the newsroom itself as well. Bud's good friend Dan Bowmar had an almost saintly look. Soft-spoken and large-eyed, he sometimes posed as a preacher. After finding inspiration in the bottle, he would wax eloquent to his newsroom comrades on soul-threatening activities such as gambling and drinking. He might reverse roles and speak on behalf of the devil, expounding on the machinations of the church.

Another friend on the paper, Joe Jordan, had a sharper, more calculated humor. One day a panhandler came into the newsroom and gave Joe a card that said the man was deaf and dumb and needed money. Joe got from his typewriter and, pointing to Dan, pushed the man over toward him. Dan, absorbed in his copy, was startled, his mouth dropped open, when Joe loudly announced, "Dan, here's some dirty son of a bitch that wants to see you." The visitor turned around and left.

Because of resignations and dismissals at the paper, Bud was rather quickly given a series of promotions. He recalled,

> By 1927 I was writing editorials in support of the Republican Party and its choice for governor. I covered the ensuing session of the legislature and, through the years, a score or so more, regular and special, and learned early the importance of liquor to legislation. I was made city editor, managing editor and finally executive editor.
>
> But titles don't mean much in newspapermaking. The man elevated in rank is likely to find himself doing the same old things almost for the same old money. Nominal promotion and financial reward don't always go hand in hand.
>
> . . . I used to write editorials, for I got a dollar extra for each one published and was happy to get it.

In his years at the *Leader*, Bud became a close observer of

Kentucky politics and politicians. He was not very often favorably impressed. Overall, he decided that "people have the habit of electing a lot of the wrong guys." The legislature, he found, was "strange assemblage composed of illiterates partly, also some very sharp and honest guys, along with others whose aims were certainly open to question." He covered sessions of the legislature for more than two decades and remembers that in the early days the sessions could be quite tumultuous. In one session the Speaker of the House was John Y. Brown—Bud said that he thought that one might question his motives but never his courage. One of the legislators dared him to come outside and have it out man to man. Brown said, "All right, come on." The challenger backed down. Then on another occasion Bud saw one of the legislators draw a pistol and threaten to shoot somebody: "Everyone was hiding behind desks by this point, myself included. They had an assistant Sergeant-at-Arms [who] tackled this guy, overpowered him and took away his revolver."

Prohibition was still around during Bud's early years on the paper. It seemed to him that nearly everyone was against it, especially the politicians. All of them were outwardly prohibitionist but taking their drinks in private. Bud tells of two politicians, Augustus Stanley and Edwin P. Morrow, who were having a debate at Mt. Sterling. They got along well and had shared a bottle beforehand. Then, as the debate got underway, Morrow was speaking and Augustus was standing nearby on the stage. Suddenly, Augustus ran off the stage with his hand over his mouth and threw up. An irretrievable situation? No—not for Stanley. He came back and said, "Ladies and Gentlemen, you will have to forgive me, but every time I get this close to a Republican, I have to puke."

Bud sent staff out to report on the effects of the repeal of Prohibition in Lexington. Beer had come in first before you could get hard liquor legally, and Dan Bowmar went around to interview people at the now-legal saloons about the advent of beer. He got hold of a man who was a gambler who operated chuckaluck games at the county fairs. "Well," the man said, "last night I drank nineteen bottles of beer and it kind of relaxed me."

A group that historians have labeled "the Bipartisan Combine" controlled state politics in those days. Pressure groups representing the coal industry, the railroads, and the jockey club combined, regardless of party, to impose their will on the politicians. But outside the workings of the Combine, partisanship could be very strong. In 1927 the Republican candidate for governor was Flem D. Sampson (called by the Louisville *Courier-Journal* "Flim Flam Flampson"), opposed by J. C. W. Beckham, Democrat. Bud was employed in writing editorials in support of Sampson, who had been backed by the paper. Both the owner of the paper and the managing editor were strong Republicans.

When Sampson won, the managing editor, Harry Jovanovie, as Republican as he may have been, regretted the loss by Beckham, a far superior man, in his view. He phoned in comments from his vacation in Florida, and a column was written that expressed those opinions. The next day, Jovanovie was fired by the owner, John G. Stahl. Bud said, "It was strictly on party lines. I don't know. I think Mr. Jovanovie was a pretty good editor really. Despite a sort of narrowness of vision, he was a totally honest man. John Stahl couldn't stand for that column."

As for Sampson, according to Bud, "He was nothing as governor. As a matter of fact, that was my first session of the legislature after he took office, and in my pieces, I wrote some editorial comments, had a column, where I was highly critical of Sampson. That seemed not to disturb Mr. Stahl [probably] because Sampson was in office [and couldn't succeed himself]."

Of all the politicians that Guthrie knew, the most interesting, if not the best, was Albert Benjamin Chandler. "Happy," as he was called, gained national fame as the commissioner of baseball, the "czar." But earlier he was lieutenant governor, governor, and senator from Kentucky. As Bud thought of him, "He was a deep fried cornball. But effective nevertheless. And he had a great memory for faces and names [when speaking, he would address people in the audience by name], and he could sing 'Sonny Boy' pretty well. He was pretty darn effective, and as you very well know, it is impossible to dislike Happy Chandler."

He was everybody's friend, whether you were rich or poor, and he had made up a Horatio Alger story of his own life, having come out of poverty to Lexington with a red sweater and a five-dollar bill. And he reminded his audiences of this frequently. Bud thought that he had been a terrific governor for his first eighteen months. He put through an election law that made it almost impossible to vote graveyards and that made chain voting very difficult, if not impossible. He had courage enough to get a tax passed on stored whiskey, despite a strong opposition in the state to any tax. At thirty-seven he was the youngest state governor in the country at the time and perhaps the youngest ever.

Bud greeted Chandler's election to the governorship with a feature story in the *Leader*, parts of which follow:

> Kentucky had a new governor today, a smiling, somewhat florid 37-year-old who won his first political campaign by singing "Sonny Boy" in the country school houses of Woodford, Scott and Jessamine counties.
>
> In the Albert Benjamin Chandler who squeezed through a packed inaugural stand Tuesday afternoon to take the oath of office there were still some signs of the old "Happy"

Chandler, the youthful state senator who delighted rural school marms and their juvenile charges by crooning in the corridors of the capitol, who took the floor too often for a first-termer, who was so hail-fellow-well-met that more restrained associates looked upon him with an indulgent condescension. . . . It was as lieutenant-governor that Chandler began that development that was to carry him eventually to the executive mansion. None were more astonished than the colleagues who had tolerated him good-naturedly in 1930 when the one-time "Sonny Boy" began to show that he was capable of convictions and determination. Behind that smiling face and beyond that geniality of nature, they found to their amazement, there lay stout opinions and there lay courage.

But a number of Chandler's actions as governor gradually disillusioned Bud. Chandler was undone, in Bud's view, by an overweening ambition. He decided that the governor should—quoting Mary Lizzie, who in turn was quoting Shakespeare—"Cast aside all vain ambition, for by this fell the angels." In December of 1935 Chandler had campaigned against the excessive number of state workers, the "weed cutters" as they were called, who were hired in order to vote for the incumbent governor. But then in 1938, while running for the Senate against Alben Barkley, he hired them all back, all ten thousand or so.

Bud recalled with some pain a particular event of that election. President Roosevelt came to Kentucky to support Barkley, and Bud sent a photographer to cover the visit. The photographer was a brash young man and naive, and as the president's car passed by him, he jumped on the car to take a picture. Bud was alarmed to find out later that the photographer had been very close to being shot by the Secret Service.

The president had come by train to Cincinnati and then by car to the racetrack at Covington to speak on behalf of Barkley. However, as governor of the state, Chandler met the train, and when they started to get into the car, Chandler jumped into the backseat between Barkley and Roosevelt. Chandler insisted that Roosevelt had asked him to sit next to him in the middle and that, anyway, as governor of the state he had a right to sit anywhere he damned pleased. The president was irritated by the matter but in his speech said that while Chandler would make a good senator, he should wait, for he was for Barkley in this particular election. However, Chandler in his Democratic primary campaign went around the state saying that the president said he would make a good senator.

In 1939 Senator Logan died, Chandler resigned as governor, and Lieutenant Governor Keen Johnson became governor and appointed Chandler to the Senate. He was elected to a short term in 1940, and in 1942 he ran in the Democratic primary against John Y. Brown. During the campaign Bud broke a story that Brown used against Chandler. A contractor in Louisville had built a swimming pool for Chandler. Bud recalled, "In building the swimming pool he had used critical materials [this was 1942 at the beginning of World War II] that shouldn't have been used at all . . . and it was a gift to Chandler. This was about the time I turned away completely from Chandler. This must have been a favor received. It is hard to imagine anyone just out of pure friendship building that pool." Chandler was elected anyway. Asked if Chandler objected to the story and became hostile, Bud said, "He never said a word about it. . . . And when I would meet him afterward and I was on his tail pretty hard by that time, he was just as friendly as could be. That is one of the virtues of the man."

When he was asked who was the Kentucky politician he most admired, who was the most decent, effective, honest officeholder in his opinion, Bud replied, "John Sherman Cooper." Cooper's lifespan, from 1901 to 1991, paralleled that of Guthrie's, and he was elected to the legislature in 1928, the same year that Guthrie started covering it for the *Leader*. Among that "strange assemblage," Bud wrote, "John Sherman Cooper from the beginning stood out." He added, "I liked him then, and I liked his subsequent career." He was, Bud thought, incorruptible—a fairly rare thing in any state legislature of that time.

Cooper served only one term in the legislature before he was elected judge in Pulaski County, where he was born and raised. Then after service in the army during World War II, he was elected a circuit judge in 1945, and the following year was elected to the U.S. Senate, replacing Chandler, who had resigned to go to baseball. He ran for reelection unsuccessfully in 1948, was appointed as a delegate to the General Assembly of the United Nations in 1949, and served as an advisor to the Secretary of State in 1950. In 1952 he was again elected to the Senate and then again failed to be reelected. He was appointed as ambassador to India and Nepal in 1955. Once again, in 1956 he ran for the Senate, winning a seat. He was reelected twice, serving from 1956 to 1973. During that time he was again made a delegate to the U.N. General Assembly. As one can see from this record, he was an unusual man, varied in his abilities and interests and certainly persistent. And he was an unusual Republican, especially for Kentucky—liberal in thought and an internationalist in his perspective.

Fishing trip on the Teton River:
Chick, Bud, and Alfred Bertram
Guthrie Sr. Courtesy of Amy
Sakariassen.

Bud at nine years old hunting
out in the country near
Choteau. Courtesy of Peggy
Bloom.

Bud's parents behind their house in Choteau. Courtesy of Amy Sakariassen.

Bud with Al Dolby, 1919.
Courtesy of Amy Sakariassen.

Bud at the sawmill in the mountains west of Choteau. Courtesy of Amy Sakariassen.

Bud on fire patrol on Sun River, ca. 1921. Courtesy of Amy Sakariassen.

Bud's first wife, Harriet Larson.
Courtesy of Peggy Bloom.

Harriet, Helen, and Bud.
Courtesy of Peggy Bloom.

Bert and Bud on a go-cart in front of the house in Lexington. Courtesy of Amy Sakariassen.

Harriet, Bert, Harriet's mother and father (the Larsons), and Helen. Courtesy of Amy Sakariassen.

Bud and his brother, Chick.
Courtesy of Amy Sakariassen.

Bert, Helen, and Bud.
Courtesy of Peggy Bloom.

CHAPTER FOUR

Marriage, Family, and Separation

S tarting in 1934 the Guthrie family would return from Kentucky to Choteau every summer, Bud to stay a couple of weeks of vacation, and Scoop to stay for the summer, with their son. This meant that Bud would be separated from his wife and child for several months each year. He hated that. But he gave in because that was what his wife and her family wanted, her health between 1933 and 1934 was not good, and at first her visits to Montana were designed to help her recover and gain weight. Money was tight when Scoop was home since, because of her persistent weakness following the birth, they had hired a woman to help her with the house and baby. Bud had insisted on it.

They started writing letters again every day—or at least Bud did, a lonely man who often complained of a lack of mail from his wife. Early in the summer of 1934, before he could leave for Montana, Bud wrote, "God damn, but it's lonely without you. Already, I have reached the point where I can't believe I was ever married.

Usually, that stage arrives just before insanity or suicide, so you can see I am taking it very hard. I am hoping, I suppose rather foolishly, for a letter tomorrow" (6/16/34).

His salary had risen to $50 a month earlier in the year, but he had to take a ten-dollar cut along with the rest of the staff, an exigency of the Depression as it cut ever deeper into the economy. He wrote Scoop in July about his financial planning for his trip in August. He would save as much as he could, coming up with $126, which he hoped would get him to Montana and the whole family back to Kentucky. But to cover possible emergencies and to give them a reserve, he planned to borrow $150 from the bank.

Before he left Choteau to go back to Lexington after his vacation, a friend gave him a bottle of bourbon. On the train, the bottle caused him to have one adventure after another: "I had the damndest time with the bottle Tom gave me that you can imagine. I never seemed to be able to get alone with the darn thing." He escaped to the men's washroom but found someone there and felt compelled to offer him a drink:

> I was husbanding a small reserve at the time I got to Chicago, thinking I'd have one drink before lunch and maybe a couple before dinner. I noticed as I sat down in the day coach, that a wan-looking sister was seated in the section ahead of me, and I heard a companion say to her, "I'll have to get off now. You take it easy, and remember that they'll meet you in Cincinnati with a wheel chair."
>
> When we were about 15 minutes out of Chicago, the girl suddenly keeled over in a faint. A woman ran to her assistance and other of us came up wondering what we could do to help. Suddenly a bright and generous idea seized me. "Do you think," I asked the woman who was holding that girl, "that a small drop of spirits would help her?" She said

she thought it would—and it did. Well, the girl had two more fainting fits before we got to Cincinnati. My first generous impulse was giving way to some misgiving, not to say alarm, for by this time the stuff was getting pretty precious. After I'd brought the invalid out the third swoon, I dashed into the toilet, swung the bottle up and downed the contents, saying desperately to myself, "Let her come out of the next one on her own power." She didn't have any more. (9/5/34)

It was almost a given in those days that newspaper men had to be tough—hard drinkers and heavy smokers who cast a jaundiced eye on the human activity around them, "Oh, what fools these mortals be" (as the heading to the Sunday comics would proclaim). Bud's wife often expresses concern about his drinking in her letters.

The upside to this toughness was a devotion by the newsmen to realism, to an honesty that was expressed in private, even if it could not always be expressed in their news writing. Bud's twenty-one years' newspaper experience became the basis for the tough-minded, realistic approach that characterized his fiction and made it so different from most novels about the West. His mindset resulted in a level of realism that jolted, if not shocked, many readers when they encountered his early frontier in *The Big Sky*. Here was not the romantic treatment that they had come to expect.

Back in Lexington he took up his tasks at the newspaper once more, overseeing coverage of city events and state politics in election and legislative seasons. And he continued to become more and more cynical. Kentucky legislators were up to the usual—yammering "incessantly over subjects often unimportant, though motives seldom unselfish. They passed piddling and unenforceable and indefensible bills. Members of House and Senate and administration accused one another . . . of dereliction, misfeasance and malfeasance, and the charges were often justified." Bud was staying, in his wife's absence, with Mary Lizzie, and that somewhat helped his loneliness, yet he could hardly wait for his wife's return. But her return seemed for a time as if it might be delayed by an outbreak of polio and their concern for Nonny. However, after consulting their doctor, the two decided that Scoop should return on schedule in early October.

In the meantime, Bud's mother had written to him, mourning the passing of summer. The oncoming cold seemed to herald the departure of the family. Bud's brother, Chick, had not been able to come home because he was stuck in Chicago working for the Associated Press. Bud had come and gone, and Jane was off to the university at Missoula. Scoop and the baby would be leaving that week. Mother Guthrie sadly observed, "For the past week the weather has been winterish but summer never seems quite gone as long as some of you are still around." She reported that Bud's father, besides his schoolwork, had the job of selling his rams. She was against it because the flock was not large enough to make the money that would justify the extra work. "This first storm gives us a taste of what's to come and I hate for dad to be wrestling around in the cold and dirt" (9/26/34).

The next year, 1935, followed pretty much the same pattern, with Bud spending two weeks in Montana and his wife and child staying for the summer. But since his wife had recovered her health by this time, his complaints about her absence that late summer and fall became more and more strident. Finally, Scoop exploded, saying that after getting his last letter she has been doing her best "to cool off": "I know you've been lonesome, and you do believe in making others unhappy about it as well as yourself. Instead of thinking so much about yourself give a thought to others and how they might be feeling. You've had me in the jitters for the last three weeks. I might have been able to enjoy a few of those days if sometime I had rec'd a letter from you saying that though I was badly missed, you did hope I was enjoying my visit" (8/30/35). She ended, "So much for another duty letter. Let's call it enough. Harriet."

This was one of the very few letters over several decades that didn't end with a declaration of love and wasn't signed "Scoop." She wrote three weeks later and asked Bud to try to find a new house to rent because the one they were in was too small. They not only had the baby, but they had a live-in helper for Scoop. Bud found a place at 511 Forest Park Road.

With the new house, they acquired a new neighbor. It was Thomas D. Clark. Clark was an assistant professor of history at the university, and his specialties were the histories of Kentucky, the Ohio Valley, and the western movement—precisely the subjects that Bud was interested in. In remembering the friendship that evolved, Bud said that the two of them spent "rich evenings, talking of old times and new books, exchanging confessions of ambitions," for both were "young and untried." For his part, Clark recalled,

> I lived a neighbor to Bud Guthrie for many years, and I suppose I never held another man in such high affection. Our families were intimate friends, and we shared our woes and our joys. Bud was a more successful newspaperman than I was a fledgling instructor in the Department of History at the University of Kentucky. Aside from our common struggle to survive in the Depression years and a family friendship, we shared a common interest of the West. He was an avid student of the West, and had been so since the day his family moved to Montana from Bedford, Indiana. We both expected to write books and to satisfy our yearning for finding answers to the exciting moments of westward

expansion in the nineteenth century. . . . Both of us gathered books on the West, and we had many conversations on the subject. When Bud began to approach the matter of writing, he engaged in long periods of reading. I used to leave my office at the University just after Bud left his office at the *Lexington Leader* downtown and I would see him bumping along on an old flat wheel streetcar reading books on the West.

Bud remembered well those streetcar rides. Along with editing, occasionally reporting, and writing editorials, he also reviewed books that matched his interests, and he would read from them on his commute of twenty-five minutes each way. Sometimes Clark would get home before he did and would be sitting at his desk, which looked out a window at the back of the Guthrie house. Clark has memories of Bud climbing up his back stairs, turning, and shouting a stream of mock insults at him, "What are you doing, you old fart? Just sitting there looking out the window! I just put out a paper—what have you done?" Then, just as often, Bud would call him on the phone to disrupt him. Since Bud's kitchen looked right into Clark's study, he would wait until he saw Clark settle down at his desk and then call. Clark recalls, "I did some sassing back." Every morning they left for work at about the same time, and Bud would always call out to him, "Hey, Prof., what's new in history?"

In 1936 the Guthrie schedule was pretty much the same. Although Bud and Scoop had made up, she still insisted on returning to Montana for the summer. In July, Bud was disappointed when his sister Jane married Bob Haugen, a man of whom he thoroughly disapproved. But worse news was to come. Bud's mother had shown signs of illness for over a year and by late summer was spending much of her time in bed as her situation worsened. The local doctors could not diagnose the basic cause of her symptoms. Bud's father wrote to Bud about "her rheumatism, with the attendant fever and heart trouble" and mentioned that her cancer spots (possibly melanoma) were "under control" (1/22/36).

For weeks they hoped against hope that she would get well enough to be sent to the Mayo Clinic, and then, when she was well enough to travel, she went by train to Rochester. A worried Bud met her there and stayed with her during the examinations and treatment. On the first afternoon at the clinic, the doctors diagnosed cancer—inoperable and fatal. Nevertheless, with only dim hope of remission, they prescribed X-ray treatments, a staggered series of which would take ten days to complete.

Bud spent as much time as the clinic would allow him at his mother's bedside. "The hours," he wrote, "were long and sad beyond saying. With false cheer I helped her to her appointments, telling her I believed I could see an improvement already." He had plenty of time to think: "In that time of waiting, day and night, I tried to drug myself with gun-and-gallop and whodunit books. I could write, I told myself finally, as well as these writers; and there must be money, which I needed, in such stuff. What about a mystery and cow-country myth in combination? So far as I could recall, the two had never been blended. All right. I'd blend them. I promised to, thinking somehow that a published book, by mere publication, would constitute a last tribute to Mother and maybe boost my bank account balance besides."

When the X-ray treatments were over, Bud put his mother on a Pullman of the westbound Empire Builder at St. Paul. Back home, Bud's father and his sister Jane took care of her. In Lexington, Bud started once again on a novel, this time with a specific plan of attack in mind. But after working on his manuscript for a while, he became disillusioned with the project: "Within a month I was bored with what I'd set down and bored more by the whole prospect—the contrived and implausible plot, the knights and knaves, and love too pure for motor impulses to pants and panties. Final tribute to Mother, this cheap lie about life? She might shy at outspoken expression, but she knew shallows from deeps. Publication? Money? Hah!"

However, he continued to work on the manuscript through the end of the year and on into 1937. On March 20, his mother died. A letter from the Mayo Clinic came to the family about the time of the funeral, expressing sympathy for the passing of Mrs. Guthrie. It went on to say that because of the type of tumor, they had feared from the first that it could not be controlled. Though stricken with sadness for her comparatively short life and the loss of her love and support, Bud forced himself to finish his project. It was called *Murders at Moon Dance*, and it would go through several revisions and bounce around from publisher to publisher for several years before it found a home.

An editor for Bobbs-Merrill, Rosemary York, came down to visit Tom Clark, whose book, *Southern Country Editor*, the company was publishing. Bud had written several chapters of his *Murders at Moon Dance* and went over to Clark's house to show them to the editor. She sat down and read through them and then turned them down. Many years later, when asked about this, Bud declared the rejection perfectly justified.

It was about this time also that Bud was involved in another project, one that displayed his persistence in the face of adversity. His disability came to him all of a sudden in 1923 when he was president of his fraternity, and he was presiding over a ceremony initiating new pledges and welcoming honorary candidates picked from the faculty. About halfway through the ceremony, he was overwhelmed by terror as his heart raced, his knees trembled, and he could not get enough air. His inability to speak in public continued: "The mere request that I speak, even though the date was distant and the attendance likely to be small, shot me chock-full of adrenaline, and I'd advance some tremulous excuse."

Determined to overcome his problem, he set out to organize a group of people equally stricken, a group wherein the members would address each other, and because they all suffered from the same affliction, would support each other. During the first meeting, they adopted only two rules: they would meet once a week, and every member would speak at every meeting. They searched for a name for the group and came up with the Lexington Speakeasy Club—a name with cachet since this was only a few years after the repeal of Prohibition.

They had members from nearly every profession and many occupations, and although as time went by more and more people wanted to join them, they had to limit the membership to thirty. Otherwise, the meetings would become too long. In a letter to Dr. Barclay Acheson, who had requested information about the club, Bud wrote in part,

> The first general session was a sort of confession meeting. Each nervous member told "How Public Speaking Affects Me." Some admitted to mental stoppage, some to fidgets, some to quavers, some to palpitation, some to shortage of wind. But by the very act of confessing, they rid themselves of some of that secret egotistic price that paralyzes initiative with the specter of failure. And by learning of the other man's difficulties, each member somehow felt less concerned about his own.
>
> As the subject next easy to discuss, the members at their second meeting talked about their businesses and professions. From there we have gone on to impromptu speeches,

book reviews, formal addresses, debates, discussions of current events and local problems, contests with other clubs. As a means of getting a man out of his tight little self, of developing freedom and a degree of histrionic ability, we have done bits of acting and recited old-fashioned declamations, with all the gestures.

The results, down to the last man, have been amazing. There is not a member of the club but has benefited immeasurably from it. There is not a one, no matter how inauspicious his start, but can give a reasonably good account of himself now before almost any audience. (5/11/40)

They determined that after their second speech no one could talk about their own business or occupation and ruled that no seasoned member could decline an outside invitation to speak. Each meeting had an appointed critic who would comment on the presentations.

Bud tells of an occasion when an outspoken, worldly man was appointed critic who would judge a young man who was given the impromptu topic, "My Most Exciting Experience." The young man went on to describe a time when he had gone to Berea, Kentucky, and fallen into a group of college students. They all climbed to the top of a hill and under a full moon lit a fire and roasted hotdogs, which they ate on buns, along with other food that students had brought. Bud went on,

The boys were mannerly, he said, and the girls correct and attractive. Later, all sat on the ground and sang songs and still later marched down the hill, where he had to take leave of them. That was his most exciting experience.

Jumping to his feet, our critic cried, "Good God! Haven't you ever had a fight in a whorehouse?"

The Speakeasy Club idea spread. At the university, male students formed a club of their own, as did a group of women, and another was established in town. *Reader's Digest* got wind of Bud's group and sent a reporter to come down to observe. The magazine asked Bud for a letter outlining the group's program and paid him $300 for it. The result of the article and his letter was an avalanche of letters of inquiry; answering them, Bud claimed, took up almost all of the money he had been paid, spending it on stationery, stamps, and a mimeographed list of procedures. Nevertheless, his letter was his first national publication, and from her deathbed, his mother wrote to congratulate him.

Possibly because he had lost so many infants to death and perhaps motivated in part by guilt, Bud's father had for some time helped groom the town cemetery, painting the fence and planting bulbs and flowers. Now, after his wife's death, he was even more engaged. He wrote to Bud (whom he called "Buddie") and Harriet on June 1, 1937:

> Janie and Bob [her husband] came Saturday evening and the next morning Chick came on the bus. It was a busy day Sunday, but one of the most satisfying I have had for a long time. I had ordered flowers, so after a breakfast at home, we went to the cemetery and trimmed the graves. We had plenty of flowers. Mrs. Larson brought us lilacs and honeysuckle and we had some of our own besides. The town is simply purple with lilacs this year. So we left the graves beautifully decorated. Then we all went to church. The service was meant to honor the old timers, but there only a scattering half dozen on hand to be honored. . . . For entertainment in the evening Chick and Bob brought the old phonograph downstairs and we played a lot of the

old records, some of them several times over. It was like living over the happy old times.

In 1937 Bud's brother Chick changed jobs, from the Associated Press in Chicago, to the *Great Falls Tribune*, now close to home and to his father. He had Sunday off and was not on duty until 6 p.m. on Monday, so that he had time to take the bus over to Choteau and back. When he was home, he and his father would often take trips into the countryside, searching out historical locations. Guthrie senior reported to Bud:

> Chick and I had a dandy trip last Sunday and Monday. Went to old Fort C. F. Smith, forty miles south of Hardin, back there for the night and next morning to Custer battlefield, which Chick had seen only from the distance. We also took in Boot Hill monument, Kelly's grave, and the Bill Hart statue at Billings. We found the cross which has been erected at the spot where Lonesome Charley Reynolds fell at Reno field. We did not have time to go on to the site of the Reno Battle on the hill. It was a very successful trip. We found also the site of the Hay Field fight, which has been marked. Chick says he is going to prepare some articles for the *Sunday Tribune*. (7/1/37)

During that summer, Nonny occasionally stayed with his grandfather while his mother visited in Great Falls or played golf. Bud's father reported to Bud that Nonny was getting to feel more at home but had not quite yet adjusted to staying with him. He took him for a ride, and they got out every now and then to explore. Nonny flushed out a young rabbit about as big as his fist. He made a lunge for it, and it jumped into an irrigation ditch, but granddaddy fished the bunny out, and Nonny got to hold him for a while. "His eyes fairly glowed," Guthrie senior wrote, adding, "The big plan now is to find him again or another like him" (7/1/37).

Bud's son's affection for animals became a problem for his parents. They wanted to be understanding parents and decided that they didn't want to discourage him. But when he walked into the house in Lexington with his first small snake wrapped around his arm, Harriet could barely keep herself from screaming. Eventually, as we have already noted, they had a large number of snakes, seventeen as a matter of fact, in a "snake house," and there was the problem of how to feed them all. They bought little copper cage traps with which to catch mice (before that, they had seen evidence of mice all over the pantry shelves). But the cages sat and sat, baited and empty. So they tried spring traps, hoping that they could get the dead mouse while it was still warm and offer it to the snakes. These traps also remained empty. Bud recalls, "No one who has not awakened morning after morning knowing he must have a live mouse by night, no one who has not driven himself out into the barren grass to look for a toad, can know the burden that settled on our house. We trapped and we searched and we searched and trapped." Finally, they bought the food. But their son was so taken by the purchased mice that his parents had to sneak them to the snakes.

Their house was on the edge of a large field behind them, and that was where Nonny (who now insisted on being called "Bert") had captured his snakes. Then, as time went by and as he got more and more involved, even reading books about them, his parents gave in and ordered more-exotic varieties by mail from Florida. Then one day Bert got tired of his snakes and turned them all loose in the field. According to Tom Clark, the neighbors, finding them under a porch or in the cellar, were not so fond of having them around. Apparently, they were used to human company.

Bud notes that they gained several pieces of enduring wisdom from their experience:

1. Once you can bring yourself to lay hand on a snake, any extravagant fear of it is likely to disappear.
2. There is nothing like a snake in the house to keep callers from interfering with your homework.
3. It is hard to catch a mouse alive.

All in all these were good times, funny times. Tom Clark remembers when Bud invited his boss to go with him to a football game. His boss was a humorless man who never cracked a smile and was a well-known teetotaler. Somebody threw a bottle at the game and hit the boss on the head and knocked him silly. Bud took him home and, in an effort to revive him, gave him a drink of whiskey and with a cloth bathed his forehead with whiskey. Then the man's wife came in and found her husband mumbling. She thought, with the smell, that he was drunk as a skunk. Bud may well have had that in mind.

But all was not hijinks at home or on the job. Bud was, at bottom, a serious, involved writer. Looking back at his time at the *Leader*, he said, "My newspaper stories I'm proudest of disclosed the high death rate among children in Fayette County, Kentucky, because of improper health methods to prevent dysentery. The *Leader*'s stories brought reorganization of the county health department and marked decrease in deaths from the disease."

Tom Clark recalled that Bud trained a lot of young newspapermen and turned them into really good journalists. And in two instances, his mentored young men "turned out to be writers of some consequence. A boy named Henry Hodge wrote a novel that was a fairly good novel." Clark recollected, "Johnny Day, Sunny Day we called him, wrote a book called *The Kentucky Mountains*, which was a very good book, and it showed Bud's influence on the writing." Clark also remembers a young woman, Elizabeth Hardwick, who lived next door to the Guthries and whom Bud encouraged. She, of course, became a tremendous success as a writer. Her first novel, published in 1945, was about a Kentucky family as seen from the point of view of a young girl. In 1949 she was married to the poet Robert Lowell.

Early in 1938 Bud read about a Nieman Fellowship program that Harvard University was going to start that September. The fellowship offered a year of free study to twelve newsmen—anything but journalism, which Harvard didn't offer. They could take any courses they wanted to take, could consult the faculty, and had use of the library; of particular interest to Guthrie was the Widener Library's collection of western Americana. The fellows would take leaves of absence from their jobs, and the fellowship would provide payments roughly equal to their salaries.

It was an incredible opportunity, especially for someone who looked on himself as provincial, someone whose views needed broadening. Bud recalled, "I felt the need of exposure, of the challenge of ideas and attitudes foreign to my Bluegrass and Montana provinces." Hearing about Bud's application, his father wrote,

> I am all for it. . . . You have reached the age when you can't make too many changes, but you are not too old to change and grow. I seemed to sense when I visited you that you were not altogether satisfied with your present surroundings. . . .
>
> I am the more favorable to the plan because looking back I can see where I have been lacking in ambition and determination myself. So, I want to see you attack this thing with all your strength and enthusiasm. You have a wife, a

brother, a sister, and a dad, not to mention other relatives and friends, who will be right behind you to help in any possible way. I have no doubt that it will open up new and larger fields. (2/22/38)

But he didn't get the fellowship . . . this time.

CHAPTER FIVE

The First Novel and Plans for the Big One

His father wrote to console him in his disappointment: "Glad you are philosophical about that scholarship. The board that made the choices overlooked their best bet." He added that he hadn't been feeling well, probably a touch of flu: "I stayed down two weekends as a precaution. Ran fever two or three days, but didn't miss any school" (4/3/38). A man of stern duty.

Then the following month he told Buddie, "Don't hurry your work on the book. Let it season. Could you enter it in some magazine contest for a prize, book to follow?" (5/1/38). Bud was still trying to polish up his Western-mystery novel, but he had also been thinking about starting a second novel. It would be honest and realistic—he was tired of Western make-believe. A clue to this was in his father's request in June before Bud would travel back to Choteau, "Bring volume I of *Trail of Lewis and Clark* when you come, and any other books you think I might like" (6/23/38). In an interview later in life, he recalled when the idea for his second novel began to crystallize: "The idea occurred to me early in 1940. It occurred to me because, so far as I knew, no honest story about the fur trade had been written, and—you say I am a romanticist— well, read the earlier stories about the fur trade if you want to run into some romanticists. They really idealized, heroized everything and everybody."

But revision of fiction past and planning for fiction future was not his only occupation. Scoop wrote him also in June of 1938, "The poem you wrote for me is lovely." Then a few days later, she wrote, "It has been a long time since you wrote anything about your book. I thought some of your leisure time was going to be taken with it" (6/28/38). He wanted to publish his manuscript, but he was getting awfully tired of *Murders at Moon Dance*.

In January of 1939, Bud wrote and published the first of many articles and editorials appearing throughout his life in various papers and journals in which he would make a conservationist statement. Appearing in the *Leader*, the article, "Faulkconer's Eagle" (renamed in a collection of Guthrie's articles, "On the Death of an Eagle"), begins,

> All night the great bird drooped in a tree, sick with a bullet in her.
>
> At dusk, a marksman made breathless by the size and rarity of her had caught her through his sights, and, wounded, she had risen clumsily and planed painfully away on pinions that had fanned a thousand miles of airways on the food-quest to Kentucky.
>
> The next morning the location of the eagle is announced to the marksman by the clamor of a flock of crows, and he finishes her off.
>
> Later, he lifted her up and spread the folded wings and

let his picture be taken thus, a hunter with his trophy, while the strong, bold head of the bird hung limp against the ruff of her breast.

Then, writes Bud, the bird will be stuffed and mounted and put in the county supply plant so that people can see what a golden eagle looks like—"that is, they will know what a golden eagle with glass eyes looks like set dead and stiff in a room." Maybe, since they have become so rare, they will never see the majesty and grace of a live eagle.

It was a strong, emotional statement from a man who, in his youth, had enjoyed the adventure of hunting so very much, bringing down ducks over the ponds and flushing prairie chickens out of the thickets in the fields near Choteau. Of course, he did it for the pot, for the fun of it, but not for vanity. His arguments for conservation became stronger and stronger throughout his life, so that he became nearly as well known for his environmentalism as for his fiction.

Later in life Bud told Bert Lindler of the *Great Falls Tribune* that his concern for the environment began while he was a newsman in Lexington, when he read *Deserts on the March* (Paul B. Sears, 1936) and *Our Plundered Planet* (Fairfield Osborn, 1948). He told Lindler, "They both got me to thinking about the welfare of the planet, and so of man."

Bud's father went to Lexington for Christmas in 1938, and his son and daughter-in-law gave him a telescope, a fitting present for a nature-watcher. Early in 1939 he wrote to his son, who had submitted his manuscript of *Murders at Moon Dance* to the publisher Bobbs-Merrill. They had asked for revisions: "Your word about the book gives me much concern. I do hope that whatever revisions and changes are made will have the book still distinctly your production. Follow suggestions of the readers, if they square with your own judgment, taste, and desires. Otherwise, tell the readers to go to hell. Your ideas are very probably a great deal better than theirs." Eventually, Bobbs-Merrill turned the manuscript down.

As usual, Scoop went to Montana for the summer, and she asked Bud to send her copies of what was now called the Lexington *Herald Leader*. It was her way of keeping track of events in what was now her hometown and keeping up with what her husband was doing. Bud had assigned to himself the reviews of any books about the West, and his wife wrote to him, "I liked your review of *Grapes of Wrath*" (6/7/39). When his wife was gone for the summer, they rented out the Lexington house and he moved into a small hotel room for the duration. During those months it was very hot, and looking back on it, Bud said he just wanted to go somewhere nice where he could sit and sweat in his underwear.

Winter and spring of 1938–1939, Scoop was pregnant; she gave birth to a girl on June 20 at the hospital in Great Falls. Bud was in Lexington and would not be in Choteau until July 17 to welcome his daughter into the world. In the meantime, until Bud arrived a month after the birth, the baby was without a name, called only "Baby Guthrie." After he got to Choteau, the baby was named "Helen," probably after Harriet's friend Helen Swanberg, who had taken her to the hospital.

On January 13, 1940, Guthrie senior wrote to his son:

Dear Buddie:

It is seven o'clock, p.m. of your birthday. I am going to write this before I go to the basketball game—Teton vs. Dutton. I recall quite vividly still the circumstances surrounding your birth—in a duplex house in Bedford [Indiana]. I believe both of your grandmothers were there to help out. It was early in the morning, around one o'clock when you put in your appearance. Well, you thrived, and in the following August you were brought away out to Montana and you didn't give a damn. Some boy! Well, son, the going since has been better for having you along. Many, many happy returns.

Starting early in 1940 the Guthries built a house of their own. Tom Clark remembered that Bud and Harriet looked around for property, bought a lot, and asked the Clarks to go out and buy the lot next to them. The Clarks drove out and found that the lots were in the middle of a rock quarry, and they didn't have enough money to buy a piece of flat ground, let alone build in the middle of a quarry. So the Clarks looked elsewhere and bought a lot; the Guthries, in turn, sold their lot and then bought another lot next to the Clarks. For several months after their houses were built, they were the only people living in that area, about two miles from downtown Lexington. The house was two-story brick with a single-story wing off of each side. Bud had his study in one of the wings, and later, after he published *The Big Sky* and started teaching at the university, he built a second study in the basement that would hold a small class. Behind the house stretched tobacco fields so that there was a definite feel of being in the country. As the neighborhood grew, mostly university professors moved in (probably Clark's influence), and with very few exceptions, it became a very close-knit neighborhood.

Tom recalled that after the Guthries had built the house on Tahoma Road in 1940, Bud got a housewarming present from the boss at the newspaper, a plant, a Virginia creeper. Bud protected it all day and brought it home and called Tom, telling him that he had very rare plant: "I took a look at it and said, 'Come on, go with me.' And he must have had a hundred Virginia creepers—it was a nuisance growing all over the place, growing in his yard. He stood and looked at the plants. He bundled up that gift that they had given him and threw it over the fence."

The upstairs window in the house looked out over the front walk. One day, some time after they had moved in, a nosy neighbor who had just moved in, who often was seen peering around trying to discover what they were doing, came up the walk toward the front door. Harriet, upstairs, intercepted him and, opening the window, began to talk to him. Bud saw what was happening. He slipped into the room behind her and, kneeling down under the window, reached up and thumbed Harriet's nose at the neighbor.

Early in July of 1940, Bud had to go to the hospital in Lexington for an emergency appendectomy. On learning about it, his brother, Chick, wrote,

> 'Twas a bolt out of the blue to learn that you'd gone under the knife. By now I trust you're able to sit up and eat something besides creamed salmon and milk toast. . . .You must be nearly ready to move into your new home. Life has surely moved for you folks—a new baby, a new home and an operation all within the period of little more than a year.
>
> Wish we were all up on Sun River now instead of where we are. It was a year ago that we made our trek into the hills and I think about that expedition often these warm summer days. (7/9/40)

At about this same time, Chick and his wife, Florence, and Jane and her husband, Bob, had also moved into new houses, the former in Great Falls and the latter in Missoula.

In December, only four years after Bud's mother died, his father was diagnosed with prostate cancer and went to the Mayo Clinic in Rochester. Bud went with him. He found the city full of "wretched memories"—at the little hotel where he had stayed before, the restaurant where they had eaten, and, of course, the hospital itself. Bud reported to Harriet that his father's spirits were good and that he didn't seem at all afraid of his scheduled operation. He told Bud, "If I knew I would go where Mommy is, I'd be glad to die right now." But, in fact, the prognosis was good—the doctors predicted he had a forty-seven percent chance to live at least five more years—which was as far as doctors could go in estimating the survival period. Bud was with his father five or six hours a day and reported "the hours drag like hell" (12/29/40). What time he had alone he spent reading in his small, dark hotel room.

After his father had recovered from his operation and returned to Choteau, the two frequently corresponded about books. Even in his retirement Bud's father was an omnivorous reader who had full access to the high school library—he even had a set of keys that would let him into the school and library during off hours. He found to his dismay that a number of the books he had ordered for the library had never been checked out. In the fall of 1942, he decided to rent his house for the winter—winter in Choteau was getting too much for him—and move in with Jane and Bob in Missoula. That gave him access to the university library as well. He read primarily histories, and when they were about Montana he would, when he could, drive out to the places mentioned in them and then report on his reading and follow-up trips to his son.

But he also read and reread literary works, starting with a rereading of Shakespeare and going on to things like Edgar Lee Masters's *Spoon River Anthology* (1915). He thought that Masters's work was "not very imposing poetry" but was still "an impressive history of a small town and community in the surrounding country"

(9/22/42). Father and son exchanged books, sometimes histories and sometimes more contemporary fiction and nonfiction. A Western novel that impressed Bud and that he sent to his father was *The Ox-Bow Incident* (1940) by Walter Van Tilburg Clark.

Clifton Fadiman had reviewed the book in the *New Yorker*, and a jacket blurb was taken from that review. Guthrie senior refers to that blurb when he writes to his son:

> How well Mr. Fadiman expresses the purpose which you have had so constantly in mind—to take the thriller and lift it onto the level where dwells literature. I am not convinced that you haven't done this better in your book, as I recall it. . . . But it [*Ox-Bow*] is stark, nothing in it that is not needed, that does not belong. . . . It may be helpful to you in improving your own story. . . . Maybe you could strip your story down to the absolutely essential elements. If I have any unfavorable impression from your story as I remember it, it is that in spots it smacks a little of "fine writing." But keep knocking along at it. (11/13/42)

Then, finally, at the end of November, Bud learned that the manuscript had been accepted for publication by E. P. Dutton and Company, and spread the news by wire. His father wrote back, "Your dad is one proud old guy, and so are Jane and Bob proud, and so will be the other relatives on both sides, when they hear of your success. Well, you deserved success after all the effort you have expended, as well as on the ground of ability. We have talked about nothing much else here."

The elder Guthrie worried whether Bud got a good contract and asked about movie rights and possible magazine serialization. At Jane's, in Missoula, he found much of his time taken up by helping her with the house and baby. However, looking forward to the next book, he told Bud,

As soon as the Christmas rush is over here I will get busy
on material relative to the Yellowstone. . . . I shall have
time for the library work soon, and shall be only too glad
to do all I can to assemble material for you and especially
to prepare a bibliography to show where material can be
found. If you have any suggestions, let me have them.
. . . To go back about the Yellowstone, I have already made
some notations in my copy of [Charles] Larpenteur [*Forty
Years a Fur Trader on the Upper Missouri* (1828)] and also
in [Hiram Martin] Chittenden [*American Fur Trade of
the Far West* (1902)]. I did this some time ago, when you
thought there was some prospect ahead. (12/19/42)

Two weeks later he reported, "I have done quite a bit of rather
desultory reading. Made a little start at the city library on the Yellowstone. Didn't locate much that was important" (1/4/43).

As for the publication of *Murders at Moon Dance* in 1943, Tom
Clark recalled, "Though this book brought a real joy at the time
of publication, I am sure that he came to look on it only as a beginning." Worse than that. He became ashamed of it and in later
years refused to talk about it to interviewers. He does write in his
autobiography, "My first book—that virginal try at free-lance pro-
fessionalism—was as unfulfilling as are most virginal breakthroughs
in whatever pursuit. In the absence of entire evidence I can't say it
is the worst book ever written, but I've long considered it is a con-
tender. Hard-cover publishers put it out under the title, *Murders
at Moon Dance*. A soft-cover house renamed it *Trouble at Moon
Dance*. Under any name, the thought of this trash troubles me.
When I see it displayed on paperback racks, where it somehow sur-
vives, I turn away."

It garnered only a few reviews. Isaac Anderson, in his "Crime
Corner" column in the *New York Times*, summarized the book as

"a combination western yarn and detective story and not an outstanding example of either." After Guthrie's death, the well-known Western writer William Kittredge was asked by the family to write an introduction to a new edition of *Murders at Moon Dance*. While he felt some obligation to the memory of an old friend, he was reluctant: "I didn't know what to say. Guthrie had repudiated this book himself."

The plot is simple and typical of the pulp Western. The setting is the western community of Moon Dance, a small cow town patterned after Choteau. The hero is West Cawinne, who solves the mystery surrounding a series of murders, kills the bad guy, wins the pretty girl, and rides off into the sunset. A central incident involves the mob violence that erupts in response to the kidnapping of a young woman. The citizens of Moon Dance suspect that someone from Breedtown is responsible—Breedtown is a shantytown outside of Moon Dance that does shelter some outlaws but is home mostly to people of mixed blood. The men from Moon Dance go on a rampage, beating and burning, and are barely turned away from lynching.

Kittredge in his introduction notes that "when people are threatened, however good they may be, they are capable of terrible things. In *Murders at Moon Dance* Guthrie graphically demonstrates the dangers inherent in the use of vigilante violence (again, revenge) to restore civil order, anticipating Walter Van Tilburg Clark's antimythological story, *The Ox-Bow Incident*." It did not really anticipate Clark's novel—that was published three years prior to Guthrie's, and we know that Guthrie read it and was impressed by it. Whether it had any influence on the writing of his own novel is an open question.

Kittredge goes on to say,

Murders at Moon Dance, if it had been written by a writer

of less accomplishment, probably wouldn't interest many beyond hardcore Western fans. But it's Guthrie at the beginning. It gives us chance to examine his first attempts at artistry, and his efforts to begin making sense of the ways our determination to stand up for justice and communality work to foster violence.

The example of his life, and his later books, are gifts to us all in our own struggle with the same huge problems. *The Big Sky* is a brilliantly articulated story about the way the impulse to violence worked out (and continues to work out) in the American West.

Just the American West? How often have our national leaders identified themselves, in dress and speech, with the lawman and gunfighter, who is, in Kittredge's words, "A man who will solve our problems with violence"?

As Charles E. Hood has noted in his thesis on Guthrie, the author's technique in *Murders at Moon Dance* "is an unhappy combination of journalese and pulp fiction." Guthrie's character names are parodies—among them Seldom Wright, Bally Buck, and Tandy Deck—apparently to show that the author does not take his narrative too seriously. In his later books, Guthrie developed the technique of including description inconspicuously in his interior monologue, into the thoughts, words, or actions of his characters. But in his first novel, his descriptions are separate from his characters as if, in Hood's words, "they are being provided by some invisible on-the-scene reporter." The result is a rather unsteady narrative with mysterious intrusions.

Guthrie's fictional town of Moon Dance is based in large part on Choteau. There actually was, however, a Breedtown, which was located on the south fork of the Teton River near Choteau. Its inhabitants were, according to Bud's childhood friend George

Coffey, Indians and half-bloods who lived in some fifty cabins. In the novel the town is burned to the ground, but in fact, it simply died out over the years. Several of the novel's characters are patterned after Choteau residents, including Judge LaFrance, who in Moon Dance is a justice of the peace and harness maker, and who is based on a Judge DeHaas of Choteau. Another childhood friend, George Jackson, claimed when interviewed that he recognized many of the locations in the book and even recognized certain opinions in the novel as coming out of discussions that he and Guthrie had had while "hashing things over" during hunting or fishing trips as teenagers.

During their years in Lexington, the Guthrie family had a routine that centered on Bud and his work. Working for an afternoon paper, he would get up early in the morning and then come home in mid-afternoon, take a nap, and then join the family for dinner. He would start on his fiction writing at night. According to his daughter, her father would dominate the dinner hour, telling stories and asking riddles. "I would fall for every one of them," Helen recalled. What weighs more—a pound of feathers or a pound of lead? Can you tell me the difference between "further" and "farther" just using two words? Further degree, farther distance. And he would always correct the children's grammar and usage. Helen remembered, "You had to speak correctly all the time. You couldn't misspeak. If you tried to tell him the house was on fire and you said it incorrectly, he would stop you in mid-sentence. It didn't matter what calamity might be taking place."

Bert, who was six and a half years older than Helen, would tease her at the dinner table: "He would say, 'Look over there, watch Dad out the window,' and in the meantime he would be dumping a piece of potato into my milk or something. Awful stuff that would make me furious. My mother would just say, 'Don't let it get to you. He won't do it anymore.' Well, bull. He would do it some more because he got away with it. But dinner hour was reserved for the family, always."

In the summer, when the family was together in Montana, they would get their horses at Tom Larson's ranch and ride up to Twin Lakes. Helen recalled they would "take a 15 mile ride, ride the horses up, and get off at the Mormon school house." She remembered, "My mother would have packed a fried chicken lunch. . . . My brother, my father, and I and some other people rode into the mountains a couple of times, into the Bob Marshall Wilderness, and one time my mother went with us."

Bert recalled his mother as wonderful, everything a mother should be. But looking back, Helen felt sorry for her to the extent that she was a victim of her time, a time before women's liberation. Before she was married, because of her father's prominence, she was known as one of the Larson girls. Then she married Bud, and when he rose to prominence, she was known as the wife of A. B. Guthrie. She was, Helen has said, "very astute, witty, very popular, and [an] outgoing person. Liked to entertain and cook. . . . She never had a job. Friends of the Library, sewing circle. Guess they were typical in those days. Would drive me nuts. She should have had a job. She was smart. She was a good editor. She looked at his stuff first."

Helen was not interested in learning to sew and cook. She was interested in literature and enjoyed talking about books with her father. While she was growing up, she recalled, "He adored me." She majored in English at Montana State University and then became an editor. Bert, on the other hand, was not interested in literary things, perhaps, as he has said, because he wasn't good at them. "My formative years were fine. My Dad was in the newspaper business. We lived in Kentucky. But then when he started achieving some notoriety with his writing, why, I wasn't interested in that at all." since he was a toddler, Bert had spent his summers with his grandfather on his ranch; he majored in agriculture at Iowa State University and then, after serving in the Army, he became a rancher.

In 1944 Guthrie was taken ill and went to a hospital in Lexington. During a two-week stay he was diagnosed as having encephalitis, sometimes called "sleeping sickness." He took a leave from his job, and he and his wife travelled to Montana, where, on the ranch of his father-in-law, Tom Larson, he rested to regain his health. He did recover, and much more quickly than predicted by his doctors. After returning to Lexington, he got back to his desk, "to assignments, colored notes [a section in the newspaper], telephone, daily copy, headlines, makeup, editorials."

At about this time, he was determined to make another, serious attempt at a second novel. He had already decided on the subject: it would be about "the mountain man in the period from say, about 1830 through the high years of his rule to about 1843, to the time of his self-wrought ruin." He wrote, "I would tell of the fur-hunters who followed hard on the heels of Lewis and Clark. . . . By boat and by horse and by foot we'd penetrate, my men and I, the surprised wilderness." A key phrase here is "his self-wrought ruin." One of his main themes in this novel, as in his other serious novels, would be that man always destroys the thing he loves. Man loves the wilderness, exalts in nature, but always manages to ruin it. So he had his theme even before he started on his first serious draft.

Bud apparently started actually writing that draft in 1944 after he came back to Lexington from his convalescence at Tom Larson's ranch. But it is clear that he had been planning his manuscript much earlier. His father wrote to him in January of 1943:

"Sure, call on me, if I can do any research for you. Specify particular points. I shall be glad to do it—more than glad. As far as I recall, you expect to cover in your book one man's life-span, beginning, you state in your recent letter, in the university library, and to clear up doubtful points" (1/18/43).

Two weeks later, he wrote, "Glad to have your outline for your new story. You had already given me the more important information about it. On the point of the railroad survey, there is the matter of date. When does the main character come west? How long is his career?" His father goes on for two pages to describe what he has found out about the various railroad surveys and accompanying treaties with the Indians. He recommends M. A. Leeson's *History of Montana, 1739–1885* as the best account of the earlier history of the state. He concludes, "Well, big success to you, son, in all you undertake; especially big success for your newest venture, the story of the man who killed his own goose" (1/31/43).

Bud went ahead with a determination to be wholly honest about his characters and what they did, to get at the whole truth—unlike the other books about the frontier, which heroized their characters and glossed over the unpleasant aspects of mountain-man life. He started his extensive research with a small but select library of early West histories. He moved on to materials borrowed from the university library, some of which were recommended by his father. Later, after the book's publication, he stated that he had done so much research that he had to take notes on his notes. By the time he was through, he had shoeboxes full of three-by-five color-coded cards.

A neighbor and close friend, Tom Clark, a professional historian, recalled,

> When Bud finally found the direction in which he wanted
> to go, he began gathering materials for *The Big Sky*. He

did his research as carefully as a historian, and perhaps even more so. He sensed in his new project its importance in opening the advance into the Far West. Again he gathered books, maps, and information wherever he could find them. I was impressed with the care with which he checked his materials on a series of maps which he kept. I am reasonably sure that he was the first man to locate precisely all of the rendezvous sites [where the mountain men gathered every year]. He came to think like the mountain men, and at times I thought he felt that he was in a way, vicariously at least, a reincarnation of Boone Caudill.

But over the months, writing at night after exhausting days of running a newspaper, the manuscript that he came up with was not at all satisfying: "After writing three chapters I suspect my imagined reader had quit me. I couldn't blame him. My copy stank."

He decided that it was past time to seek help. Some experienced writers may advise to just sit at your desk in front of your typewriter, and something will come out. But what? What if it is terrible? He needed someone with a knowledgeable eye who could point to what he was doing wrong. There were so many possibilities, and he was not aware of any of them. But help would come soon.

Two old friends were nagging him to reapply for a Nieman Fellowship—John F. Day, whom Bud had hired when Day graduated from college and who went on to *Time-Life*, and Paul J. Hughes, from the *Louisville Courier-Journal*, whom he met when they were both covering the legislature at Frankfort. Both men were recipients of the fellowships and raved to Bud about the opportunities—the courses, the contacts, the books, and even the good conversations. Maybe most of all was the "opportunity for a man to draw back and have a cool look at himself." So he reapplied and then faced the selection committee of two in Louisville.

The interview with Arthur Schlesinger Sr. and Louis M. Lyons (director of the program) went well. But Bud thought the interview was too short and too convivial—probably just a courtesy to the two former fellows who had recommended him. Nevertheless, after a few weeks of thinking the worst, he found that the committee had approved him.

The most important factors leading to his eventual success as a writer were his capacity for hard work, his unflagging persistence, and his tenure as a Nieman fellow for a year at Harvard. And the latter made all the difference. Bud has declared, "It was the big break." Tom Clark recalled, "I remember so well the afternoon when I came home from work and the great mother's helper, Guthrie, yelled over that he had been given a Nieman Fellowship and was going to Harvard. This was a major landmark in his life. There he came into contact with several people who either impressed him or gave him real assistance. Among those were Frederick Merk, Arthur M. Schlesinger, Sr., and Ted Morrison. Too, he met and formed a fast friendship with Bernard DeVoto. These new friends and the environment surrounding the Nieman fellow had a marked influence on Bud."

In the fall of 1944, Bud, Harriet, and the two children, now ages five and eleven, left for Cambridge in an old Nash Rambler. It was a difficult trip, especially at the end, when they got to Cambridge. They couldn't find the Commander Hotel, and no one they stopped to ask knew where it was. They drove around in circles until they finally ran across it. They had a reservation for only two days and, in that time, had to find housing in a very tight housing market.

Lists of vacancies were provided daily by the university, offering far fewer places than could accommodate those looking to rent. It was a race. Harriet studied a city map and took up the competition by car or with cab drivers; she sometimes even went out by foot to scout out a place. Meanwhile, Bud, happy to give up the duty to his wife, looked after the kids and fed the pigeons in the Commons. First, much to their relief, she found a room with two beds in a dilapidated house, which kept them off the street for a few days; then a small apartment with floors slanting off in all directions that they had to vacate after a month; and finally an apartment owned by a retired school superintendent that they could have for the nine months they would be in Cambridge. But it was a close thing. The apartment owner was very reluctant to rent to a family with children; however, being the son of a school superintendent, Bud had much to talk about to his presumptive landlord and made a good impression.

CHAPTER SIX

The Big Break—the Nieman Fellowship

The first few weeks in Cambridge were a nervous time for the Guthrie family. Not knowing where you can lay your head is one thing, but not knowing whether or not your wife and children are going to have a roof over their heads for the night is yet another. However, as it turned out, the Harvard experience was well worth the initial anxiety. Everything— classes, faculty, and library—was open to the Nieman fellows. But beyond these opportunities, there was also association with the other nine fellows, all of whom were interesting and, in their own ways, distinguished.

Among them was one of the best rural newspapermen in the country, Houstoun Waring, editor of the *Littleton Independent* in Colorado. Then there was Nathan Robertson of *PM*, who Guthrie considered to be "so far to the left as to affront reason." He recalled, "Though never winning me over, he made me re-examine and alter my thinking." Kendall Foss, from *Time* magazine, had a "well-informed mind, by far the most intricate and involved to be found in the group." Also among them was William H. Clark of the *Boston Globe*, a reserved man with a quiet, dry wit. Guthrie observed that "unlike some or even most of the rest, he was a conservative." These were only some of Guthrie's colleagues, whom he described as "keen newspapermen," one and all. (As a commentary on the time, we can note now that were no women included, although there were many distinguished newswomen scattered around the country.)

The director of the Nieman Fellowship program, or the curator as he was called, was Louis Lyons, a former newspaperman. He was a patient and thoughtful man who became a friend and advisor to Bud and the others, and knowing Harvard, he knew where and how and to whom to direct them. In his initial interview with Guthrie, Lyons recalled that Guthrie told him he wanted to write a novel and had a few chapters already written: "Then 43, he had done some fiction 'pulps,' he said. In applying for the fellowship, besides indicating the studies he wanted as background for his newspaper work—which is the purpose of the fellowships—he proposed a major piece of writing. This was accepted. To his studies in international affairs, he added Frederick Merk's American history course—The Western Movement—then the broadest sweep of American history at Harvard—and a writing course with Theodore Morrison. Merk's course gave him background, in addition to his own Montana youth and Kentucky milieu."

To help Bud with his research, Lyons promised to arrange for him to have a carrel on the same floor as the western Americana collection in the Widener Library. When Bud told him that he needed help—"What I am hoping for is a coach"—Lyons suggested that he talk to Ted Morrison, who he thought would be a good advisor. Morrison was head of the writing program at Harvard.

When Bud met with him, he found Morrison to be a tall, slim, handsome man with a short haircut, tweed coat, and khakis and a quiet Ivy League manner. Bud notes that he was friendly but reserved. Morrison agreed to advise him on his project and asked him to bring him the pages that he had written.

Bud recalled that when he saw him later, after Morrison had read his manuscript, his advisor told him,

> The best part . . . were the bits of internal monologue, the passages in which I held closest to my protagonist. "Internal monologue" was a phrase new to me. As he went on, I recognized that "best" was a relative term. Best of a bad lot. My distance from my character necessarily would vary, he said, but did I want to divorce him completely, as in my descriptions? Would an unlettered country boy have thought of "cirrus" clouds and "sluggard" suns? (God Almighty).
>
> I had written of the boy, "He was hungry." Well, maybe all right, Morrison said. Sometimes the quickest and flattest way of expression justified itself in the context, though it had no appeal to the senses and smacked of authorial intrusion besides. But what if I substituted for that dead declaration of hunger: "He thought of the corn dodger and spring greens Ma might be fixing"?
>
> I make Ted sound blunter and more positive than he was, and I have shown only a few, ready grains of his seeding. He was always considerate, kindly and tentative in his words of disturbance and never authoritative, being the first to admit and announce that if a thing worked, then it worked, and that was all there was to it.
>
> Lesson One, I thought as I came away from that first meeting with him. Food for thought. I had a time digesting it.

Morrison was the right coach, although it took about six weeks for Bud to figure out what he was talking about. Morrison was wise enough to know that a writing teacher cannot dictate, he can only suggest, and suggestion can seem very vague to a bewildered student. Bud recalled, "I would go home after a session and torture my brain. What was it he meant? What really was wrong, what really had he suggested?"

His mental turmoil ended when a sudden insight came to him after he and his wife went to a movie in Boston, an incredibly bad one. Reflecting on the movie, which was terribly overacted, he realized that one of the things that his coach was trying to tell him was that he was showing off, or as he put it later, "hamming" it up. Then Morrison led him to realize over time that as a newspaperman, he brought several handicaps to his writing of fiction. He needed to get rid of "journalese," language and patterns of language that he had developed as a newsman, and in that connection he had to learn to show and not tell, which, as he said, is "a difficult achievement in any case and more difficult in the case of a newspaperman who had spent his life telling."

These were points that Morrison drove home—as he recalled, deciding that Guthrie faced one serious obstacle when he began writing *The Big Sky*: "As has happened before and since, his very success and distinction as a journalist did not stand him in good stead when he turned to historical fiction. He had to learn, or revive his knowledge of, the crucial differences between these two forms. But he had *The Big Sky* in him, and after a time it began to write itself naturally."

These lessons dictated that Bud had to forget himself. He had to let his characters tell their own stories, and while identifying with them, he had to let them act on their own as they would. To do that he had to inhabit his characters, to merge with them, and to lose his own identity for a time. He had to leave his present time and place and go back in spirit to the time he loved, the time he was writing about. He recalled, "When I rewrote the first chapters of *The Big Sky*, I don't think I used a word of the same prose, although some situations were the same. When I finally was satisfied with the first chapter, it had been rewritten 12 times."

But according to Morrison, it was more than just a matter of rewriting the first chapter over and over again. The big change in the direction of Guthrie's writing of the manuscript came when Morrison pointed out to him that, with the appearance of Jim Deakins in chapter 3, a rightness came into the manuscript that hadn't been there before. There was a naturalness in that chapter that led Morrison to recommend that Guthrie go back and try to emulate it in the preceding chapters. And so the rewriting began and went on until Guthrie was satisfied that he had brought the early chapters into harmony with the method and tone of chapter 3. It wasn't easy.

Morrison's help, however, did not end with bringing that moment of enlightenment to Bud. Morrison commented on every succeeding chapter, even after Guthrie left Cambridge to return to Lexington and they had to correspond by mail. He was a remarkably selfless man.

Further evidence of that selflessness came after Bud made a suggestion. He realized that although the Nieman program was wonderful, it had a rather glaring omission. Within the program they would expand their horizons, but there was nothing in it that helped the newsmen become better writers. When Bud expressed this concern to Louis Lyons, Lyons agreed. How about a weekly seminar? Maybe Ted Morrison would conduct it? Incredibly, as Bud recalled, "Morrison would. Without extra pay, at the cost of his own work as poet and novelist, without much recognition except from all nine of the ten of us who participated, he gave what he had to give. It was not insubstantial."

Morrison himself has written that he considered the request a "flattering but alarming privilege." He could remember that in the seminar, what he called a "shop course," they considered magazine articles, editorials, short stories, and verse. He added, "Undeniably the lucky excitement of this first seminar was the chance to hear a succession of chapters of Guthrie's novel, later published as *The Big Sky*. Guthrie's extraordinary talent for fiction, a talent as natural as water finding its level, has been widely recognized; he has permanently enriched the record of America in his novels. But I should like to pay him a tribute on another score, too, as a generous human being, interested not only in his own success but in the success of others, notably newspapermen."

Guthrie told a reporter after he had finished the novel, "I work painfully. . . . I bleed." Ambitious, hardworking, anxious to learn, Guthrie pushed on with his manuscript: "Word by word and line by line my manuscript proceeded. Not in bursts, though, for me, writing is a slow and painful business. It demands concentration and search and presents the obstacles of dissatisfaction with what could be said better. And there's no immediate reward in putting words on paper. The reward, great but fugitive, is in having written, in having found the word, the line, the paragraph, the chapter that is as good as ever you can make it. I spent a full day on one line of dialogue and knocked off satisfied."

He never outlined, thinking that he would be imprisoned in an outline. Rather, he let his characters carry him forward—his "characters made themselves what they were." They assumed a kind of vitality and life of their own as they began to assert themselves. He remembered, "In my first chapter of *The Big Sky*, I hadn't even thought about Jim Deakins. Or Teal Eye. Don't call this inspiration; rather it is an inner organization of the subconscious reserved for writers."

In the constant labor and lonely business of writing, how can one force oneself daily to face the typewriter? Guthrie's solution was threefold. He could adopt the technique that Hemingway made famous (although it has certainly been used by many others): if you know where you are going, leave something as a start for the next day. His second method was to gain momentum in the morning by retyping the last page of what he had written the evening before. And, third, he would fool himself by telling himself that he would work just a half hour. That would help him start, but he would seldom stop after just that half hour.

He was doing so well with his writing during his Harvard year (he had finished two fifths of the eventual manuscript) that his Nieman was extended for two months. The extension was granted at his request so he could attend the Bread Loaf Writers' Conference, run by Morrison, in Vermont. He and Harriet decided that she and the children would go on to Montana. Bud recalled, "The two months I spent there were lonely. Family gone, Nieman friends gone, classrooms, professors, seminars gone. There remained, not for me to impose on overmuch, Ted Morrison, Louis Lyons, Benny DeVoto, Charlie Morton of the *Atlantic Monthly* and the few non-academic friends we had made. There remained the Widener Library and the typewriter with its demands on me." He moved into a residence hall and spent the first part of the summer in Cambridge, and then in August went to Vermont for the conference.

Referring to the seminars at Harvard that Bud had suggested, Morrison recalled, "His contribution was to offer for my comments the evolving chapters of a novel he was writing. Not often in a lifetime, I venture, does a more exciting project cross a teacher's desk. I formed my own judgment as the manuscript progressed, but I wanted a professional check on my enthusiasm, and I naturally thought of Bread Loaf as a testing ground for the still unfinished work. Guthrie came to the Conference as a Fellow in 1945, and I turned his script over to William Sloane, a staff member then conducting his own publishing business."

The Bread Loaf Writers' Conference started in the 1920s as a summer session for high school English teachers to help them update their knowledge and skills. By the end of the decade, it was drifting more and more toward a conference that emphasized creative writing. Ted Morrison became director in 1932 and set about inviting not only prominent writers to serve on the staff, but also editors, publishers, critics, and literary agents. In his mind the conference should be practical, to help writers write better, but also get published.

The conference had teams that specialized in fiction, nonfiction, and poetry. A poet and fiction writer himself, Morrison felt deeply that there should be a crossover—that fiction writers could learn from poetry and vice-versa. The activities at the conference were both educational and social. There were meetings of the conference staff and attendees as a whole, usually for the purpose of listening to a guest lecturer. There were meetings of the fiction, nonfiction, and poetry staffs and students, where individual works were read aloud and discussed. And there were private, one-on-one tutoring sessions between staff members and individual aspiring writers. The social events ranged from softball games and tennis matches, to hikes in the surroundings countryside, and evening social hours and parties. There were also plenty of opportunities for the fellows and students to talk to staff members, sometimes at length and frequently.

Bud was particularly drawn to conversations with Bernard DeVoto and Robert Frost. He had become acquainted with both of them at Cambridge, and he acknowledged that he was initially awed by their reputations and was hesitant to approach them. By appearance, DeVoto was intimidating. Short and stocky, with thick glasses and a pugnacious, square face, he was vocal and opinionated. He was, of course, by this time a famous historian who specialized in the very period of American history, the western movement that Bud was writing about. He remembered his thoughts about DeVoto at the conference:

> Except for a couple of casual encounters I hardly knew him at that time. A difficult man, a curmudgeon, given to extremes and tantrums, he made me uneasy, and uneasier still because he was an authority on the early West, a student with knowledge undoubtedly far beyond mine even in application to the limited years I'd researched. Fortunately, I didn't know that in a sense I had stolen his subject, and was writing the kind of novel he had long wanted to write and perhaps would have written already but for a growing shakiness of faith in himself as a writer of fiction. . . .
>
> Another man might have resented my usurpation of his western preserve, might have cried down through vexation the kind of a novel he'd had in mind before. Not DeVoto. He read *The Big Sky* in manuscript and promptly beat all the drums to promote it.

Frost was also difficult. Even with the fame that had come to him by this time, he was a very insecure man. Unlike in the photos of later years, when he looks short and stooped over, he was at this time tall and robust, a big, rumpled-looking man with a shock of snow-white hair and a face with large features. Bud remembers that he "could be and often was the captive of fierce and aberrant passions. . . . Staff members with experience of him walked on tiptoe, wondering whether this or that would enrage or please Robert." But he and Bud got along well—he was always friendly and kind. Bud suspected that might be because, as a fiction writer, he offered no competition. Bud found Frost to be a great conversationalist, not talky but often hitting the target with a cryptic comment. He talked, Bud recalled, "about and was wont in his inquiring way to enlarge on little things."

Toward the end of his time at Bread Loaf, Bud was asked to meet with Bill Sloane. Bud went to his appointment with some trepidation. He knew that Morrison had given his manuscript-in-progress to Sloane for his opinion of it. At five o'clock that afternoon, Bud found Sloane sitting with the manuscript before him. The editor lit his pipe, paused, and asked Bud how near he was to being through. How long would it take him to finish? Bud wasn't sure because he had to go back to work at the *Leader*. Then Sloane told him that the manuscript was very good, in fact, really great stuff, and offered him a five-thousand-dollar advance. Bud was stunned but also jubilant—he had never contemplated that amount of money in one pile before. He rushed to find the single phone at Bread Loaf in order to wire his wife: "Swinging on a star. Five thousand in advance."

After the conference was over, Bud stayed several days with the Morrisons at their small farm just outside of Bread Loaf; Frost's summer home was only a few hundred yards away. After Frost's wife, Elinor, died in 1938, Ted's wife, Kay, became Frost's secretary and manager for the remaining twenty-five years of his life. She assured him of the hospitality and friendship at the conference for as long as it lasted. The Morrisons had arranged for Frost to buy the Homer Noble Farm, which they had been renting. They stayed the summer in the main farmhouse, while Frost stayed in a cottage on the farm just up the road.

Sometimes Bud trudged up to Frost's place, and occasionally Frost would come down to the Morrison's. Once during a heavy rainstorm, Bud was surprised when Frost showed up at the door in a slicker, rain hat, and gumboots. They all sat by the fire and shared a long afternoon talking and exchanging stories. Talk sessions with Frost at Bread Loaf or the farmhouse sometimes lasted until the early morning; sometimes they were cut short when he would suddenly depart—no one could guess why. Had someone said something to offend him?

Frost's poetry was Guthrie's favorite—interesting, because Guthrie's father, of another generation, loved it, and for a long time Bud couldn't imagine why. Later in life, the three photos on Bud's office wall were of Morrison, DeVoto, and Frost.

During all of this, of course, World War II was going on. Bud had to scrounge up extra ration stamps in order to get the tires and gas that enabled the family to drive from Lexington to Cambridge. Slightly illegal, it made him feel guilty even though it was necessary. But he felt even worse when the foundation had to raise the age limit because so many young men had to go to war. He had been too young for the first war and too old for the second. After the conference and his return to Lexington, he got news from his wife of Choteau's celebration of the end of the war (V-J Day, the surrender of Japan, came on September 2): "Choteau began celebrating the minute the news came over the radio and they weren't to be outdone. Everybody in the neighborhood rushed uptown and joined in the big parade. All the church bells were ringing, the siren was blowing and they even got out the fire truck. It was no time until almost every establishment was displaying a big flag out front. Many, especially the young girls with men overseas, were wild with joy. It was quite a show just driving up and down the street seeing how different ones were taking it."

Once he had returned to Lexington, Bud went back to work at the *Leader* as its executive editor. Although he considered his pay to be low (as was the custom on most newspapers at the time), he was grateful to the paper because the management had been generous in so many other ways. The paper had paid him in full during the months of his illness, given him four-week vacations, had cosigned his mortgage at the bank when he bought his house, and had given him his Nieman year off with pay to supplement his fellowship. So even though he knew that, with the approval that came with his advance, he would eventually leave newspaper work, he was compelled to go back—and go back with gratitude.

On his return, his boss, General Manager Fred B. Wachs, told him to manage his schedule to leave time to work on his novel: work an hour or two, or half a day, whatever time it took to give needed direction to the staff and then go home and tackle the typewriter. He would still receive his salary. This incredible generosity suggests indirectly a number of things about Guthrie at this stage: that he was a very capable manager, that a number of people had faith in his writing ability, and that he was a very likable guy.

Tom Clark recalled, "When he came home *The Big Sky* to all intents and purposes had been finished. He had signed a contract with Henry Holt, but in the interval Henry Holt was sold to Texas millionaires, and Bill Sloane, now editor of the Rutgers Press, and a group had withdrawn to form their own company. One of the books they took with them was *The Big Sky*. In many ways this no doubt was a fortunate thing. The new publishers pushed their best book, and with good results."

By "finished" Clark meant that the manuscript was on its way. It was still only about two fifths completed when Guthrie got to Lexington, and it would take more than another year to finish. But while he was in the last stretch on the novel in September of

1946, a nervous constriction of the throat manifested itself so severely that it led him to go once again to the Mayo Clinic. He wrote to his father:

> My wire to you told just about all the Mayo verdict as to my health. Lungs, gall bladder, stomach, gullet, throat, blood, heart and kidneys, all were examined and found to be normal. My trouble appears to be entirely of nervous origin. Dr. Brown said I was like an engine on which the timing had slipped, with the result that the engine ran badly although every part was of itself all right. To my relief, he told me that functional irregularities like mine NEVER led to organic troubles. He offered no cure for my condition, and very little medication. He said I had an unusually good understanding of the case and that, largely of and by myself, I would find the remedy for it; that is, that I would find the way to tranquility, which itself is the cure for nerves. Well, maybe so, though tranquility is mighty hard to catch. Anyhow, I have been feeling much better and more assured as a result of the examination. (9/24/46)

He also reported to his father that he had reached an understanding with the *Leader* about his tenure. He would stay on until the first of the year or shortly thereafter in order to get things in shape so that his departure would be painless. He wanted to leave it a well-functioning newsroom.

That November he finished *The Big Sky*, or as he put it, the manuscript got itself completed:

> Hours and weeks and months of slave labor went into it. Working, I could look back on what I had done with some satisfaction, but what remained to be done appalled me.

. . . I had a theme, not original, that each man kills the thing he loves. If it had any originality at all, it was only that a band of men, the fur hunters, killed the life they loved and killed it with a thoughtless prodigality perhaps unmatched. Yet in the absence of an outline the typewriter was errant or balky. It produced pages of junk or no pages at all. I cursed it day after day.

When the end of the writing did finally come, he was exhausted. Taking the manuscript to New York, he felt numb to any reaction to it that might come from the editors. As a matter of fact, his mind was elsewhere. He was thinking about the Oregon Trail and a new book, which became *The Way West*. He had become a writer.

But he needn't have been concerned about the publisher's reaction, in any event—the manuscript got an enthusiastic reception, as did he when he arrived in New York. But back from New York in Lexington, he was still unsettled in his mind, still looking for tranquility, and as he surveyed his life on his birthday in January, he was not at all satisfied with himself. Even though they were together in Lexington, he wrote to his wife:

Dear Mrs. Guthrie:

Forty-six seems a good age for a summing up, and I seem a good subject.

Looking at myself, I am painfully conscious of failures to be the man and husband and father I ought to be. I know that I don't give enough time to the children, or patience, or understanding. I know I don't get the enjoyment from them that I should. I know I have failed you many times, in little things and big. Sometimes I wonder that you have retained any respect for me at all; if you have, it is out of your own generosity of judgment.

I have had a lot of fun with whiskey in my life—and a lot of woe. Looking back again, I believe most of the unkind and foolish and regrettable things said and done have been said and done when my alcoholic content was high. I know very well that the payment, in remorse and lowered health, has far exceeded the fun. More, as I grow older I appear to be losing both physical tolerance for alcohol and reasonable judgment as to its use. It is a condition I can't explain; I only know that it exists. I am not fearful of becoming an alcoholic. Neither my constitution nor my temperament would permit of that. But I am concerned that I show so little sense.

At forty-six, I hope to do better. I shall try to do better. I shall do better. I am not making any high resolves or imposing any Spartan limitations on myself. I am just promising to do better. I realize, in the very act of promising, that I shan't be able to execute my intentions entirely. No one does, I think; certainly I never have. In some, I hope, large degree I shall do so, however. And when and if I fall short now and then of the standard I should like to set, will you remember that not always do I understand myself? At times there is so much inexplicable unease in me, so much of fret and ferment, that I behave in ways that shame me later. I am afraid that inward restlessness, aroused by causes I am in the total dark about, has increased as I have grown older. I am afraid it is the reason of my drinking too much on occasion. Alcohol does give some momentary relaxation. But there are other ways, and better ways, of arriving at tranquility—and I propose to find them.

There are many other things in my mind and heart, details and ramifications and additions to what I have said—but you know now all that I am feeling. With your intuitive understanding you don't need a bill of particulars.

So I shall close this summing up with a re-expression of the large and essential truth. I want you always to love me, for I shall love you always. It is because I shall that I want to meet your hopes and expectations. Above everything I want you to be happy in your life with me; unless you are, there can be no happiness for me anywhere.

Yours, with a stricken conscience, Bud (1/13/47)

Although he continued for some time in emotional turmoil, his manuscript went ahead at his publisher, William Sloane Associates. Without any major revisions, Bud's typed pages went quickly into galley proofs. He sent a set of them to his father, who was staying with Bud's sister, Jane, in Missoula. She recalled, "I was in the hospital having a baby when *The Big Sky* was about to be published. Dad brought some of the proofs with him to the hospital, and I remember he went, 'tsk, tsk,' at some of the risqué parts because he didn't think that anyone in my condition should be reading them. But he was very proud."

Asked for a blurb for advertising purposes, Benny DeVoto wrote to Bud after sending a statement to the publisher: "Quite simply, yours is the best novel I've read in at least ten years and there was no reason why I should not say so. It is a gorgeous job and I congratulate and envy you with a full heart. What I cannot understand is how a man with so little fiction behind him can be so technically expert" (12/26/46). This was the man who for years had taught fiction writing at Bread Loaf.

The title of the book was for a time a puzzle that searched for a solution, something that would be just right. Bud and his wife and other members of his family, his editors, and even Ted Morrison racked their brains for something but came up with nothing. Finally, Bill Sloane said forget about it for now—just send me some autobiographical notes. And it was from these notes that Sloane came up the title. Bud had mentioned his father's first day in Montana, when he stood under the big sky and exclaimed, "By George, I'm free." You have got your title, Sloane told Bud, and from Bud's father came not only the book title but, afterward, the state motto of Montana.

Explaining how he was led to write *The Big Sky*, Guthrie told an interviewer just before publication: "The West has always interested me, both as a place to be and one to read about. I have known a good many Indians, too—Crees and Piegans and part bloods. They have been workmates on Montana sheep and cattle ranches. I have hunted arrowheads at buffalo runs and lugged sun-bleached bull skulls home from the prairie and imagined the wallows occupied again and the plains brown with humped backs. From my father I learned to enjoy history of the westward movement particularly."

CHAPTER SEVEN

The Big Sky Triumph and Tracking *The Way West*

*T*he Big Sky was published in the spring of 1947. It was an immediate success, and the success almost overwhelmed a troubled author: "I wasn't prepared for the praise the published book got. Me, an important new author? Me, a fresh voice out of the West? Me? I read the reviews and looked at the pictures and, though pleased, felt somehow diminished while my family rejoiced. Though my being had gone into it, the book wasn't mine now, and what comments were made about it were like voices heard in the distance. Here I was, apart from it, and tomorrow I would fall on my face."

As *The Big Sky* began to catch on as a result of almost universal critical praise, Bud received a flock of invitations. Bookstores wanted him for signings, periodicals for interviews, literary groups and community organizations for luncheons and cocktail parties. It was exciting but troubling for someone who still had some fear facing an audience. He thought it was his duty, for the sake of sales and out of courtesy, to accept as many invitations as possible. Later, he decided that had been a mistake and that he should have stayed where he belonged—with his typewriter.

Nearly every major periodical reviewed the book, as did newspapers large and small across the country, and most praised it, some extravagantly. Book review sections in several newspapers gave their full front pages to *The Big Sky*, while the *Saturday Review of Literature* put Guthrie's picture on its cover. Many reviewers wrote that the book was certain to become a classic; many said that it should win the Pulitzer Prize. Joseph Kinsey Howard said in the *New York Times Book Review*, "Until—and unless—a better one comes along, *The Big Sky* is the outstanding novel about the time and country with which it deals." In the *New York Herald Tribune*, Dorothy Canfield Fisher wrote, "A monument of a book! One of those monuments made out of rough boulders, native to the spot, rolled together to serve as a pedestal for a towering bronze figure of epic size." And the *Atlantic* review praised the novel, writing, "There are passages of sheer poetry that suggest Carl Sandburg while remaining entirely Guthrie; passages that one is tempted to quote at length for the sheer joy of transcribing them." *Time* magazine said, "Author Guthrie's mountain men—buffalo hunters, trappers and guides—are seen, smelt, and heard with a consistency and solidity of understanding that makes most other writing about them seem perfunctory or fake."

There were a few reviewers who pointed to what might be called "technical faults" in the novel. Margaret Marshall, in the *Nation*, regretted that Guthrie applied a realistic technique to material the reality of which cannot be captured by the documentary method. His "mountain men would be more believable if they were more legendary. . . . The spirit of the West, whatever it was, has escaped him—partly I think because he used a realistic trap." And in the

New Yorker, J. M. Lalley also criticized the book: "His purpose is to portray these trappers, or mountain men . . . as they really were, which requires as much attention to their barbaric vices as to their romantic resourcefulness and fortitude. But Mr. Guthrie comes very close to defeating this purpose by employing in his descriptive passages a prose that is startlingly like the costumes of his characters—a sort of sturdy buck-skin dialect lavishly embellished with poetical foofaraw."

But Bud's friends were universally pleased with the book and the author's achievement. Tom Clark recalled, "We were so proud and thrilled at Bud's success. He made the rest of us piddlers seem like country boys with ink on our fingers. The book had a wonderful sale, and the movie contract lifted the Guthries well out of the doldrums of [their] depression."

H. G. Merriam, Bud's creative writing teacher, felt that the book would be the last word on its subject. In an interview he said, "It will be hard for anyone to write a better novel about the mountain man than *The Big Sky*. It is the definitive book. Do you know what I mean by that? I mean that nobody's going to write a better one."

Such applause from critics and friends however appreciated were not regarded by Bud to be the apogee. "The best compliment [he] ever had" on *The Big Sky* or on any of his other books was given to him by a passing acquaintance in Lexington. He congratulated Guthrie on the publication of his book and remarked, "You know, to look at you, a man wouldn't think you could do it."

While there was a generally positive critical response to the novel and good sales, there was also a puritanical reaction from some readers who objected to Guthrie's realism (a realism about sexuality, violence, and language that seems very tame today). Tom Clark recalled the reaction by some in Bud's hometown: "Bud's good Indiana Methodist conscience bothered him a bit in staid old Blue Grass Lexington where so many damn fools, ignorant of the realities of the opening of the West, tittered behind the stairway like a bunch of snaggle-toothed boys about to turn a back house over on Halloween."

Periodicals that reviewed the book for libraries where cautious. *Booklist* warned, "It is a lusty, brutal story of frontiersmen who could not live except in wild free places untouched by civilization. Read before purchase." And the *Library Journal* also put up warning flags: "A story rough as the men it characterizes, with frontier frankness and language and situation which may offend. Men will enjoy it."

But there were many reviewers who praised the story's realism:

> There is much drama in the book, much violence, much cruelty. Fighting brawling, Indian raids, scalping, casual murder, drunkenness, gambling—the full record is there, realized as fiction with great skill.
>
> One has to be a student of the fur trade to appreciate how true it is to history, and how much of what history has come to understand about the era has been worked into it.
>
> But, for all its violence, "The Big Sky" is suffused with the beauty of the country and of the deep, rewarding companionship of men bound together by their way of life, and at times it has a poignancy that is overpowering.

At the time of the publication of *The Big Sky*, Guthrie was described by a fellow newspaperman writing for the *Louisville Courier-Journal*:

> Guthrie is of average height, thin (he lost 30 pounds writing

"The Big Sky"), with a walk reminiscent of a cowboy's tee-tering on his high-heeled, spurred boots. Twenty years in a news office haven't relieved him of the wiry strength he acquired on Western ranches in his youth. His features are regularly cut and blue eyes look out from large, round glasses.

At Harvard, his fellow Niemans used to remark on the trick he had of opening his eyes wide in astonishment at even the most obvious statement. Guthrie could listen to a 15-minute monologue, lift his eyebrows several times, never say a word and convince the monologist that Guth-rie was the most delightful conversationalist he had talked with in years.

Although he would go on to write ten more novels, one of which would win the Pulitzer, it was *The Big Sky* that brought him into the company of the Western American literature immortals. Wayne Chatterton, in *A Literary History of the American West*, said about the novel: "Today it is a worn thing to praise the big-ness, the openness, the spaciousness of this novel. Among the nov-els of the early West it shows best the power of fiction to be big-ger and truer than real people, place, time." And in summarizing Guthrie's overall contribution as a writer, he said that "more than any other western writer's, his prose has the quality of 'curious fe-licity,' Coleridge's term for those writers who can use the limited number of words in any language to create new, startling, fresh-seeming effects—the sense that words have never before come to-gether in these peculiar ways."

In February of 1947 Bud resigned from the *Leader* and went on to teach a course in creative writing at the University of Ken-tucky. The advance on his book was largely gone, royalties had not yet begun to come in, the movie sale was in the future, and he worried about covering the family expenses. Also, it was a flattering offer and a challenge to his confidence in his public-speaking ability. He continued to teach periodically at Kentucky until 1952, and starting in 1948 taught a summer course at the University of Montana. Tom Clark said that many of those who had Bud as a teacher in Lexington looked back with fondness on their experience: "I see people occasionally [many years later] who reminisce about his course in writing." Some of his students became successful writers and attributed their success to Guthrie.

An unexpected and nearly overwhelming result of the publication of *The Big Sky* was fame. And when the money started to come in, the Guthries' social calendar began to fill. They went regularly to the races; they were invited to join the Lexington Country Club, and Harriet was thrilled. There were formal dances not only for the adults but for the children as well. Bud, although less social than his wife, had a tux made and with some reluctance joined in with the Lexington upper crust, which in the past he had sometimes mocked.

In 1947 and for many years after, when Bud went to Montana in the summers, most likely he would not be in Choteau but at Twin Lakes. The property, which Guthrie called "rock and jackpine land," contained two cabins and some rickety outbuildings, property that Bud had purchased early that summer. The main cabin had been a sheepherder cabin and was without running water, electricity, or a bathroom. There was a wood stove for warmth and cooking. The lakes were really just ponds filled by outflow from the Teton River, and because nearby ranches had priority water rights, the lakes were often, in dry years, low. The section he had purchased was twenty miles west of Choteau, with a view of the eastern front of the Rockies, and from there one could pack with horses up into the mountains. It became Bud's favorite place to be.

He and Harriet were familiar with the property because they had visited the dance hall there, run by a local bootlegger, when they were dating. (The dance hall, by this time, had burned down.) Bud found out the property was for sale for $10,000, but he didn't have the money, so he borrowed $7,500, interest free, from Harriet's sister, Alva. After the success of *The Big Sky* and the onset of royalties, he was able to pay her back.

That summer of 1947, some of Bud's friends from Kentucky came to visit the Guthries at Twin Lakes. According to Tom Clark, "Bud pulled out all the stops to give [them] the Western treatment and they are still talking about that wild experience. . . . He got them a little bit tight, and Bud was a big sombrero Westerner with them." Among the visitors was Dan Bowmar, Bud's colleague on the *Leader*. Bud got him up very early in the morning in his pajamas and gave him the tour, never allowing him to change into his clothes and keeping him in his pajamas all day.

Bud's colleague on the *Herald-Leader*, Joe Jordan, recalled on his trip west, "One hot day he induced me to go to the virtually inaccessible Mount Moriah cemetery, atop of [a] lofty crag with (estimated) 70 degree sides, and sit there panting while he stood, uncovered and reverent, meditating as he gazed at the graves of Wild Bill Hickock and Calamity Jane."

Other visitors to Twin Lakes during this period were the actor George Montgomery and his wife, Dinah Shore. Montgomery was from Montana, and his father had been a longtime employee of Bud's father-in-law, Tom Larson. The actor was interested in the possibility of buying the movie rights to *The Big Sky*. Their stay was not very successful, either for the purchase or for a vacation, because Dinah hated Twin Lakes. With an outhouse, no electricity, and no running hot water, it was too primitive, and she complained constantly. Bud's daughter recalled, "She was a huge pain in the ass."

A frequent visitor to Twin Lakes was Bud's friend since childhood, George Jackson. The two of them were often up there alone together in the summer and sometimes winter. One winter, as told by Bud's niece Peggy Bloom, the two of them were snowbound in the cabin:

> My uncle [was staying] at Twin Lakes when it was still very primitive, I am not sure if there was even electricity. I don't think so, but he went up there with his friend, George Jackson, . . . and it was just a horrific year for snow and they got snowed in, day after day, and there were plenty of provisions so they were reasonably happy.
>
> About the sixth or seventh day George got up, rubbed his eyes, looked out the window and said, "Well, Bud, what are your plans for today?"

Early in 1948 Bud heard that his publishers were in trouble: "While I prospered, my publishers were going broke, not because they weren't good publishers, but because they had begun business just prior to a slump and had no backlist—like, say, a cookbook—to sustain them. Under their pressure, in six months of such effort as I'll never be able to muster again, I wrote *The Way West*."

Guthrie had thought about writing this novel for some time, perhaps since his childhood reading of Francis Parkman's *Oregon Trail*, and planning for it more specifically during his last months of working on *The Big Sky*. In November of 1947, he wrote to Bernard DeVoto:

> Yep, I'm a professor now and even a doctor, I'll have you know, according to the easy promotions that prevail hereabouts. I have just one class, and it meets just twice a week, so the job is hardly onerous. I'm enjoying it and learning one hell of a lot more than my students, I'm afraid.

Benny, give me one bit of advice, will you? If you planned to write a novel about the Oregon Trail, as I do, what year would you choose? I'm inclined toward the earlier years, but haven't done enough reading and thinking yet to make a considered choice. (11/15/47)

When he finally took up the project, at the behest of his publisher, it didn't matter how much he thought he knew—he realized that he faced a daunting task of historical research before he could write. What things must the historical novelist know? Looking back, Guthrie wrote,

> He must know not only the broad outlines, the social conflicts, the political, military and economic concerns and consequences of his setting; he must know how men talked, what they wore, with what techniques they fashioned their lives, how they regarded and how they met the questions that still may bother us today. . . .
>
> Even an acquaintance with the sticks and stones of history isn't enough. The fictionist in history must be able to read between the lines of his sources, which, in American literature at least, tend to be restrained, staid, proper, in accordance with an old conviction that a lot of what went to make life wasn't fit for print. He must fill in, synthesize, guess intelligently, for what he's trying to tell about is life as it was lived, not alone as it was reported.

With this book, as with *The Big Sky*, Bud insisted on as complete a realism as he could achieve. To get at the "sticks and stones of history," he turned to journals and diaries written at the time: "The day by day journals are prime sources and better by far than the journals written out of memory." And the overland diaries recorded little things: "Rained today. Made twelve miles. . . . Oxen sore-footed. . . . Mosquitoes bad. . . . Thought about my sister, Susan, since it was her birthday, and wished much to see her. . . . Water warm and foul to taste. Some of company suffering from the flux. . . . Wood so scarce we are having to use the dried dung of buffalo and, with custom, have come to think nothing of it. . . . Today the Sabbath, but we nevertheless [work], halting in time for a brief service, led by Brother Clark." His most useful journal source, Bud said, was that of Joel Palmer, who went across the plains in 1845, and wrote that he "deliberately made it that year because [he] didn't want to get involved in the Mexican War."

But historical research in books was not enough as far as Bud was concerned. He wanted to see the Oregon Trail country for himself, do research on the ground. He said, "I would call this psychological preparation. I thought I needed to do that before I undertook the book. I took notes." He took two trips to experience the trail and scout the topography that summer, the first with his son. He wrote periodically to his wife, who was in Montana during the trip, and they had arranged various towns where she could write ahead to "General Delivery" for him to pick up her letters. He wrote to Scoop nearly every day and sent letters from Collensville, Illinois (6/16/48); Lawrence, Kansas; Grand Island, Nebraska (6/18/48); Central City, Nebraska (6/1948); and Old Fort Kearney, Nebraska (6/20/48).

In his letter to his wife from Grand Island, Bud wrote,

Today was one of our best days, though not our longest in miles by a good deal. How we got this far I hardly know. We spent nearly three hours at the offices of the Kansas State Historical Society, where we were treated with every courtesy and where I found an old-newspaper and western-

Americana library the like of which I hadn't seen before. I feel I must go back there when I really get to digging on the Platte book.

Well, we headed away from Topeka at about noon and traveled dirt and gravel roads a good part of the afternoon, wanting, as nearly as possible, to follow the exact route of the emigrants. I think we came as close to it as anyone could by car. . . .

Both of us fine. Nonnie has been doing a good deal of driving, and doing it well. I am getting eager to reach Scottsbluff and so have word from you. Wasn't that where you were going to write me? (My memo is in the car.)

Love to you and to our baby, Bud

That night they stayed in a motor court (the early motel). They had planned to camp out at night, but it was simply too cold for their bedding. The next night they stayed in a private home on the outskirts of Central City, Nebraska, and Bud wrote,

My dearests:

Well, here we are at about the place we stopped last night— but we've seen much since then. . . .

We ran into a bunch of U.S. Army engineers, who told us how to reach the junction of the two rivers [the Platte and the Missouri], the only hitch being that the man who owned the land was very touchy on the subject of trespassers. We decided to tackle him anyway, but found him not at home. Reluctantly, his women-folk allowed us to drive across the farm.

Well, we stood right on the point dividing the two rivers—and it was an awesome and rewarding sight. Nonnie took pictures, which we are hoping will turn out well.

Tomorrow we'll head west again, making slower time because there will be more landmarks to be seen. . . .

Love from us both, Bud

A few weeks after his return to Montana, Bud was joined by his longtime friend Randall Swanberg of Great Falls, and they drove to Nebraska (it was, for Bud, "back to" Nebraska). Swanberg recalled that Bud took notes on the physical terrain and went to various points along the trail route just to see what a person might see from there. Swanberg helped Bud by taking notes on plant and bird life—Swanberg was much better than him at botany and zoology, Guthrie recalled. According to Swanberg, Guthrie was "meticulously accurate" in his use of information gathered during research trips. As an example, Swanberg pointed out that "if Bud writes about a man in a rifle pit, with a gumwood flower by his shoulder, that gumwood flower will be in season."

Bud and Randall traveled up the Sweetwater, over the Old South Pass, and on to Fort Bridger. At that landmark for the wagon trains, Independence Rock, Bud looked at the names and dates chiseled into the great stone spire by the pioneers of the mid-nineteenth century. Among many others he noticed one inscription, carved in 1848, which bore the name "Deakins," spelled the same as for Jim Deakins of *The Big Sky.* He was astounded.

Bud was almost obsessed with accurate detail, a concern illustrated by the way he took notes. In an article in *Holiday* recalling his research travels for *The Way West,* Guthrie discussed his note-taking: "It is in my notes where I, a Montanan, saw the first insect I'd call a horsefly: Kearney, Nebraska. Where I saw the first Magpie: Roubidou Pass, a few miles from Scott's Bluff. Where I first noticed sagebrush: Bridgeport, Nebraska. Cactus was blowing pink and yellow west of Casper, Wyoming, which should be spelled Caspar after Caspar Collins, who lost his life fighting Indians not far from the town that, honoring him, misspelled his name."

The Way West was easier to write than *The Big Sky* in one respect—the wagon-train trip gave Bud a framework. In an interview, he recalled that the day-to-day progression of the trip, in addition to the predetermined time span, were factors in the book's relatively quick completion. But it was, nevertheless, a period of intense concentration, finding and reviewing notes and then writing and rewriting until he was satisfied with the results. Tom Clark, his neighbor in Lexington, recalled, "We watched Bud dig and sweat through *The Way West*. He had resigned his regular routine job at the newspaper and now gave full time to writing. I am fairly certain that in dealing with the experiences of emigrants on the Oregon Trail he wished to some way relate himself and his family. His family had gone West at a later date, but in many ways to no less harshness of nature and social conditions. Bud grew up against the background of an emerging West around him, and with so many of the old landmarks so readily in sight."

Clark adds that his research for this book was just as careful as that for *The Big Sky*, but the spirit in *The Way West* is gentler. And that may have come out of the inclusion of women in the latter book. Bud was worried about his ability to write about women. How could he get into their minds, how to understand them? He found, however, that "the buds of the opposite sex that abide in all can be awakened, can be brought at least to some bloom if imagination works hard enough."

Another type of character presented a challenge. He wanted to include in his novel a preacher in the group that he would follow to Oregon. But with a troubled history within the fundamentalism of a Methodist upbringing, one that had turned him against all organized religion, he was unsure how to conceive such a character.

His temptation was to pick out a preacher figure he could mock. However, years before he got to *The Way West*, he had spent ten cents in a used bookstore for a pamphlet by a minister who had written about his life on the Oregon Trail in 1841 and 1842.

In thinking about writing his new book, he realized that the minister of the pamphlet, Joseph Williams, was the model he could use for his own preacher. "Here he was, with his narrow morality and his conviction that a personal god kept score on curses, carnality, and skepticism. I would make fun of him." But in the end, he wasn't able to. His preacher grew away from him. Brother Weatherby, as Guthrie called him, came to draw on his admiration.

The most admirable trait of the original Joseph Williams was courage. "Penniless," Guthrie wrote about him, "at the age of sixty-four he had traveled a course that few men but rough trappers and traders had traversed before him. He never complained." Demonstrating qualities that Guthrie himself aspired to—toughness of character, endurance, and single-minded devotion to his calling—Williams provided a basis for a fictional character that the author was forced to admire despite himself.

The author was able to draw on Joel Palmer's and Joseph Williams's diaries for details about daily life on the trail. Although these details were all important to Guthrie, most readers probably wouldn't even appreciate them. His intense search for them suggests that he worked as much as a historian as he did a novelist. In his thesis on Guthrie, Charles Hood quotes from one of Williams's diary entries, recorded as the wagon train went along the Platte River, to show how the entry paralleled material in the novel:

Thursday, we traveled up the north side and of the south fork. Here we saw thousands of buffalo, all along the plains. Our hunters shot down one bull; they thought it unnecessary to kill any more. Here we saw packs of wolves, which followed them. This morning there was a great alarm given that the Indians had driven off some of the oxen, and our men went in pursuit of them, and brought them back. One man said he saw an Indian, and shot at him; but some did not believe him. All this time, I had to stand guard every fourth night. The Indians still come to trade with us. Here we have nothing to make our fires but buffalo manure. This morning a large buffalo bull came near us, when we were marching along, and seemed regardless of the bullets; but after about fifteen or twenty were shot into him, he fell. We started across to the north fork, about two miles to the northwest, and then traveled about twenty miles up the river; staid there on Saturday night. Here an awful circumstance took place: A young man by the name of Shotwell, shot himself accidentally, and died in about two hours afterwards. I was called upon, by his comrades, to preach his funeral, which I did.

(It is unlikely that Williams is making a joke with the name "Shotwell.")

Several of the items in this entry are reflected in *The Way West*: Indians driving off stock, pioneers using buffalo chips for cooking fires, and a preacher presiding over funerals of men along the trail.

If the many false starts and frequent revisions made *The Big Sky* a marathon, the pressure of his publisher's need for a new title from him made *The Way West* a long-distance sprint. Yet, many reviewers thought that the second major work was better in several ways than his first. He finished the manuscript in the spring of 1949, and that summer went to Missoula to teach a short course in creative writing. During a pause in the conference, he and the director, Joe Howard, went downtown to get a bite to eat. They stopped off at Bud's hotel, where a telegram was waiting for him. It said that his novel had been taken by the Book-of-the-Month Club. Bud recalled that Joe let out a whoop and couldn't wait to get back to the campus and announce the happy news.

Having a book chosen by the Book-of-the-Month Club can be a blessing and a curse. The choice guarantees a large printing and circulation of the book, but at the same time it tends to suggest to reviewers that it is in the "best-seller" category rather than the serious-literature category. However, Bud was lucky in that most reviewers took the book seriously, which may have been in part the result of the halo effect that spread over from *The Big Sky*. Many writers have difficulty following up on a successful first novel—some write an obviously inferior second one, while others are simply paralyzed.

Edward Weeks wrote in his *Atlantic* review: "The second novel is always more of a test than the first, and this is a better book—broader in scope, deeper and more versatile in its characterization and with more power and beauty in its feel for the country." Agreeing with this sentiment, Walter Van Tilburg Clark in the *Saturday Review of Literature* wrote, "We say not only that "The Way West" is no jaded follow-up, but that it is even, in conception and manner, a better book than *The Big Sky*." And the *New York Times Book Review* stated, "Even more successfully than its predecessor, 'The Big Sky,' Mr. Guthrie's second novel, repossesses the past and gives a sense, not of fiction, but of the Western experience itself as it was totally known a hundred years ago by the men who underwent it, who chose it, and who were re-created by it as Western Americans."

Several reviewers based their criticism on what they claimed was Guthrie's obvious intention to write a novel that would be purchased by Hollywood. This may have been an offshoot of a prejudice against Book-of-the-Month Club selections, in this case the conviction that Guthrie's book was a jaded retelling of a stereotypical story with stock characters. As the *Catholic World* put it, "If there had never been a westward emigration in this country, it would have been necessary for the novels, radio, comic books and Hollywood to invent one. Incidentally, a lot of popular westania [sic] does use stock characters and situations. In his novel of the 'On-to-Oregon' wagon train, Guthrie adheres to the pattern." The reviewer suggested that the role of the "natural born leader of men named Lije Evans" would be "just the part for Joel McCrea."

Other reviewers had other suggestions. The *New Yorker* stated that "Lije is Henry Fonda to the life, and 'The Way West' also provides roles as juicy as Brown's Mule plug for Walter Brennan, John Wayne and Ward Bond." The reviewer, Brendan Gill, ended this caustic essay with "Hollywood canner of celluloid, meet Bud Guthrie, hewer of rhetoric!" *Commonweal* observed that "all the elements usually required of a film epic are here." However, other reviewers, conscious of the temptation to dismiss the book as fodder for Hollywood, went out of their way to point out how the novel surpassed the popular Western.

Time listed the Hollywood stereotypes that were absent from the book: "In all the body-torturing, spirit-testing haul from Independence to Williamette, there is not one Indian attack, not a single war whoop or flaming arrow, not one hot-blooded, devil-may-care hero to turn in an impossible rescue, not even a big-breasted heartbreaker in low-cut linsey woolsey to take strong nation-makers from their plain wives and set them at each other's throats."

The *Herald Tribune*, with its own list of missing stock Western situations, concluded, "The On-to-Oregon company was thoughtfully assembled on the Missouri's banks to reach the Columbia safely, and it did so with no eye cast at a distantly future Hollywood."

In the spring of 1949, Bud received a letter from the University of Montana asking if he would appear on campus to accept an honorary doctorate of letters and then make a short speech. He accepted and appeared at the ceremony but later found that a mistake had been made. Instead of a doctor of letters, he received, with cape and parchment, a doctor of literature, a step above letters. But by the time the mistake had been discovered, everything had been prepared, and the committee decided to go ahead. Bud remarked with a smile, "My degree has been framed, and, when occasion offers, I wear my cape proudly, for I am unique: the one and only Doctor of Literature by inadvertence."

Toward the end of that year, the Guthries returned to Kentucky. He found himself either "lazy or exhausted, one or both." After his royalties were hit hard by the taxes he had to pay, he felt it would be foolish to go ahead immediately to make more money. Yet, in the spring of the following year, he did take on an assignment from *Holiday*, the first of several, and found that he needed some information that his friends in the newsroom could look up for him. He telephoned, and the friend who answered said, "Congratulations, Bud." "On what?" he asked. "You've won the Pulitzer Prize. Just came in on the wire." Less than an hour later, confirmation came in a telegram from the president of Columbia University, Dwight D. Eisenhower.

Bud's neighbor Tom Clark remembered "how elated" he and Bud's other friends were when Bud won the Pulitzer Prize. Clark recalled, "This seemed to me to be a wonderful realization of those dreams we had in our earlier years, and we vicariously shared the joy of the prize."

Bud's brother, Chick, wrote to him from Minneapolis, "Jeez! My heartiest congratulations, you intellectual son-of-a-bitch (to quote George Jackson). The news editor of the Star came running into my sanctum yesterday afternoon bearing the news. 'They cheated him out of it once,' he said, shaking my hand, 'but not twice.' . . . Nothing's pleased us more in a long time" (5/2/50).

In an interview Guthrie compared *The Big Sky* with *The Way West* by saying, "The two novels are quite different in tone. 'The Big Sky' was largely negative. They were a people who destroyed, and only that had meaning and zest for them. 'The Way West' is affirmative; they were the people who were going to make homes. It is a kind of affirmation." His neighbor in Great Falls and a fellow writer, Dan Cushman, put it this way: "*The Big Sky* was properly wrong. It was a big, sprawling, wonderful success. It doesn't have the progressive art form that *The Way West* has got."

But Bud's friend Tom Clark stated the difference between the two books more succinctly when he said, "As purely a personal opinion, I have always felt *The Big Sky* was a more spirited book, but *The Way West* the work of a master stylist."

CHAPTER EIGHT

To Hollywood and *Shane* and the Move to Montana

Bud's concern about his speaking disability and his resulting interest in public speaking went beyond the Speakeasy Club and led him to become a leader in organizing the Lexington Public Forum. Throughout the forties he was instrumental in bringing a series of lecturers on a variety of subjects to the city. He had become something of an expert on public speaking, and his own ability had progressed to the point where he could speak with some confidence. According to contemporaries he was not a particularly impassioned speaker but always managed to convey material of interest in a voice that was clear and deliberate. He had overcome his demons.

Evidence for this came after the successful publication of *The Big Sky*, when he agreed to go on the lecture circuit. A New York lecture-management agency, Lee Keedick ("Manager of the World's Most Celebrated Lecturers"), had contacted him in May of 1947. They knew of Bud because he scheduled lecturers as president of the Lexington Public Forum, and Keedick wrote to ask if he could stop by and see him in Lexington. He would like to add Bud to his roster of speakers.

Bud waited until the next year to sign on and gave a half dozen lectures each year for three years, traveling to places like Chicago, Indianapolis, Nashville, and Louisville, speaking at colleges and to civic groups and women's clubs. His fees ran from $150 to $300, but he had to provide for his own travel and hotel expenses. By early 1951 he had been summoned to Hollywood, and realizing that his lecturing activities were not adding substantially to his new income, he quit.

During 1950 Bud was busy, nearly overwhelmed as one thing piled up on another. Early in the year his sister Jane's son, Bobby, was diagnosed with childhood schizophrenia and was, at Bud's suggestion, sent to the Brown Schools in Austin, Texas. The school specialized in dealing with children who had mental and emotional difficulties. Because Bud was paying for his nephew's treatment, the staff reported to him in some detail about Bobby's condition and progress. He, in turn, followed that progress closely.

At the same time, Bud's dad, staying with Jane in Missoula, was experiencing declining health, and it seemed clear that he would not be able to return to Choteau and live by himself. Jane, working as a teacher, would be unable to care for him. Bud, once again, came to the rescue and took over making arrangements for his father to stay in a nursing home in Missoula and for the Choteau house to be sold. The whole family was worried about the father's ability to make the adjustment.

Then, in the summer of 1950, Bud joined the writers' conference at Missoula with Joe Howard, who ran the show, and with Benny DeVoto and Helen Everitt. Also that summer, he joined Benny DeVoto in a memorable adventure—to follow once again the Lewis and Clark path along the Missouri River. The trip was arranged by Bill Lederer, who later wrote *The Ugly American* and who, along with Bud and Benny, was an alumnus of the Bread Loaf Writers' Conference. DeVoto was a novelist and editor but was best known for his histories, a trilogy chronicling the impact of the West on American culture: *The Course of Empire* (exploration from the sixteenth to the nineteenth centuries), *Across the Wide Missouri* (the Rocky Mountain fur trade), and *The Year of Decision: 1846*.

Guthrie was concerned with much the same territory, although he planned a series of novels that brought the history of the West forward into the twentieth century. In an interview in 1949, he outlined his plan: "I want to write a series of at least four panels on the Western movement. In them I want to try to interpret American life to the American people. It disturbs me to see people highballing over the trails without any idea of what they're doing. You know about my first two books. The third will be the story of the cow camp and/or gold camp days. Maybe both. I'm not sure. The fourth book will be the interior Northwest from the turn of the century to the present." In fact, he ended up with a series of six books, covering the stream of western history from the mid-nineteenth to mid-twentieth centuries.

Bud only half-seriously suggested that Lederer might have arranged the trip not only with thoughts of their friendship but also with the thought that "an outing with us would give him the real secret of authorship." Both Bud and Benny were Pulitzer Prize winners. Lederer, a commander in the Navy at the time, had obtained the sponsorship of the Air Force and the Army Corps of Engineers, and the three writers would travel 1,400 miles by plane, boat, car, and foot, retracing the Oregon Trail and looking at flood-control projects on the Missouri River.

The military's motive was to obtain for the Corps of Engineers' activities the endorsement of these influential writers who, in their work, had focused on the Missouri. Both Bud and Benny were chary of the Corps—particularly Benny, who had written in opposition to its dam building—but they set aside their reservations when Lederer assured them that the Air Force part of the Missouri trip would be taken whether they went along or not.

On the first leg of their trip, they flew over the Oregon Trail, and as Bud later wrote, found themselves "looking down . . . on landmarks [they] had looked up to before, traveling in minutes, traveling in one short afternoon distances translated into so many days and so many weeks and so many months by long-dead Oregoners whose vanished ox trains labored below . . . and were gone with the turn of a prop." He added, "Mountain men, home-seekers, small- and great-souled missionaries . . . these we knew. Ours was a time of union with all them."

After several flights over segments of the trail where they found "known places again. Known stories. Old history come alive. Past into present. The forgotten remembered," they asked if they could borrow a small boat. They wanted to get the experience of traveling at least a portion of the river "in a manner approximating that of travelers long before [their] time." In the boat and going down the river, they could identify with Lewis and Clark, seeing what they saw, running aground as they did, and getting sunburned and calloused. As they drifted on, they knew where they were in the old sense, but not in relation to the towns that had grown up along the river during the more than a century since the explorers had passed.

Bud recalled, "Like proof of our antiquity, a little boy appeared. He sat on a high bank, fishing all alone, his eye fixed on the red bobber below him. We pulled closer, and Benny yelled, 'Say, son, can you tell us where we are?' To the author of *Across the Wide Missouri*, the boy yelled back, 'Mister, you're on the Missouri River.'"

The trip was both bitter and sweet. It was sweet in bringing them back to the landmarks of the Oregon Trail and in bringing Bud and Benny closer together. It also gave Bud a deeper appreciation for DeVoto's fierce adherence to his ideals, particularly in environmental matters. But the trip was bitter in that much of what the engineers and reclamation people proudly proclaimed along the way as "progress" was to them, for the most part, simply depressing. As he reported, "By plane and flatboat, by plane again and car and launch and steamboat, we reached St. Louis, that one-time gateway to the West, passing fabled rivers on the way whose convergences were drowned or would be drowned by dams."

Early in 1951 Bud's life took another turn. Unexpectedly, he was offered a job in Hollywood to write a screenplay for the Western novel *Shane*. At $1,500 a week it was an offer he couldn't refuse, even though he had no idea of how to write a screenplay. During his first weeks there, his daughter, Helen, wrote him, "Write me about all the movie stars you happen to see or talk to" (1/31/51). And his brother wrote, "What a life! . . . We trust that the movie town won't swallow up the author, although I'd probably be willing to prostitute my art for the money they pay out there" (2/5/51).

Howard Hawks, with Ed Lasker, had bought the rights to *The Big Sky*, and because Hawks was impressed with Guthrie's ability to write Western dialogue, had recommended him to the producer-director of *Shane*, George Stevens. Bud recalled his first meeting with Stevens:

> The studio and the director, George Stevens, wanted to produce a superior western, within the western's limits. The Robin Hood Idea, you know. Well, it worked out very well. But I like to think we added to the Myth. My first morning

with Stevens I said, "Do you know one thing, George, that offends me? You see all these western pictures, people getting shot down—I ain't never saw a funeral! Those bodies still lying all over the landscape? And he said, "By God, that's a good idea. We'll have a funeral!" It wasn't in the book, though. The book is a very thin book. Just a short story. So a lot of improvising had to go into it.

Another suggestion that Bud made may have had even more of an influence on the tenor of the movie and its ultimate success. In regard to what would be the central conflict of the movie, he told Stevens that "there was no complete right or complete wrong in the stands taken by open-range ranchers and homesteaders. Each side had its case." And again, Stevens agreed. Perhaps as a result of this understanding between writer and director, the movie was imbued with that pervasive sense of ambiguity that lifted it above most other Westerns.

The author of the novel was Jack Schaefer, who Bud thought had betrayed some ignorance of the Western lore that he himself was familiar with but, at the same time, showed that he knew a lot more about some things than Bud did. (Bud did not know that, when he wrote the novel, Schaefer had never been farther west than Toledo, Ohio. All his knowledge of the region had come from many years of reading about the West.) However, Bud did admire his prose and was attracted by two elements in the novel that he found very engaging. One was that the story was told from the point of view of a little boy. The other was that the triangle, which involved the homesteader, his wife, and Shane, was kept innocent by the admiration of each character for the others. In that regard, Bud commented that "you would hardly have thought that situation had much appeal to the industry."

Maybe there was a confluence of taste in prose because Schaefer was also a newspaperman; certainly there was a confluence in their interest in history. In an interview, Schaefer has said that *Shane* was written while he was employed in Norfolk, Virginia. Recalling the Depression, he said, "I taught nights in a prison; mornings and afternoons I worked for a newspaper and edited a small weekly magazine. . . . When I was through working I read books on American history to relax . . . and felt most at home west of the Mississippi River." Then he wrote that in 1945, "Primarily as a means of relaxation I started writing fiction late at night. I began writing a short story about the basic legend of the West. It kept growing and wound up a novella."

When he was through, he didn't know what to do with it. Finally, on impulse, he sent the manuscript to *Argosy*, a men's adventure magazine. And he was lucky. He sent his single-spaced typescript without a return envelope; such submissions are usually just discarded. The publisher, however, took it home with other manuscripts by mistake, started to read it, and ended up deciding that the magazine would use it.

It was published in 1946 as a three-part serial under the title *Rider from Nowhere*, with lurid pulp-Western illustrations and captions. By 1948 Schaefer had left his job as a newspaper editor, revised his manuscript, found an agent, and had his novella accepted for publication by Houghton Mifflin. It came out in hardbound edition in 1949. It was not a best-seller but has been a persistent and steady seller over the years, going into many editions. There is a parallel between Schaefer's career and Guthrie's—the newspaperman who works overtime to produce a successful novel that leads him to quit his job and become a freelance writer.

The novel, while it used many typical mythic elements, was by no means a pulp Western (despite *Argosy*'s illustrations). The critic

Ann Ronald points out, "From its inception, Schaefer meant the piece to be a literary endeavor, 'classical in form,' he said, 'stripped to the absolute essentials.' Indeed, he speaks freely of the conscious artistry he brought to the novel, designing its narrative technique and shaping its story line so that layers of meaning gradually are revealed."

Westerns, as pointed out by John Cawelti, have always had a cultural ambiguity, celebrating both the individual cowboy and outlaw, and the community of settlers. *Shane*, both the novel and the movie, raised this ambiguity to a new level. As Matthew J. Costello has noted, "[The producer-director] George Stevens saw the western in terms of mythic traditions of heraldic bravery and chivalry, yet offered a more starkly realistic portrayal of western life than had previously been achieved." The critic goes on to point out that this disjunction of myth and reality in the film forces the audience to see "Shane as a mythic and chivalrous figure through the eyes of young Joey Starrett. This contrasts with the realism of the muddy streets, the meager constructions in the town, and the drab work clothes of the settlers." (Contrast this drabness with Shane's buckskin outfit decorated with fringes.) Much of the realism of the movie had its roots in the novel: "One of Schaefer's most important accomplishments in *Shane* is that the background seems to be a real frontier and the people real people."

Another congruence between Schaefer and Guthrie was their environmentalism. On Schaefer's part, this concern was apparent even in his first novel, *Shane*, as Gerald Haslam has pointed out: "The environment itself is a dynamic force to which the characters must respond and within the framework of which they must interact. Indeed it sometimes appears that the interaction occurs as much between character and environment as between character and character."

In any event the two writers had careers very much alike, had a similar fondness for reading history, and had a similar concern about human degradation of the environment and the slaughter of fellow mammals. It was, after all, in *The Big Sky* that Guthrie put forth the theme that man destroys the very things he loves, whether beaver, fellow humans, or the wondrous wilderness and the freedom that it offered. It was a felicitous joining of talents—Schaefer, Guthrie, and, of course, George Stevens—that produced a classic motion picture. (And the casting was fortuitous. The unlikely Alan Ladd—unlikely because he was short and blonde and in life not very heroic looking—did a bang-up job as the troubled Shane. Jean Arthur played Mrs. Starrett, the farmer's wife; and Van Heflin, Mr. Starrett, the farmer. Brandon de Wilde broke your heart as the young boy who idolizes Shane: "Shane! Shane! Come back!" And Jack Palance was unforgettable as the vicious hired gunfighter, Wilson.)

Since its release in 1953, the movie has been reviewed in hundreds of newspapers and magazines and analyzed by dozens of film scholars. The evaluations of it have been overwhelmingly positive, which pleased Bud very much indeed. He looked back with pride to say,

> Not for more than a year did I see "Shane." It had been kept in the can, as they say, until "High Noon" passed into the sunset, a matter of timing. When I did see it, I sat stunned and incredulous. I hardly recognized my own stuff. It was, if not the best, then high among the best of all the westerns I had ever seen. My conviction was supported by the reviews it received, by the gate it drew and by the inclusion in the five nominations for the Academy Award, which I think it deserved. I speak with modesty,

for it was the genius of Stevens that made the film what it was. Under a grade-B director it would have been a grade-B picture.

In 1953 Bud was nominated for an Academy Award for his screenplay. But the next year, when the award was presented, it went to Daniel Taradash, who wrote the screenplay for *From Here to Eternity*.

The critic and novelist Mary Clearman Blew has written—perhaps surprisingly—that she feels *Shane* was Guthrie's masterpiece. In its spare elegance it was a departure from the sprawl of *The Big Sky* and the ruminations of the *Arfive* series—"its glorious Wyoming mountain peaks and plains, so sweeping and lush and somehow unassailable, in contrast with Guthrie's obsession with the disintegration of landscape; and most of all, in place of the romantic despair that characterizes all the novels, the film's theme of courage as affirmation of the human condition and sacrifice as the basis for hope. Where the novels bear out Guthrie's apocalyptic vision—each man destroys what he loves best, he said famously—the film reaffirms decency, loyalty, community . . . the sacrifice of the gunman sustains the community."

The year before, 1953, when their daughter, Helen, was set to go to high school, the Guthries moved to Montana. (In the meantime, son Bert, who had graduated from high school in Lexington, was at the Lawrenceville School in Lawrenceville, New Jersey, for an extra year of preparation for college.) Montana had been calling the Guthries back for some time—it had always been what they considered home. But, in fact, *they* didn't move—Bud wasn't with them. He was in Hollywood working for Hecht-Hill-Lancaster where he was writing the screenplay for *The Kentuckian*, one of his several sojourns during this period to write for the movies. (It was released in 1955 and starred Burt Lancaster (who also directed), Dianne Foster, Dianna Lynn, John McIntire, Una Merkel, Walter Matthau, and John Carradine. Lancaster became one of the few close friends Bud acquired in Hollywood.) In Bud's absence Harriet sold their Lexington house and arranged for the moving van. They had planned their move for over a year and had their eye on a house in Great Falls (530 Third Avenue North), which they purchased. During the summers, they would stay in the cabin at Twin Lakes.

Thomas Wolfe famously said you can't go home again, and it is true. Home is never the same as you remember it, and sometimes it's radically different. Despite spending most of his vacations in Montana, Bud was startled by the changes he found on moving back. In Choteau, faces he knew well were gone, strange faces had taken their place, and people and events from the past had been forgotten. Even the surroundings seemed different. The mountains, woods, and fields seemed smaller, less vital, than he remembered them from his childhood.

And once he became a resident, he became more aware of the social and political conditions in Montana. He observed now with eyes schooled by years of close observation of Kentucky politics. Looking more closely at his home state, he found much of what he saw depressing. For one thing, the climate was not particularly hospitable to intellectual pursuits, regardless of the surprising number of professional writers in the state. The salaries at the state university had been the lowest or among the lowest in the country for decades. For another, social differences, in religion, lifestyle, or behavior, were often suspect and unwelcome. Bud reflected that the sparse distribution of a relatively small population over a big area— 147,138 square miles—led to a lack of communication, which, in turn, distorted and confounded Montana politics and gave rigidity to choice. Widely separated farm families and tiny communities were beyond the reach of daily newspapers, and in Bud's view, radio and television (beyond the reach of many) hardly filled the vacuum. He felt that a population joined by good, independent newspapers was essential to an open-minded democracy.

Bud had a temper, but it did not come out so much with people as it did with issues. His daughter recalled,

> He was passionate about issues—"rotten sons of bitches" who took the wrong side of a political issue. . . . He considered running for office at one time. . . . He wanted his pal Randall Swanberg, a prominent lawyer in Great Falls, to put his hat in the ring, but he wasn't going to run as a Republican or Democrat because he had issues with both parties. . . . And he didn't want to call himself an independent. He wanted to start his own party, and he wanted to call it Sons of the Wild Jackass. At the last minute Randall lost his nerve and couldn't quite file for father as a son of the Wild Jackass.

The Guthries were in Great Falls almost a decade, from 1953 to 1962. Bud worked in a studio behind his house on Third Avenue North, but now that he had no regular routine dictated by a job, he was often at loose ends and, much to Harriet's discomfiture, would wander around the house. The social environment had changed. Instead of having his newspaper buddies, he now found friends and renewed old friendships among a number of local writers. The closest relationship was to Joseph Kinsey Howard, whom he had known for several years because Howard's mother had purchased a cabin on the Circle 8 Ranch a few miles up the road from Twin Lakes. It was Howard who may well have filled Bud in on recent Montana politics and who certainly influenced him to more fully commit himself to environmentalism. Bud had been concerned about conservation, partly as a result of his association with DeVoto, but Howard really fired him up.

Another writer friend in Great Falls was Mildred Walker Schemm, who from 1934 to 1972 published thirteen novels, four of them about Montana and the West. During her life she felt some discouragement, and at times even despondence, about her lack of fame and the relatively poor sales of her work. It is to her credit that she could remain a close friend to a writer who had become so very prominent and who had produced several best-sellers. The Schemms also had a cabin within a few miles of Twin Lakes, and Mildred and her daughter, Ripley, had known Guthrie for many years. Ripley's brother, George Schemm, a neurosurgeon, became a very close friend of Bud in later years.

Also in Great Falls were the writers Dan Cushman, Norman Fox, and Robert McCaig. What did these writers talk about when they got together? Ripley, referring mainly to her mother, Howard, and Bud, has said they talked about their work but also about how the reviewers got it wrong. Ripley quotes from her mother's journal: "We didn't get together in any writing group but we were all starting and all working. We all knew that writing was a solitary business but the awareness of the others writing was important to us."

Bud always spoke well, publicly and privately, of his fellow writers, and he wrote blurbs for them, including this one for one of Walker's novels: "In *If a Lion Could Talk*, Mildred Walker after ten years of silence has come out with a novel that surpasses her others—which is no small thing to say of an author so skillful." However, Walker wrote in her journal, as paraphrased by her daughter: "DAMNING & PATRONIZING descriptions of novel in both PW [*Publisher's Weekly*] & *Kirkus Review*. And NO reviews." She notes "a few people . . . find it good. . . . Bud Guthrie, Helen Taylor, and my brother George and I."

Now in Montana, Bud realized once again that individualism had become a kind of religion, a religion based in part on the myth of the lone horseman, the very myth Bud had used in writing his motion picture. Bud's niece, Peggy Bloom, recalled her uncle talking about the cowboy ethic, "[And] he says it often. 'If a man owns a piece of property,' Guthrie says crankily, 'he thinks it is his to do with as he damn well pleases.' He drums his fingers on the table. 'Bit by bit we are destroying the wilderness, and if we can't address the population problem we are headed for catastrophe.' That was a theme."

Influenced by his conversations with Joe Howard, Bud came to realize that this adherence to a radical individualism was encouraged by a social rigidity, a rigidity that was historically reinforced by the laissez-faire philosophy of two corporate giants, Anaconda and the Montana Power Company, which virtually ran the state for many decades. (One reason that Bud did not look for his first newspaper job in Montana was that it was a state of small weekly papers, and Anaconda had owned most of them.) And as Bud has said, for reinforcements the two corporations looked to the cow counties east of the Continental Divide, where a belief in individuality and man's rights extended to and made personal the impersonality of corporations. It was a conflict seen in microcosm in *Shane* and would be central to his next novel in his series about the West, *These Thousand Hills.*

One of those people east of the Divide who was a rancher, politician, and devoted right-wing conservative was Tom Larson, Bud's father-in-law and one of his favorite people. That Bud loved Tom, a man who hated President Roosevelt and the New Deal and worked to kill just about every liberal bill that came up in the legislature, is testament to the breadth of his sympathy. It's also testament to Tom's likeability. Bud understood where his friend's conservatism was coming from, while at the same time he was aware that there was so much to admire about him. Born in Norway and living there until he was six, Tom had courage and a driving desire to get ahead in a new land:

He brought with him curiosity, wit, a willingness to take chances, an expectation that excluded both despair and regret and an assurance far more becoming than cocky. He was nineteen when a bartender asked him if he was of age. "I've had the seven-year itch three times," he answered, and the bartender drew him a beer.

In those early years he did what jobs he found available, always with an eye fixed ahead. Although he didn't arrive from Minnesota until 1895, Tom lived the life of a pioneer in the Choteau area. At one time or another he drove a stage, bought, broke and sold horses, served as county assessor, and had a country store. His aim was to establish a ranch, and he filed on a gravel bar on public land, a parcel that others scorned. He started with horses and sold rough-broken ones in markets in Indiana and the Deep South. As his acreage grew, he went on to raising sheep or cattle depending on circumstances. At the same time, with a partner he undertook the construction of large irrigation canal from the Muddy River to the area near the town of Brady, a town that he founded. Those who sought land were eager to pay for water rights on the canal, and Tom, who at one time owed the bank a worrisome $70,000—a huge amount at that time—ended up with a tidy profit. He had guts and was willing to gamble.

Although he was, according to Bud, "a poor politician, having little memory for names and no room in his character for blandishments, deals and evasions," he spent a record twenty-one years in the Montana Senate. It seemed as if he got to know just about everybody in Montana even though he had trouble with names, and everybody got to know him. "Some quality," Bud recalled, "or qualities—sense of humor, incorruptibility, geniality, slowness on his part to take offense—saved him from assault and made him a friend of friend and foe alike."

Perhaps what endeared him to Bud the most was his sense of humor. Like Mary Lizzie he was a character, and also like Mary Lizzie he had a profound effect on Bud's life. His tales of the old days were a major contribution—in spirit if not always in substance—to Bud's next novel. Bud said of him, "In his spur-of-the-moment facility for saying the unexpected, for putting wit and essential sense into a capsule, he belonged in the company of Will Rogers, Charlie Russell and other gifted old-timers now mostly dead."

Bud called him a good drinking man, but far from being a drunk. They had a tradition of going out on the town together at least once during Bud's vacations from Lexington. On one occasion, late in the evening, they decided they had had enough to drink. As they were about to leave, a group of friends came into the saloon, and before they could decline, they had drinks in front of them. The next morning Bud said to Tom, "Pretty rugged." Tom nodded and asked, "How many did we have after we quit?"

As his granddaughter, Helen, recalls, Tom did almost all of his wheeling and dealing in the local saloons. So he would come home for dinner, take a short nap after dinner, and then go back uptown to one of maybe three saloons. He would do his hiring and firing and visiting and conduct his business—sell three cows, maybe do some other transactions—and that was how business was done.

Helen tells another story about Tom that has been passed down in the Guthrie family. Tom's wife, Helen's grandmother, was just a simple Norwegian lady who was not very artistic, but she tried. One year she put up a Christmas tree in the hall where the coat tree had been. She tried to make it pretty, hanging lights, balls, and tinsel all over it, adjusting things here and there to make it look as attractive as possible, and she did all this while her husband was down at the saloon conducting business. He came home late that night and threw his coat over what he thought was the coat tree. Helen continues with the story: "She [grandmother] got up the next morning to make him his cornmeal mush . . . and here was her pretty tree with his heavy old winter coat smashed all over it. Broken balls and all that stuff. And when he came down to breakfast, she said, 'Hmmm, Tom, you came home with a pretty heavy load last night, didn't you?' He said, 'Yep. Should've made two trips.' And that was all that was ever said about that."

Of all the stories Bud told about his father-in-law, one stands out as particularly characteristic. Tom walked out of a saloon and paused to look across the street at the construction of Choteau's most ambitious building. A passing preacher stopped and asked Tom, "Do you go in there often?"

"Often as I like," Tom said.

"To drink?"

"When I feel like it."

The preacher pointed to the cigar. "How many of those do you smoke a day?"

"Many as I want."

"Brother," the preacher said, waving toward the construction across the street, "if you didn't drink and didn't smoke, maybe someday you could put up a building like that."

Tom puffed on his cigar. He asked, "Do you drink?"

"Of course not. Never."

Tom took the cigar from his mouth. "Ever try one of these?"

"No, Brother. It's wrong."

"Well," Tom said, "if you change your ways, maybe someday you can put up a building. I'm putting up that one over there."

He was, too. It remains the most substantial building in Choteau, though built in about 1917.

Ted Morrison, Kay Morrison, and Robert Frost at Bread Loaf, Vermont.
Courtesy of Ted Morrison and College Archives, Special Collections,
Middlebury College, Middlebury, Vermont.

Bud and Bernard DeVoto at Bread Loaf. Courtesy of Ted Morrison.

Autograph party for
The Big Sky—Bud,
Bert, and Harriet.
Courtesy of Amy
Sakariassen.

Bud in the house at
Great Falls, Montana,
posing with the keel
boat model used in
the movie of *The Big
Sky*. Courtesy of Amy
Sakariassen.

Bud with George Jackson (middle) and a customer at the barbershop in Choteau. Courtesy of Amy Sakariassen.

Second from left, Bill Lederer, Bud, and Bernard DeVoto on a trip to retrace the Oregon Trail, 1950. Courtesy of Amy Sakariassen.

(*Opposite top*) Bud with his daughter, Helen,
on the Ohio River near Louisville, Kentucky.
Courtesy of Amy Sakariassen.

(*Opposite*) Circle 8 Ranch, Choteau, Mildred
Walker Schemm (fourth from left); Bud Guthrie
(sixth from left and standing); Joseph Kinsey
Howard (eighth from left, holding hat); and
Dr. George A. Sexton (far right). Courtesy of
the Montana Historical Society, Helena.

Still from the motion picture *Shane*, featuring
Alan Ladd as Shane. Courtesy of Bison Archives,
Hollywood, California.

Bert, Harriet, and Bud at Twin Lakes. Courtesy of Amy Sakariassen.

The Wilderness Riders, Fritz Gannon, Shirley Gannon, Bud, and Randall Swanberg (foreground). Courtesy of Amy Sakariassen.

CHAPTER NINE

Bucking the Myth

These Thousand Hills

G uthrie's third novel in his series was the tough one. He had to wrestle directly with the myth. He got to the point in his historical progression that he was writing about the period of the northwest that embodied that myth—the open-range cattle ranch. Here were the cowboys, the guns, the cattle, sheep, and wild horses, and the struggles over land and water that we are all familiar with. Underlying these struggles were the conflicts accompanying the settlement of the area, between those who wanted to keep the area untamed and those who wanted to farm the land and build new communities. All these things had been part of the real West—but their reality had been debased by being incorporated in the myth and by being romanticized by pulp literature. If you use many of the same materials, how do you keep your novel from sounding hackneyed, like a pulp?

He struggled with this problem during the latter part of 1952, then again from 1953, after finishing the script for *The Kentuckian* in Hollywood, and until 1956, when the book *These Thousand Hills* was published. In an interview Bud commented on his writing process: "I may rewrite them [a dramatic scene] four of five times until they fall into the tone and accent that I want. No, my first drafts of all my chapters—I never accepted the first drafts. My first drafts are awful. I wouldn't show them to anyone. But somehow having done them—that's the hardest part, doing the first draft. I can sit down rather happily and shape it."

And in another interview he talked about his insistence on perfection: "I'll never be prolific. . . . I can't let a thing go until it's right—not just right, but right with me. Every chapter, every paragraph, even every line must be the best I can make it."

In writing *These Thousand Hills*, there were many false starts and much discarding of material. Bud's fellow writer and friend Dan Cushman remembered his struggle: "God knows how much good fiction went into the waste basket. He worked it to death. . . . When you do that, you lose its virility. By the time it was rewritten, it was pallid—like a piece of meat after a raccoon gets through washing it in the creek. . . . Bud must have thrown away about 200,000 words—gutsy stuff. I'd like to have what Bud threw away from that book."

During the entire period of writing, Bud was sending chapters to Ted Morrison for comment—he even sent alternative passages for Ted to choose. Although he made suggestions, sometimes a lengthy list of them, his responses were usually approving and encouraging, as when he wrote in February of 1955: "The first thing I have to say is that you are writing as well as ever, and I think better than ever. By writing I mean the whole business of word and phrase and sensory detail and dialogue exchange, everything that goes into the language texture. The second thing is, I think the book is on the move and under way and taking on the dimension and the humanity that properly belong to you as the writer you are"

(2/18/55). But despite this encouragement, Bud became more and more self-critical and doubtful. Success weighed heavily on him, and he had become a perfectionist. As Dan Cushman said, "Bud is afflicted by his own success. . . . [P]erfection is his albatross."

But his struggle was not just with the novel. There was the beginning of a long internal conflict over the grip the demon rum, or more specifically the demon whiskey, had on him. Nearly every close friend that Bud had had over the years was a drinker, many of them heavy drinkers. They ranged from his colleagues on the *Leader*, to his dear friend and sometime landlady Mary Lizzie, to Benny DeVoto, George Jackson, and Tom Larson. For him his drinking was not only part of his rebellion against his strict Methodist upbringing but had become the gateway to friendship and fun. And it may be that his frequent exposure to the heavy drinking in the Hollywood scene of the time increased his appetite and capacity for liquor consumption.

One of the results of this drinking increase was a troubled marriage. Harriet began to catch up, and in Great Falls the two of them began to fight frequently. Their daughter, Helen, remembers that when she was living with them she would hear screaming fights, and she would go upstairs to their bedroom and yell at them to knock it off so that she could sleep. "You two shouldn't be living together," she would say. "How can you live together and scream at each other that way?"

Bud was often in Hollywood and making a lot of money, and that became worrisome to his family. His brother, Chick, wrote to him: "Know you're carrying quite a load, what with Hollywood commitments, the novel, etc. You indicated to Florence [Chick's wife] that you were through with Hollywood, at least until the book is done. I hope you stick by it. People keep asking me when your next book's coming out. I know it's not easy to turn down that heavy movie scratch but I don't like to see Hollywood dominating you" (9/14/54).

The money was a bone of contention. Bud had been very careful with his money but now became careless, and over the next few years, gave away a lot of money; Harriet went on shopping sprees. During these years in Great Falls, Bud often went to Hollywood for periods of weeks. He not only wrote screenplays, but also treatments, acted as a consultant, and on at least one occasion even worked as a script doctor. When he was not away, Harriet often traveled, sometime to her parents in Choteau, but more often to the South or Midwest to visit friends and relatives. There seemed to be an unspoken agreement between them to be together as little as possible. It was one solution to the constant friction.

Their daughter recalled,

When he started working at home, he would work for an hour or so and then he would trail her [Harriet] around the house. This was particularly true in Great Falls. And finally she couldn't stand it anymore because he would write and then he would fidget. Walk around the house, trail her around the house, and she would be trying to sew, clean house, or cook or something, so she made him rent space at the Rainbow Hotel. This was in Great Falls. Well, that didn't work worth a damn because the ladies who went there to Silk and Saddle [a bar restaurant]—it was a racing motif—would go there for lunch, and then they didn't want to use the public bathroom, so they would go upstairs to father's room that he rented to use his bathroom. Well, he would start visiting with the ladies, of course, and the next thing you know, he would be downstairs buying them an after lunch drink or something. So he was not very productive, but at least he was out of her hair.

In his autobiography he admitted that he was glad of interruptions, "They take me from the typewriter, and I find excuses for not coming back."

One of the ways besides travel that Harriet was able to get away was through the twice-a-week meetings in Great Falls of her bridge club, a club of eight or ten women that included several of her longtime friends, such as Helen Swanberg and Helen Sexton. In the summer they might meet at the Sexton cabin on the Circle 8 guest ranch, two miles from Twin Lakes, and hike into the Glacier National Park. They called themselves "The Menopause Marchers."

Helen's husband, Dr. George Sexton, was a longtime friend of Bud's, and when Bud was at Twin Lakes and George at his cabin, they were neighbors. One day Bud and George Jackson were putting in a new concrete foundation for the outhouse and had put the Guthrie dog, Coney (Coney Island Hot Dog), in one of the outbuildings, out of the way—it was never really involved in the prank they had planned. When George Sexton drove in to Twin Lakes over the hill, Bud came staggering out toward him, "Oh Sexton, Sexton, oh God, I don't know what we are going to do. What we are going to do? God, get a rope!" George looked at him blankly, "What's wrong?" Bud explained that the dog fell down in the hole of the outhouse. George said, "Let's see, how are we going to do this? Well, we are going to have to take that outhouse up, get down in the hole on the rope, and get the dog out of there." They got the outhouse off its new foundation and then Bud turned and said, "You're the smallest man, George."

On September 1, 1954, Alfred Bertram Guthrie Sr. died in Missoula. From Minneapolis, Chick wrote to his brother,

> I am glad, though, Bud, that you got back to the hospital

before Pop died. It makes it seem a lot better, somehow, even though he wasn't aware of your presence. . . .

It was difficult to sleep after getting the word. It brought back a lot of memories. With all his anti-socialness and temper Pop was a very lovable guy and in many ways a great one. I wish that I possessed more of his rugged fortitude and moral honesty. (9/2/54)

The Great Falls newspaper announced, "Pioneer of Teton County, A. B. Guthrie Sr., Dies." The *Choteau Acantha* began its obituary, "A. B. Guthrie Sr., 83, first principal of Teton County Free High School, former Acantha publisher, county official and civic leader, passed away at 10 p.m. yesterday from the infirmities of old age" (9/2/54).

Bud reported to his brother on the funeral: "Janie and Bob came over for the funeral, and we, together with George Jackson, Tom and Mom Larson, sat in the family section. As perhaps I told you, Harriet was in Kentucky at the time of Dad's death and could not get back in time for the services" (9/8/54). The next day, having had a report from his sister on Bud's condition as observed at the funeral, Chick wrote to Bud that she had said he was "under heavy tension with the novel and all and were not looking so sharp." He added, "Take care of yourself, boy, and taper off on the fire water. We don't want anything happening to you" (9/9/54).

Bud and Chick were very close, although during this period they did not see each other much. From the letters it is clear that Chick was supportive, not jealous of his brother's success, and was very pleased that Bud had taken care of their father and had handled the details of the estate. However, after a tentative request by Chick that he or his son get "some little thing that belonged to dad," Bud replied with a very angry letter. It was an irrational letter that suggested that Bud was not, indeed, in good shape emotionally. Chick was taken aback:

> Your letter gave me quite a turn. Hell, Bud, I have nothing to be critical about. I have only thanks and gratitude and thought I had got this expression across in previous letters. . . . I am not dissatisfied in the least with any of your actions anent [about] the estate. I hope you will believe that, God dammit, and won't dismay me with any more letters like the last one. I've always rated you as the big guy in my life and have rejoiced at your success. I am not an ingrate, I hope. . . . The last thing I want, though, is a hassle over who gets the fur-lined shaving mug or the gold toothpick. (10/4/54)

Fortunately, the misunderstanding didn't last, but it was another symptom of how troubled and pressured Bud's life had become. Fame and money, or lack of it—and add to that alcohol and self-doubt.

Meanwhile, he was still researching for his novel as he was writing. He felt a particular burden to make it as factual and as real to its time and place as possible in order to avoid or at least mitigate the clichés. As an example of his attention to detail, one aspect of his research was to find out what hymns his characters might be singing in a frontier church in the 1870s. Randall Swanberg remembered, "For sixty days he studied old Methodist hymns. He could sit and sing those hymns—thirty or forty of them. Bud has a tin ear—can't sing worth a damn—but he knew them."

Looking back, Bud said that *These Thousand Hills* was his most difficult and least successful because "it dealt with the cowpuncher and had to avoid, if it could, the stylized Western myth." In an interview he was asked if this lack of success might be attributed to a romantic viewpoint, and he responded, "No, I don't think so. If I do have a romantic view, it doesn't embrace the myth. The myth I dislike. The truth I like. The myth is invulnerable—imperishable. It exists. In *These Thousand Hills*, I opposed it by trying to show, actually, what the day of the cattleman was like. The book wasn't very successful. The gun and gallop jobs still sell, to publishers and to TV audiences, and studios and all that. It's indestructible."

As before, he worked to discover as much first-person reporting on the period as possible. He wanted to find and verify details. In a foreword to *These Thousand Hills*, Bud describes the various sources he used for the novel—an unusual step for a novelist to take, and one that suggests how concerned he was to convince the reader of the work's base in reality. He writes that he was lucky enough to be born at a time when, as he grew up, he encountered the vestiges of life as it was lived in the late nineteenth century. And he had friends among the old timers (certainly Tom Larson was among them) who could remember those early times. But beyond these aids, there were the written records: the cowpuncher chronicles of Teddy Blue Abbott, the humorous and authentic Montana stories by Con Price, the stories by the artist and sculptor Charlie Russell, and the books by James Willard Schultz, who lived among and wrote about the Indians.

After the book was published, a mutual friend of Bud and Con Price took a copy of *These Thousand Hills* to Price, who by this time was a very elderly gentleman, and reported back to Bud that Price was amazed by how much that "young whippersnapper" knew about early-day ranching.

The diaries of Abbott were particularly valuable to Bud, giving him insight into the character of the Montana cowboy and details of the life on the trail and in the cow towns. Charles Hood quotes from Abbott's diary to show how Guthrie used it:

Eleven men made the average crew with a trail herd. The two men in the lead were called the point men, and then as the herd strung out there would be two men behind them on the swing, two on the flank, and the two drag drivers in the rear. With the cook and horse wrangler and boss, that made eleven. The poorest men always worked with the drags, because a good hand wouldn't stand for it. I have seen them come off herd with the dust half an inch deep on their hats and thick as fur in their eyebrows and mustaches, and if they shook their head or you tapped their cheek it would fall off them in showers.

Then Hood quotes from Guthrie's writing about the cattle drive from Oregon to Montana in *These Thousand Hills*:

From a rise a mile or so ahead of the herd, the point was all that Butler could make out, the lead cows and the riders at the sides and behind them nothing but a long, thick, creeping worm of lava dust. . . . It was hell for men behind, hell for swing and flank and double hell for drag, and the riders would be riding masked by their bandannas but still with dust in mouths and noses, dust in ears and hair, on cheeks and lashes, dust powdered, layered, streaked by tears and slaver, dust in the deep-split lower lips that were better left unlicked.

There is a lesson here of how a skilled writer of fiction can take reality and make it even more real.

Abbott also wrote in his diary about a cowpuncher who gave all his money, a hundred dollars, to a prostitute in Miles City and moved in with her in a little shack behind a saloon. She kept him all winter, and when she had "company," he slept in the shack's kitchen or in the saloon. In Guthrie's novel, the protagonist, Lat Evans, moves in with Callie Kash, a prostitute in Fort Benton. His falling in love with a prostitute and his later marriage to a schoolmarm were often cited in criticisms of the novel as western clichés. One critic called the book disappointing in comparison to Guthrie's previous two novels, describing it as "an excursion into banal melodrama."

But these relationships have a deeper significance than their use by others as stereotypes. They set up an internal conflict of allegiance in the protagonist that is at the center of the novel. Beginning in nascent form in *The Big Sky*, there is the theme of the contrast between the psychological turning inward on the self and the psychological freedom offered by nature on the frontier. More fully developed in *The Way West*, the theme becomes the conflict between a conscience informed and shaped by a somber and rigid Calvinism and the psychological freedom offered by space and land under the big sky. It was a conflict at the heart of Guthrie's own experience and one that he brings to Lat Evans in *These Thousand Hills*, and to that extent, the novel had some aspects of autobiography.

Lat is a rebel, but his rebellion is moderated by his religious background, whether he wills it to be so or not. Bud recalled that he was a rebel when he got out of college, but again that rebellion did not go too far. His close friend Randall Swanberg has pointed out that Bud was a "rebel against convention, particularly religious convention and cant." Yet, he was not a flouter of those conventions that governed his own behavior. He observed that "Bud like[d] to be outrageous," but was probably "more prim in his relationships with women than most," adding that, in 20 years, he had never seen Bud "make a pass at a girl," noting "and he has had chances." Lat treats Callie pretty much as though he was married to her, and when the chips are down, he is chivalrous, at some cost to himself, by showing loyalty to her.

Like Guthrie, Lat had grown up with frontier Methodism, and although he, too, rebels, and in his case does so by leaving the homestead in Oregon and seeking freedom in Montana, the strictures of his parents' religiosity linger in his consciousness. Nevertheless, he falls in love with Callie Kash, who later nurses him back to health after he is badly wounded by renegade Indians, and loans him money, which eventually enables him to start the ranch he had aimed for. He owes her much but leaves her behind to marry a respectable, religious-minded schoolteacher, Joyce Sheridan.

The two women represent the two sides that pull on him, the respectable (the residue of his background and the pull of his ambition), and the free and independent life that is the promise of this new land. In a larger sense they also represent the new West versus the old: the settlers with their communities, and the lone cowboy, trapper, and prospector who are being displaced. Lat starts out as the lone cowboy and ends up a pillar of his community, a member of the school board with the possibility of running for the state Senate.

Lat's conflict involving the two women comes to a head when he is faced with a choice. Callie is witness to a murder committed in her establishment. If Lat agrees to testify for her when the murder comes to trial, he may hurt his wife and his standing with her and thereby ruin his marriage. If he protects his and his wife's respectability by staying out of it, he will have betrayed someone who was dear to him, who nursed him when he was near death, and who was in part responsible for his current success. The choice in his mind was not between right and wrong but between two rights, or as Lat puts it to himself at the end of the novel, "to be right for the right reasons."

While Callie doesn't have a heart of gold, she is a gentle, caring person conscious of the fact that she is trapped by circumstances in the role of prostitute and feels tortured by her circumstances and her role. But for many critics, her character was too close to the heart-of-gold stereotype. Yet, her character as developed by Guthrie is as an individual with thoughts and reactions, and it has, as outlined above, a purpose with many dimensions. A conventional plot used in an unconventional way for much more than simple entertainment. However, even his friend Dan Cushman, who had followed the composition of the novel, felt that Bud had tried to use the clichés for his own purposes but, in his view, failed and ended up having the clichés use him.

There were other friends, however, that thought that the novel was a success. Randall Swanberg in Great Falls wrote, "Bud's style grows. In *These Thousand Hills*, I think the writing is best. The scene of the buffalo dying alone on the prairie is sheer poetry. Bud had a feeling of failure about *These Thousand Hills*, but it was a lighter, smaller book than the others. He wanted to demonstrate the importance of a whorehouse in early western history. When you've said it, you've said it." Swanberg also noted that he felt that Bud "drew heavily on his acquaintances" for the characters in the novel, including using him as the model for a lawyer in the story (Bud denied that he did).

And as always, his family was solidly behind him, as witnessed by this note from his sister Jane: "By now you've received at least two fan letters from friends of mine here. . . You're more than due for one from me too. I've delayed writing because I scarcely knew how to express what I felt about the book. To me, parts of it were truly great writing" (12/3/56). And Tom Clark wrote from Lexington: "I would like to know all about your writing. I enjoyed very much your last book. I read it without putting it down. I read it and looked out the window and wished I could go across the driveway and chat with you. More especially I have wished on many occasions that I could go and throw you down on your living room floor and beat you up" (12/30/57).

Perhaps the best assessment of the place of the novel within the series of three novels came in a review of *These Thousand Hills* by Walter Van Tilburg Clark in the *New York Times Book Review*:

> It would appear, then, that Mr. Guthrie has sought to embody the spirit of each era of his series in the kind of man created by that era and most important to it. It would also appear that he has sought to give the very form of each book a reinforcing likeness to that spirit—for "The Big Sky," a world vast, loose and scenic; for "The Way West," a world narrow and moving, and for "These Thousand Hills" a world tight, various, uncertain and contentious. And if "These Thousand Hills" does not move with quite the certainty and power of its predecessors, it seems likely that the difference results, not from any faltering on Mr. Guthrie's part, but from the nature of his materials.

But Bud did falter in the process of composition, with many stops and starts. Some measure of how unsure he was about his work is reflected in the number of people he had reading it for him as he proceeded with the manuscript. He enlisted not only Ted Morrison but Dan Cushman and another writer in Great Falls, Norman Fox. And it was Fox, by the way, who came up with the book's title. Toward the end of his manuscript, Bud had written, "Below him lay the lovely land and the birds of the field and the beasts of the forests that were his, and the earth and the fullness thereof and the cattle on a thousand hills." The passage came from the Bible, the Book of Psalms. Norman Fox suggested the title "A Thousand

Hills," which is what it remained for some time, and then Bud changed "A" to "These" just before publication.

In the summer of 1956, revisions of the manuscript were not yet completed, yet typescript copies were being circulated to every major film studio. Twentieth Century Fox sent the story editor Arthur Kramer to Great Falls in July to present an offer for an option on the book, but Guthrie held off making a deal. Then he and George Jackson were at the Twin Lakes cabin in the late summer to close up for the year—putting the canoe away, storing the lawn furniture, stacking the wood and chopping kindling, putting out poison baits for the mice, hanging out the blankets for airing, and taking a survey of the outbuildings and locking them up. Before they could get to their chores, the phone rang. His Hollywood agent was calling to tell Bud that Twentieth Century Fox had offered seventy-five thousand dollars for the movie rights.

Bud wasn't sure and still wanted to hold off. What if, when it came out, the book was successful? He might be able to get more, a lot more. He took the plunge, and in a somewhat shaky voice, he told his agent, Ben, that he would settle for a flat hundred thousand. Ben seemed to think that the figure was impossible, and George sighed and said, "Goodbye to a fortune, Buddy." But rather than helping with the chores the next day, George insisted on staying near the phone. He was worried—here was a guy who made a living by cutting hair at $1.50 a head and was probably thinking how many haircuts he'd have to do to get to $75,000.

When the call came, it was late in the day. George, smoking one cigarette after another, drummed his fingers on the kitchen table-top. The studio had agreed to Bud's figure. Bud recalled, "George clapped his hands as I replaced the receiver. 'God dammit,' he shouted. 'I knew you'd make it. I just knew you would.'"

He over-celebrated that night.

The pot was sweetened considerably when Fox promised Bud an additional seventy-five thousand if he would write the screenplay. As seemed to be his practice in negotiations with film companies, he hesitated for some time and then, finally, in December accepted the assignment.

Early in 1955 Ted Morrison wrote to Bud to ask him to participate in the Bread Loaf Conference that summer. He had asked him before, but Bud had refused, reluctant to leave Twin Lakes during his summer stay and wanting to keep his time for his ongoing manuscript. However, this request was different. Ted was an unusual man, in many ways a great man who was selfless in helping not only Bud but many others, often at the expense of his own writing. Ted had decided not to be the director of the conference anymore. He had suffered several tragedies, including the death of his son, who was killed while working on his car's snow chains at the side of a road during a storm. Ted was stricken, and decided he needed to change the direction of his life. He decided that the conference took up too much of his time—he wanted just to write and teach.

The officials at Middlebury College asked him to give them a two-year notice, which he gave in the winter of 1954–55, hoping that he wouldn't have to direct the conference beyond one more year. He wrote to Bud, "I need staff members for the Conference, and I always want you, as you know. . . . This may be my last year. Now certainly this doesn't give me a claim on anyone else's plans or convenience, and I don't want it construed that way. But I can't help thinking how cheerful it would be if you were around to hold up my failing hands in my last or next- to-last appearance (as Director, at any rate)" (1/27/55).

Ted had done so much for him, getting him through his first big book, and helping substantially with subsequent books as well, how could Bud refuse? Even though he was just beginning to enter the home stretch on his manuscript of *These Thousand Hills*, he went to the conference to serve on the staff in the summer of 1955 and then went the following year, too. Besides doing something for someone he had owed so much, another, incidental benefit of his service was that he was able to see DeVoto (who was not on the staff, but a featured speaker) and Robert Frost.

In this period, the early and mid-1950s, Bud lost two of his dearest friends, both unexpectedly. And in both cases, Bud tried to pay his respects by writing something. Joseph Kinsey Howard was not only a friend but in several ways a mentor. Howard, who died in 1951 at the early age of forty-five, had a small cabin near Guthrie's at Twin Lakes, and he and Bud got together often during the summers. Reflecting on the relationship, Bud said, "Joe and I were very, very close friends. We shared a common interest in the West. He was influential, I suppose, in that we encouraged each other."

Joe, as everyone called him, was a journalist and historian of Montana and the Metis Indians and was doing research in many of the same areas as Bud while Bud was working on *The Big Sky*. Dan Cushman, a friend to both men, has said, "Joe Howard meant more to Bud than any other writer. His novels were not printed— he was Great Falls' Keats. He hung over Bud, helped show the way, raised obstacles." On Howard's death in 1951, Bud helped scatter his ashes from Flaptop Mountain above the Circle 8 and Howard's cabin.

He may not have published his novels, but he wrote a history, *Montana: High, Wide, and Handsome* (1943), which when it came out was very controversial in taking the monopoly practices of Montana corporations to task. It is still considered a classic. Several years after his death, Joe's wife got in touch with Bud to write a foreword to a new edition of *Montana: High, Wide, and Handsome* to be published by Yale University Press. Bud worked on the foreword during the first few months of 1957, and the new edition was published near the end of the year. In his foreword, Bud said,

Dear Joe,

They want me to write a piece about you and your first book.

I wish I could talk it out in the way that you and I used to talk in those long bull sessions in Lexington and Missoula and Great Falls, not to mention the Teton canyon where the sight of your old cabin always reminds me of them.

He went on to say, "When Joseph Kinsey Howard died in August of 1951, I said that Montana had lost her conscience. Who but he could push and lead us to a recognition of our shortcomings? Who could tackle prejudice and privilege and so awaken us to them? What voice would speak for the neglected, the oppressed, the victimized? Or for our misused inheritance of soil and water and timber?"

The other death of a close friend was that of Bernard DeVoto in November of 1955 at age fifty-eight, leaving, as Bud said, "a real void" in his life. Bud had seen him in good health only a few months earlier, at Bread Loaf, and once again the death was a shock, and Bud agreed to deliver two memorial lectures at Bread Loaf in August of 1957. He planned one lecture to treat DeVoto as a historian and the other to treat him as "the absentee westerner devoted to the preservation of western resources."

In order to gather material, Bud wrote to DeVoto's wife, Avis, and to Helen Everitt, Lovell Thompson, and William Sloane, asking for anecdotes revealing illustrations, observations of Benny, and any memorable sayings. He also wrote to a friend in the Forest

Service, Chalmer K. Lyman, asking, "What has happened to the Forest Service and to government lands in general since DeVoto was inveighing against the raiders? Is the Service still under fire?" Bud explained, "I want to discuss his work and to tell what has happened since, either as a result of or in spite of his efforts." Lyman replied that in general the Forest Service was in good shape, no doubt due in part to DeVoto's efforts in its behalf.

By the time he was ready to deliver his memoir of DeVoto in August 1957, Bud had decided to combine his topics and deliver just one speech. It was in many ways a personal tribute, reflecting his values as much as those of his subject. In an obituary editorial, the *New York Times* noted that only a few days before his death, DeVoto had published a collection of his essays, *The Easy Chair*, taken from his column that ran for twenty years in *Harper's Magazine*. In the collection DeVoto wrote, "No one has got me to say anything I did not want to say and no one has prevented me from saying anything I wanted to." "That," the *Times* added, "expressed the spirit of DeVoto, a great American, and the spirit of the America he loved."

In his speech, "DeVoto—A Memoir," Guthrie said, "If you were to ask me what Benny's greatest contributions were to America I would have to say the quickly forgotten but enduringly effective journalistic pieces, like 'Due Notice to the F.B.I.' Even more important are the articles that sought to preserve our West. Benny was a journalist and a pro. He would like to hear me say that."

CHAPTER TEN

Down in the Dumps—Drink and Divorce

Bud finished his manuscript of *These Thousand Hills* in the early fall of 1956, and it was published in November. He spent much of the first part of the following year in Hollywood, working on a screenplay for the motion picture version of his book. In an article on Guthrie's work in Hollywood, James V. D'Arc reviewed his progress: "In the first half of 1957, Guthrie did produce a treatment, and then a screenplay. However, the first script at 176 pages was much too long. By August, it was down to 159 pages, still too long, but at a more manageable length. However, comments on it from the producer, David Weisbart, were only 'guardedly complimentary,' indicating that the screenplay needed further work, and Guthrie struggled through several revisions during succeeding months."

His brother wrote to him in April 1957 to rib him a bit for living the high life: "I understand from Janey that you are rotting away in solitude down in that drab and disgusting land of glamor with little to do but gaze out of your hotel window and wish you were in Montana. That is somewhat hard to believe for one as garrulous as you, but by now, if my information is correct, you have been relieved by visits from Harriet and Helen" (4/25/57).

No high life—his work on the script was not a happy experience. Looking back, he has said, "Friends ask me why the writers of novels don't re-write them as screenplays. It's silly for studios to engage somebody else. I tended to think so myself. I learned better when I came to California to make a screenplay of my book. . . . I was too close to my novel, too committed to words and pages and characters and the turns of the story to use a knife, to divide and discard and reassemble and reduce to the size of a short story a full-length book, as movie makers must do."

As he tried to shrink his book to the dimensions of a play, he found that the necessity was too much for him. He gave up, and the studio brought in a script doctor under long-term contract, ostensibly to "collaborate."

Bud's reaction was, "We didn't collaborate. He took the screenplay. Well, what he made of it offended me. Granted my script needed help, but what he did to it, it didn't need! So I refused any credit. That's the second time I've turned down credit, which is, you know, heresy in Hollywood. But I don't want my name on something that I can't be reasonably satisfied with." Reviews of the film were generally positive, although it did not make much money at the box office. One reviewer—there is always one—wondered why the studio bothered to buy Guthrie's book if they were going to produce such a formula Western.

As disappointed as Bud was initially with the movie project and his inability to come up with a satisfactory screenplay, he changed his mind after seeing the finished picture. There is something noble about his confession to producer David Weisbart, considering his sweat and tears in trying to come up with a producible screenplay and his resentment after he had to admit defeat and turn it over to a contract writer. In his letter he wrote that the film "astonished" him "agreeably" and went on, "Though I went to it prepared to be disappointed, I came away pleased. I count it a superior western. . . . The picture is awfully tight. With a little more leeway I think it would have emerged as one of the very best pictures of its kind, past and present, though I still wonder why some of the changes were made. But I am not kicking. I'm confessing to a mistaken prejudgement."

But he did not refer to this change of mind in his autobiography and declared that "the film version [of *These Thousand Hills*] lost the values I had struggled for in my novel." Still, he does say in more general terms, "Though neither my books nor my screenplays, save *Shane*, came out as I hoped they would, I have no personal quarrel with Hollywood. I met nothing there but consideration, kindliness and generosity and would be false to myself were I fashionably snide." He expresses no great admiration for actors and actresses (too often "uninformed egotists"), although he notes that it was a pleasure to work with Burt Lancaster as producer and director on *The Kentuckian*.

The movie of *These Thousand Hills* was released in 1959 with a screenplay by Alfred Hayes that was based on Guthrie's novel and possibly to some extent on his previous screenplay. It was directed by Richard Fleischer, and the lead was played by Don Murray, who had recently appeared in *Bus Stop*, opposite to Marilyn Monroe. Also starring were Richard Egan, Lee Remick, Patricia Owens, and Stuart Whitman. James V. D'Arc, who has written about Guthrie and the movies, has pointed out that it was originally budgeted as an "A" movie, but "became a glossy-looking 'B' production although filmed on location near Durango, Colorado, in CinemaScope and color." The movie had favorable reviews, but generated only modest box office returns and has had little play in recent years on television.

The next big project for Bud was *The Big It and Other Stories*. While he was still working to gather, arrange, and edit the stories in the spring of 1962, he got a request from Wallace Stegner to read his book, *Wolf Willow*, in galleys. He and Bud had become acquainted at Bread Loaf in 1946, when Bud was a fellow and Wally was on the staff. Wally's book was a memoir of growing up on a homestead (summer) and in a small town (winter) in Saskatchewan, just north of Montana, at about the same time that Bud was growing up in Choteau. Bud's collection had several stories set in "Moon Dance," his fictional name for Choteau. After reading the galleys, Bud wrote

Dear Wally:

Damn it! You've beat me to the punch—to a lot of punches.

The manuscript I'm just completing has much in it about my old hometown of Choteau. A good many of our experiences were the same, as are a good many, now, of our reflections. I was particularly interested, since it's a point I've hammered, in your observations about the isolation of minds from the surrounding history. I have argued that the man without knowledge of what happened before him right here where he operates is cut off from the melancholy but altogether good sense of being part of the flow of time and experience. So he is cut off from degree of fulfillment and, standing apart and alone, seeks blind ways somehow to place himself. I'm not expressing myself very well, but feel I don't need to. Anyhow, this is only in introduction to what Jake Vinocur, of Montana's English department said very well after I'd spoken this same piece. "Lives without context," he said.

Bud was not only working with stories he had written based on his own growing up in Choteau, but had in the back of his mind the idea of writing his own memoir. When he finally got around to writing his autobiography (his next book project), he spent several pages devoted to his conversation with Jake Vinocur. Following Vinocur's statement "Lives without context," Bud asked him, "Maybe I follow you, . . . [n]o thought about precursors and successors, about relationships in the human adventure, about kinship to the dead and unborn and all that goes with it?" But Jake was silent, perhaps thinking about what Bud had said.

Bud's autobiography, which he called *The Blue Hen's Chick* (a title I'll explain later), was his attempt to find and confirm his own context. And writing the autobiography, bringing order to his memories, allowed him to go on to write the fourth book in his series of six historical novels, *Arfive*. This was the most autobiographical of the series, dealing with the small town Montana of his childhood. Indeed, Bud said later, in an interview, "I wrote *The Blue Hen's Chick* because I thought I couldn't write the book I am writing now [*Arfive*] if I didn't. I wanted to get things in order."

As early as August 1959, Ted Morrison had written Bud about Bud's future plans: "I'm delighted by all your news; as far as I'm concerned, your letter made the best mail of the summer. Your autobiographical excursion sounds like a first-rate project to me, a natural for you and for a lot of readers. I'm glad Mary Lizzie will have a chance to figure. And I'm glad the fourth panel in the Western series lies beyond and in view" (8/30/59).

While Bud had no trouble placing articles, writing and publishing many during the 1950s, he had some trouble getting his short stories accepted by periodicals. Guthrie claimed that the problem was primarily the decline of the market for stories in mass-circulation magazines, a decline that started just about the time he started to freelance after the publication of *The Big Sky*. During the next decade and a half, many of his best stories were rejected repeatedly before they were purchased. He and, more importantly, his agents were persistent. Looking back on that time, he commented, "It's true that many of the stories in 'The Big It' never found a market in magazines. Granted the possibility that they just weren't good enough, it still remains that the sun of the article stands at high noon. Write a how-to or how-come piece, an article on 'I Made Love to a Gorilla' or 'The Lesson of a Drippy Nose' and you've got the editor's attention. This trail, blazed by the *Reader's Digest*, is thick with followers. The result: scant space for fiction." The irony of this is that the first piece that Bud published nationally was in *Reader's Digest*—on his Speakeasy Club back in the 1930s.

But another reason that at least some of his stories had such a hard time finding homes may be that they are so idiosyncratic. Several of them, as collected in *The Big It*, are frontier yarns, displaying Guthrie's funky sense of humor, hardly fitting for the *Atlantic* (although one was published eventually by the *Saturday Evening Post*). He said in the foreword to his collection that he had "a tall time writing the tall stories." Four of the thirteen stories are tall tales, two are about mountain men, several are retellings of folk stories or those he heard from old timers, and others are autobiographical to some extent. Of the tall tales all are humorous and have punch lines. All the stories are set in the West, and almost all take place in the distant or recent past. He seemed to have patterned these stories after Mark Twain's folksy tales told with humorous exaggeration, such as "The Celebrated Jumping Frog of Calaveras County."

One of the humorous yarns is the title story "The Big It"—an odd title, and even odder as the title for a book. In the story the townspeople of Fort Benton come into the possession of a small brass cannon, the "Big It," on the back of a mule, and they decide that they will impress the local Indians with their firepower. They face a gathering of Indians that seems a bit threatening. The men carefully aim the cannon to fire across the river to make a large hole in the far bank and tell the Indians to watch their big medicine.

But as the fuse fizzles down, the mule is frightened, and, according to the narrator, it begins "buck-jumpin' around in a wheel, the cannon bobbin' its big eye at one at one and another and all of us innocent bystanders while the fuse et down toward the charge." Everyone except the Indians runs for cover. Finally, the cannon slides down to the mule's rear and fires off harmlessly past the mule's tail into the ground. The narrator asks Chief Two Plumes, who with solemn dignity had been watching the proceedings, how he liked them: "He answered, 'How?' and let the rest of it wait, but in that Injun eye was a gleam. Then he said, 'Paleface jack-ass poop.'"

One of the mountain man stories is a retelling of the famous story of the ordeal of John Colter, who escapes from Indian captivity by diving into a river and staying out of sight under water by breathing through a reed. Guthrie's character, John Clell, swims underwater and makes his getaway by finding the opening of a beaver lodge and swimming inside. The story ends once again with a punch line. After waiting for the Indians to leave, Clell walks for seven days back to the fort. He realizes that his friends would know why he wouldn't eat prairie turnips after living on raw ones for days, but what they wouldn't understand "because he didn't try to tell them, was why he never would hunt beaver again."

Two of the autobiographical stories are based on Bud's father. "The First Principal" is based on an actual fistfight between the father and a cowhand who considered school teaching a sissy job. The other, "Ebbie," referred to earlier, is the sad story wherein the father clubs the family dog in a fit of temper and blinds her. Charles Hood has summed up the powerful effect of the emotions that are exposed: "With great sensitivity, Guthrie relates the agony of the remorseful father who must destroy the dog, the grief of a son who doesn't understand, and the touching loyalty of the dog who loves her master even after he has blinded her."

Published in February of 1960, *The Big It and Other Stories* won praise from critics. It was offbeat, containing nothing like the *New Yorker* story that had become the literary standard, and that alone seemed to recommend it to many reviewers. As W. H. Hutchinson commented in the *San Francisco Chronicle*, "It is to the publishers' everlasting credit that they were willing to put these vagrant, off-trail sketches between boards for the joy and edification of the bookish public."

The major negative voice in the reviews was that of Henry Nash Smith, who reviewed the collection in the *New York Herald Tribune*, saying such things as, "Two stories in the book ["Independence Day" and "Ebbie"] suggest that Mr. Guthrie's impressive talent might have undergone a different and perhaps more interesting development if he could have ignored the demands of the slick magazines."

His friend, the Montana writer Dorothy Johnson, wrote to Bud, "Who, I want to know (but don't tell me), is this Henry Nash Smith who reviewed your new book with so little understanding in the *Herald-Tribune*? I was just about to write you a fan letter about it, with particular enthusiasm for "The Wreck." That one almost wrecked me emotionally. Mr. Smith probably likes stories in the *New Yorker*. I can't stand them" (5/22/60).

Bud replied, "Bless you! I have had harsher criticisms than that of Mr. Henry Nash Smith but never one so stupid. All I know about Smith is he wrote a nonfiction book called THIS VIRGIN LAND. I hate to have to acknowledge it's a pretty fair work. Anyhow, it's a lot more important to me that you like my book than that Smith doesn't" (5/25/60).

Smith was the author of *Virgin Land: The American West as Symbol and Myth* (1950), which became a landmark study of western history and culture as a part of the development of the country as a whole. Smith starts with the changing vision of the West, mysteriously unknown and then romanticized, as an impetus toward the growth of the nation toward the Pacific, a movement that was eventually thought of as its manifest destiny. Smith goes on from that vision of the West, as mysteriously unknown, to Jefferson's dispatching of the Lewis and Clark expedition, to the growth of the hunter–trapper mythology, then to the cowboy icon, and finally to the farmer, the settler in a land advertised as fertile, though it often wasn't. In a more limited scope, Smith's study roughly parallels the fictional treatment of that history in Guthrie's series of books. Both saw the meaning of America in terms of the western movement.

Appreciative reviews of the collection of stories from the *Saturday Review*, the *New York Times*, *Library Journal*, and *Kirkus Reviews* raised Bud's morale, but problems with his publisher eroded it. William Sloane Associates went out of business after Bud published *The Way West*, and Houghton Mifflin had taken over publishing his work. His new publisher was reluctant to publish a collection of stories because such books, at that time particularly, usually did not sell well. The publisher acceded to publishing the stories as a favor to their author, who had previously produced best-sellers.

After Bud had difficulty finding his book in bookstores, he wrote to his publisher and found that it had printed only four thousand copies. As he wrote to Ted Morrison, he had told his publisher "far in advance that it would sell five thousand copies in Montana alone." Bud added, "In four days the edition was sold out and Houghton Mifflin was tardy and stingy in bringing out the second, third and, by now I guess, the fourth printings. We couldn't find a copy in Philadelphia, New York . . . and later, Lexington and Louisville. There are no copies in Montana, either. All this in spite of reviews that made the book better than it actually is." Bud thought this behavior insulting and couldn't figure out the logic of not printing more, at least the second time around.

A more serious source of concern was the impending breakup of his marriage during the latter part of 1962. Concern about money was part of the conflict. One way or another, Bud and his wife had spent enough so that despite all the Hollywood income, they were almost broke. In his letters he joked about bankruptcy. His plan to become solvent again depended in part on the sale of *The Big It*, and when Houghton Mifflin messed that up, he had reason to be furious. Nevertheless, Bud never changed publishers or agents during his entire career (only going temporarily to an independent publisher to put out a collection of children's stories that Houghton Mifflin would not handle).

Although Bud was loyal to agents and editors, after he became famous, he began to stray from his wife. Close friends have testified that he never visited a prostitute, never had an affair, and never even flirted seriously. But the last two claims were not true. Randall Swanberg may have testified that "in twenty years" he had "never seen him make a pass at a girl," although he "had chances," but

Swanberg was the husband of Harriet's best friend, Helen, and may have seen Guthrie only on his best behavior. (Some evidence for Bud's straying came in his giving the name of one of his woman friends, "Callie," to the character in *These Thousand Hills*.) Helen and Bert have said that, at about the time of *Shane*, after he received the Pulitzer, his celebrity ruined him. Bert has said, "That was one of his big failings—he couldn't stand success. He didn't know how to handle it." He became, in Helen's words, "a womanizer." This was true most of all in Hollywood, since friends in Great Falls seemed to have been largely unaware of it.

His daughter recalled, "My mother kind of looked the other way, if she were aware of it at all. Later on, I think it was a little more obvious. I am sure there were many things she was unaware of at all. I remember being at a cocktail party with them in Southern California where he was snarfing after another woman. I found it embarrassing in the extreme. She [Harriet] seemed to be pretty much oblivious to it."

Nevertheless, he was in love with Harriet and stayed in love with her, but frequent, violent arguments made it difficult for them to continue to live together. Jane thought that one of the reasons for their breakup was that Harriet didn't know when Bud was working. Jane said Bud would "sit at the kitchen table, ostensibly doing nothing. . . . Sometimes he [was] working while he [was] reading 'who-dunnits.' He [was] reading the words, but in the back of his mind he [was] working."

According to Charles Hood, Bud's close friend George Jackson recalled in an interview an incident that illustrated Guthrie's ability to work out writing problems while doing something else:

Jackson was having "eye trouble" [he was almost blind], so he closed his barbershop and visited Guthrie at Twin

Lakes. Although Guthrie was supposed to be writing, Jackson found his friend was fixing the fence, cutting wood and doing other chores. On the second day of Jackson's visit, Guthrie still had not written a word. He was playing solitaire, Jackson recalls, when he suddenly "shoved the cards away. He pulled out his typewriter and typed for about three quarters of an hour. Then he got up and said, 'Well, I whipped that sonovabitch.'" Jackson had not suspected that Guthrie had been working on that passage all the time. "In the back of his mind, he was kickin' it over."

Moody, preoccupied, sometimes deeply depressed, and doubting his ability, Bud was not an easy man to live with. Swanberg observed that sometimes Bud got "very depressed," and thought he was "not worth a damn." And in an interview Bud stated, "I don't often re-read anything I've written but when I do I have the terrible suspicion sometimes that I can't write that well anymore." As time went on he became melancholy and saddened by growing older, and drank too much. His friend Marguerite Hanusa in Choteau observed, "When they moved to Great Falls, Bud was a celebrity. This led to drinking and more drinking. . . . The trouble was with his wife. . . . They reached an impasse. It was hell for them. He had always loved her very much. It was a bad experience."

Harriet had always been more social-minded than Bud, and in the early days this helped him get out and meet people. But then as he became established, he no longer needed so much social activity, but Harriet did. As his sister, Jane, pointed out, they would go to cocktail parties, where Bud would be uncomfortable, drink too much, and then say things that he would be sorry for the next morning. She remembered one occasion when her brother left a party and walked many blocks home because he couldn't get his wife to leave.

In the end, he was the one who instigated the divorce in early 1963 (it became final in May). As Helen recalled, "That did not serve my mother well. Her exact words were to me, 'Buddy left me like a dead skunk.' And then she really went downhill from there. He didn't do a whole lot better." As it developed, the divorce was a long-term emotional disaster for both Bud and Harriet.

They sold the house and, in June, Bud went to Lexington and left Harriet, who moved into a condo in Great Falls. Bud was lonely and depressed and wondered what he was going to do with his life—whether he was through as a writer. Harriet drifted, got into relationships that were disastrous, and fell into financial difficulties. They had needed each other as stabilizers, something they lost as their boats collided in the dark, shuddered, and sank.

Bud withdrew into himself, declining speaking engagements, and after a spate of article publications in the mid- and late fifties, turned down almost all writing assignments of articles and reviews. In his state, it was perhaps natural that he turned inward to self-examination and that that, in turn, led to his actively considering an idea that he had had for several years—an autobiography. As we noted earlier, he was convinced it would help him re-examine and evaluate his life and help establish the groundwork for his next novel, which would be his most autobiographical, the one in his series dealing with his own time. Chick felt that he had turned to work, developing "a slavish devotion to writing," as a result of his loneliness.

But Bud did not want to write the book just as a project of self-discovery. He had a whole list of memorable characters he wanted to write about: Mary Lizzie, Joe Jordan, Dan Bowmar, Happy Chandler, Tom Clark, Tom Larson, and George Jackson. As in his novels, he was an observer. What was important was character—the quirks, oddities, misbehavior, humor, and loving warmth and giving of so many of the people he had encountered. That to him, even more than what he thought or felt, or his accomplishments, was the story of his life. For the most part, life had been fun, and now it was no longer fun.

After a stay in Lexington, where he sought out consolation from old friends, Bud moved on to Los Angeles where he lived with Grace Givens in a mansion in Westwood from 1963 to 1964. She was an older lady who had been a family friend in Choteau, had married and moved to Los Angeles, and now was a widow. She already had one roomer, John Marko, who was an interior designer and artist and who kept up Grace's yard and flower garden in lieu of paying rent. Marko became a good friend, and Bud took him several times to Montana. He gave one of Marko's paintings to his sister for Christmas in 1963 (it was a view of the trees at Twin Lakes), and Janie wrote on Christmas Day to thank him for the gift:

> It set me thinking of times past when you surprised me with something delightful. You may not remember the five five-dollar gold pieces in a white box all lined in white velvet, but I'm sure you do remember the complete riding costume you got for me—and probably at a time when you could poorly afford it. How very proud I was!
>
> I am sitting here in the living room watching the fire in the fireplace and wishing I could express without sounding maudlin all the thoughts I'd like to put on paper for you. You will have to settle for the statement that I'd never have had you one jot different from what you have always been. You have added so much of zest and interest to my life. (12/25/63)

At Grace's, Bud worked on his autobiography, but he was nearly without funds. His arrangement with Harriet was that she would get half his income, but although he continued to receive royalties, he was without work, and his daughter was worried about both his and her mother's ability to survive.

Helen recalled that her father "gave an awful lot of money away. He gave it to women—money flying all over the place. He had no money sense whatsoever." So she called up his agent in Hollywood, Ben Benjamin, and asked him if, were she to come down to live with her father and keep him on the straight and narrow, could he find him work? He said, "Yes, I can." Among Bud's many projects over the next few years was a treatment for Columbia Pictures of David Lavender's book *Bent's Fort*, which was never produced. He had an extensive correspondence with the director Tom Gries and, for him, did a treatment of a program for a television series called *Sun Prairie*, which also was not produced. And he was a consultant to Gries for his movie *Will Penny*.

Much of *The Blue Hen's Chick* was written in Kentucky, and in the first few months Bud was in Los Angeles. Thereafter, he spent a full year revising the original manuscript, and in the fall of 1964, Helen helped her father read the galleys. In January of 1965, Bud wrote to Harriet, giving her an accounting of his finances: "I am sending you my check for $707.87, which represents one half of what I have received in Houghton-Mifflin royalties. . . . I am not wealthy, but I am not broke, and things are looking up for both of us. I just received the illustrations for the dust-jacket cover of *The Blue Hen's Chick*. I think it's wonderful. I also think the book will do very well, and of course you have a half interest in it" (1/16/65).

The autobiography was published in March 1965. Its title comes from an exclamation of delight by Mary Lizzie after Bud had won six hundred dollars at the races when he was in Lexington years before. For Mary Lizzie, he had shown that he was the rare and chosen one, and the conceit tickled his fancy. And so he came up with a title, which, like his title for his short story collection, no one at first glance could understand. But these were phrases that had meaning for him, and after all, these were his books.

The Blue Hen's Chick is an informal, freewheeling book, full of personal anecdotes, and fun to read. There is humor, and much of the humor is at the author's own expense, but there is sadness as well. Nevertheless, the effect of the whole is of a relaxed story of a man who was at ease with himself and enjoyed life, and in reading it, it is hard to realize just how troubled and unhappy he must have been at the time he wrote it.

In his book Guthrie tells of his family's arrival in Montana from Indiana, of his boyhood in Choteau and surroundings, of job-hunting during the Depression, of his life as a newspaperman in Lexington, of his time at Harvard and Bread Loaf, and of his return to Montana. Along the way he tells stories about his friends and about encounters with public figures as a newsman, and he tells about his struggles to research and compose his novels. All and all, as many reviewers noted, it is unpretentious and candid.

Once again the reviews were positive, among them those in the *Saturday Review*, the *New York Times*, *Harper's*, and surprisingly, the *New Yorker*, which had been critical of his previous books. In the *Saturday Review*, Robert L. Perkin summarized the book by saying, "The method is loosely chronological, the mood one of gentle philosophy tempered by virile prejudices, and the manner is broad brush. Guthrie sketches his life not as a narrative but as a series of vignettes, many in continuity, but some, one suspects, slabbed in just because the flavor is right." Those anecdotes just "slabbed in" are the basis for the few complaints registered by reviewers. Bud could not resist a funny story that he heard as a newspaperman in Lexington or a funny incident he heard about or witnessed in Choteau, especially if it were a bit off color—whether it had any bearing on the narrative of his life or not.

CHAPTER ELEVEN

Living with Janie and Courting Carol

If there was any indication of Bud's troubled spirit at the time he wrote the autobiography, it comes in the concluding chapter. Here he sits, looking out the window of his Twin Lakes cabin and reflecting on his surroundings. But the mood is not just reflective—it is also melancholic. He seems to be contemplating not only nature around him but, now that he is alone, what he has lost, where he is now, and how he can go on. Some in the Guthrie family feel that the book was for Bud the summing up of a life at what he had come to believe might very well be the end of that life—or, at least the end of his career. But there is in the ending to the autobiography the suggestion that out of communion with place, his place, he may find salvation, the strength to continue. As he looks out, he concludes,

> Suddenly the yard is bare, abandoned by the birds, left vacant at the last by the chipmunk after he had flirted

goodnight from the woodpile; and I feel deserted and thrown in on myself, as if I were the last of life.

Westward, astride the backbone of the Rockies, the sun sets through the mist. Time to have a drink. To have two, maybe. Almost time, as old-time camp cooks used to say, to burn a mulligan.

End of an April day.

Bud made an attempt to overcome his loneliness by moving in with his sister in Missoula. He had written his brother in early 1965 from Grace Givens's house in Los Angeles:

> I expect to stay here until early summer. There is a possibility then that Janie and I will share her house. I am not sure. I have a friend here who is anything but a mistress, but is damn good company. I am debating what I should do. I like to have a settled home. And somehow—don't count this as sex—I want a woman in my life.
>
> For the rest I am doing reasonably well, turning out a piece of prose once in a while. (1/16/65)

His move from Los Angeles came at just about the same time as his autobiography was published in mid-1965. Jane, too, had divorced. Both Bud and Chick had tried to talk her out of it, although Bud had never liked or approved of her husband. Bob was, by all accounts, a good man, quiet and cordial, a professional photographer. But Bud just ran all over him. He respected strength—wanting to be looked straight in the eye and responded to by left hook to left hook. Bud's niece, Peggy, felt that he was hard on the husbands of his womenfolk. When Helen brought her new husband, Hub, to meet Bud and the family, Hub was out one morning hitting golf balls on the lawn. When he came in for a cup of coffee, Bud asked, "Why don't you go out there and find your lost balls?" And Hub replied, "They are not making father-in-law's balls like they used to." Peggy added that Bud "particularly liked other people who were witty, that gave him competition. He enjoyed good wit."

He could be, according to Peggy, wonderful, kind, but he could be cutting, and that was especially hard for the people closest to him. One night when she was in graduate school, she and a group of her friends came in late at night, and as usual, Bud was still up. There were three women and three men, and Bud got up from his chair, didn't say hello or shake hands, just said to one of the men, "Don't they teach you in graduate school to take your hat off in the house?"

Janie had several times offered her home to Bud, and after he arrived, she gladly took over the burden of keeping her brother on "the straight and narrow." The next four years were a somewhat happier time for him, although he still battled with alcohol and too often lost.

When with company at Twin Lakes, he seldom drank hard liquor but kept a beer in hand, one after another. Peggy Bloom recalled, "For all the times I saw Buddy, I never saw him drink to the point where he didn't have control of himself. . . . At twin Lakes he would have a beer going all the time, but the beer probably lasted about an hour, so I figured he always had a three beer buzz going on . . . and he just let it finish, sit there at the table and talk to everybody and sing." On the other hand, a favorite story among those who knew Bud tells of the time when his neighbor Alice Gleason, of the Circle 8 Ranch, was driving into Choteau for groceries. She saw Bud and George Jackson fishing on the Teton, and they flagged her down. "Oh, oh, wait Alice, Alice, we need some things from town—can you pick them up for us?" She said, "Sure, let me make a list." She got out a pencil and paper and asked, "What do you need?" Bud paused, glanced at George, and called out, "Bread and bourbon."

In Missoula, staying with his sister, Bud found himself oppressed by the gloom of so many gray days, and he missed the wind and broken clouds of the area around Choteau. There the sun might shine through even in the winter. Walking around to look at the interior of Jane's house, he noted that John's painting of Twin Lakes, which he had given her was hanging in the dining room. Soon after he arrived, he was settled into the back bedroom, and soon after that, he arranged to do his writing in the finished basement. Peggy recalled that it "was kind of cavy, the way basements are, but maybe that was good for him, to kind of go down there and concentrate." The basement room had its own furnace, lots of shelves for his books and papers, and good lighting, and he was perfectly happy to take possession and do his work there. He set up his typewriter and spread out his papers on the ping-pong table. Peggy recalled,

> Buddy always stayed up so late, so late. He was just a night owl, maybe one or two in the morning. That was okay. It was just different because my mother was teaching fourth grade at Washington School, and she needed her sleep, so she would be in bed by 10 p.m. anyway. So I think that Friday night was kind of the night when the two of them would decide on what groceries they needed, and brother and sister would head to the grocery store, get the food. Then they'd stop by the bottle shop, because in Montana you couldn't buy liquor in the grocery story, and they'd come home and have two or three martinis on Friday night and two or three on Saturday night. And that was a big deal because on the weeknights my Mom walked pretty straight and narrow as far as partying because she had to be up the next day.

Both Peggy and her mother thought that "in many ways Bud needed that regimentation. Maybe he was too adrift down in California, and maybe he came up as sort of a chance to introduce a little structure in his life." Peggy added, "I think my mother was lonely, and I think Buddy was just adrift, so here they were the two together, always compatible, never any discord." She added, "He did pay Mother rent, and that helped Mother with her house payments. It wasn't a lot, but they split the groceries, and my Mother would never have charged him a dime—she just enjoyed his company so much, but still it helped because she wasn't a fat cat."

She also remembered, "Every day Bud ate the same thing for lunch, he'd have a can of Deviled Ham Spread, and then he would have Ritz Crackers—he would get out a roll of Ritz Crackers. 'This is the perfect lunch, baby; there's no dishes.' His nutrition was just wretched. It is amazing he lived so very long." Bud took over much of the cooking. It had become a hobby—he even subscribed to gourmet magazines in order to collect the recipes. But most of his dishes were not very fancy. His preferences had been developed by his mother's cooking. Among his favorites were tomato aspic salad, Lipton pepper steak, beef lyonnaise, pot roast, and two of his favorites, zesty meatballs and corn dodger. His recipes for the latter two were,

ZESTY MEAT BALLS

Brown meat balls in ¼ c. oil. Remove and sauté 2 medium-size onions. When tender add:

1 c. applesauce

½ c. tomato sauce

1 t. horseradish

Place meat on sauce and cook slowly until you are hungry.

BUDDIE'S CORN DODGER

1 c. corn meal

½ t. salt

½ c. boiling water

1 T. melted shortening or enough so
    patties mold well in the hand.

Cook in greased skillet until patties are nicely browned on both sides. These are compatible with beans.

He specialized in beef and almost never had vegetables. At a dinner party, his blessing or toast was invariably, "To whatever gods there be, thanks for good company."

His routine during the week tended to be deviled ham, crackers, and beer, and then at night he would move into a couple of Wild Turkeys and some beef, and call it quits. Sometimes he would write for a couple of hours in the morning or at night. He loved to call people on the phone. He would sit down at night after a couple of drinks and then get on the phone. Peggy recalled, "His bills were just colossal. But that didn't bother him. Money never seemed to bother him. He would phone and bring everybody up to date." And he kept in touch with Hollywood.

But it wasn't just a beer at noon and Wild Turkey at night. Left alone during the day—Janie would be at work and Peggy was away attending Smith College in Northampton, Massachusetts—Bud began hanging out in downtown Missoula, becoming a famous habitué of the Florence Hotel bar. The Montana writer Bill Kittredge recalled that when he got to Missoula in 1969, Guthrie was legendary around town as a drunk—gossip that was no doubt generated by his fame. But it was obvious that living with Janie had not entirely solved Bud's need for structure in his life or totally relieved his loneliness.

While he was in Missoula, he spent his longest period between publications of a novel, apparently treading water and hoping for motivation and inspiration to carry him ashore. Ostensibly, he was working on *Arfive* (which did not until much later get that title), but his work on the manuscript was spasmodic, and it wasn't until after he left his sister's house and remarried that he found shore at last and was able to finish the project. Since Peggy was an English major aspiring to become a writer herself, Bud felt free while at his sister's house to discuss with his niece his work on his novel, his scenes and characterizations. As far her own writing was concerned, "There was never just a straight 'Whoa, that was really good.' It was always measured somehow. Praise was metered."

Although it is but a small part of Bud's total published writing, the composition of poetry was something he turned to frequently. Sometimes it was a way to express his emotions, as in his poems to Harriet before they were married and living at a distance from each other, and sometimes he seemed to use verse-writing as recreation, as expressions of his feeling for nature, and, occasionally, as an expression of something that struck him as humorous.

As in his fiction, his verses tended to be very traditional in form, with a steady meter and regular lines that rhymed. He admired E. A. Robinson (as did Walter Van Tilburg Clark, who wrote a lot of poetry) and then later, the work of Robert Frost, after he met him. Later in life, as we will note, he became a close friend of the renowned poet Richard Hugo, whose free verse and tough working-class imagery baffled him. The two had discussions in which Hugo tried to instruct him in modern forms and Guthrie tried to argue that more traditional poetry like Frost's should be his model.

Bud had memorized a wide variety of poems, from Tennyson and other major British poets, to the Americans Robinson and Frost. He also loved light verse like that written by Robert Service ("The

Shooting of Dan McGrew": "A bunch of the boys were whooping it up in the Malamute Saloon," and "The Cremation of Sam McGee": "There are strange things done in the midnight sun"). At a party or just on the inspiration of a moment, he might recite a poem or two.

Of the few poems he published, three came out in *Harper's Monthly* in 1964 before he moved to Missoula, and two of these involved Twin Lakes ("Twin Lakes Hunter" and "Twin Lakes Winter"). The cabin continued to be very important to him, although it is doubtful that he got a lot of writing done there. After the divorce he divided the weeks of summer with Harriet, which cut down his time there considerably. When he was at the cabin, Jane and Peggy would go up to stay for several days, usually over the fourth of July, which was family reunion time. Peggy recalled,

> There wasn't anybody just my age to pal around with, but I used to sit through the conversations, the adult conversations. . . . The thing I do remember from my sitting and listening is the poetry that often was quoted. Buddy had a great memory, and he would bring poems from his youth, or he'd say that reminds me of this limerick—something— magic things, flotsam and jetsam, that were just coming, and I always enjoyed that.

One summer Jane and Peggy drove to Mexico for a vacation, leaving Bud to look after the house. Jane bought a sterling silver fruit compote bowl from a silversmith in Guadalajara. On their return to Missoula, she showed her treasure to Bud. She expected him to say something like "That's beautiful," but instead, without hesitation, he recited, "There once was a lady named Alice, who peed in the Archbishop's chalice. It is my belief she peed for relief and not out of Protestant malice."

But Peggy recalled that he was often sad, "Often his conversations would be fairly weighty, kind of gloom and doom—as he often said, 'I am usually angry at somebody.' It would be politicians or some issue that he was thinking about, maybe writing about, and to a child sometimes that is not as much fun as other things. But as I grew older, I realized that his great sense of fairness often led him to these positions. . . . [But] he was always a great entertainer. He would have full court and we would listen."

Bud loved his sister and loved his niece (both were diminutive and he lovingly called them his "midgets"), and although he was happy to be living in his sister's house—it was a lifeline for him—he was not a happy man. Not distraught, simply not functioning well. Although he often thought about his new novel, he did not often sit down to work on it. And as time went by he drank more and worked less and less. He could be grumpy, even angry, anger not expressed so much toward individuals as about causes, but for the most part he could hold his liquor and put up a good front. That isn't to say that he had entirely lost his sense of humor.

Helen recalled flying with him back from the coast, where he had been working as a consultant on a movie project. It was a Western Airlines flight with the seats configured to face each other, and they were looking at strangers across a table. Bud had had a couple of drinks and needed to use the restroom. The flight was bouncing around, but he managed to navigate down the aisle. And then, coming back from the toilet, he looked down at the people across from them and at all the other passengers in the vicinity, and in a huge booming voice said to Helen, "Well, Baby, I just peed all over the Comstock Lode." Looking back, Helen could only shake her head and say, "He was on. He could be on and usually was when he was around me."

Gradually, over the next few years, however, his situation would change dramatically when he met someone who would help him pull himself out of the slough of despond. She would be a very unlikely rescuer.

When he got an offer from Rand McNally in 1966 to write the introduction to a coffee table book, he was inclined to turn it down. But the book did pique his interest, since it would be a collection of photos tracing the journey of Lewis and Clark, a topic he certainly knew something about. The Rand McNally editor in Chicago, Herbert William Luthin Jr. who was in charge of the project, had been impressed by Bud's writing. He got in touch with Bud, and when Bud sounded reluctant, arranged to come out to Montana to present the project to him and presumably to talk him into writing the introduction. Bud seemed to Luthin to be the perfect choice, not only because of his writing and research on the early West, but also because the photographer and editor for the book itself, Ingvard Henry Eide, was also a Montanan.

That Herb Luthin's wife Carol would go with him to Montana was largely an accident. Although she was a college graduate, she was basically a 1950s-type housewife, the mother of two, and she almost never went on business trips with her husband. She recalled,

> [Herb] said he was coming out . . . to Montana, and I said I would really like to go too. I had never been West. So we were invited to come to Bud's cabin at Twin Lakes for this meeting. And we flew out. This was when I introduced myself to Bud as the daughter of an Army engineer because I had read *The Blue Hen's Chick*, and I was aware of his feelings. And Montana was really a mind-blowing experience for me. It was just incredible to me. I had never been anywhere like that, and it just answered something.

In early September, the Luthins were at Twin Lakes for four days, one of those days traveling up into Glacier Park for a picnic. About her experience in Montana, Carol has said, "I loved it—it felt really wonderful to me." Bud took them over to Great Falls to catch the plane, and once on the plane, Carol found herself crying, "I cried all the way to Billings. For no reason, except I was just desolated to be leaving. I do not know why I cried—I just cried. . . . There was no involvement with Bud, nothing like that."

After Carol sent a thank you note, something of a correspondence began, and in a letter back to Carol, Bud wrote that he would be coming through Chicago in late October. To return his hospitality, the Luthins invited him to stay with them. After they brought him home from the airport, Carol's son, Bill, said to Bud, "That's a really nice tie." Bud stopped, smiled, took off his tie and said, "Here, boy," and gave him the tie.

Later that evening, while sitting around the kitchen table talking, Bud was talking about a friend of his: "You know, I simply don't have any respect for a man who would never say he was sorry." It was for Carol a moment of sudden insight. She thought, "I was married to a man who would never say he was sorry. And I thought, my God, there are people in the world who think differently." She has reflected, "My marriage was not a happy marriage. It was in many ways an abusive marriage. . . . [Herb] would come home from work and drink two martinis and anything could happen. . . . It was quite frightening, quite horrible."

Her parents didn't know; nobody knew. She was in a situation where she was sure the response would be, "Don't whine and complain. Try harder. Make it work." Her parents were pillars of the Methodist church (she had that in common with Bud, but didn't realize it) and were very conventional. Carol felt she simply could not raise the issue of a possible divorce with them no matter how badly her marriage was going.

In the meantime, Bud had said to her during his visit, "You know it would be really nice if you wanted to . . . if you would like to correspond or we could correspond when I am writing this book. It kind of steadies me down to correspond." Carol thought that would be "really nice." "He was," she thought, "such an open, friendly guy." She didn't think that he had his eye on her at this point, but she was sure that he sensed her marital situation. Even while he was visiting in Chicago, Bud went back to work on *Arfive* and had explained to Carol his plan for the book and the trouble he had had developing it from autobiographical materials.

The correspondence lasted from 1966 to June of 1970 and got more and more heated and personal as time went on. Eventually, they were writing each other more than twice a week, sometimes almost every day, and they developed, in Carol's words, "a great fondness for one another." It was a courtship by letter—in looking back, Carol counted the number of times they saw each other before they were married, and it was only five. And their meetings were always in public places, with a group at Twin Lakes or at the Chicago train station and once at Carol's parents' home in Davenport, Iowa.

One needs to realize in order to understand what happened that, despite his background as a hard-drinking, heavy-smoking, cynical newspaperman, he could also be charming. From Kentucky he brought with him the manner of a Southern gentleman—not part of a façade, but rather an expression of something that had always been in his character. Kindness and consideration were even more a part of his character than his cynicism and occasional combativeness. And he seemed to have a special talent for charming women. He liked them and he liked talking and listening to them, even when others might not take them seriously.

On the other side there was Carol. She was slim, brunette, and beautiful—Bud thought of her as "elfin." She was intelligent and had a good sense of humor—something required of those around a man who was frequently joking. There is little doubt that he fell for her before she even considered him as a possibility. There was a considerable age difference. She was thirty-eight and he was sixty-eight. To win her seemed impossible, and his feelings for her began in his mind as a kind of fantasy, something to dream about, not as something that might actually develop into something real. The fantasy was fed by a relationship that developed at a distance, in letters. Letters gave him the courage to say things to her that he might have been reluctant to say in person. We might stop to reflect that his courtship of Harriet was also largely by letter—words had a special power for him and he was a powerful user of words.

A week after the Luthins' original trip to Twin Lakes in early September of 1967, Bud began his correspondence with a letter to Herb. He had finished a draft of his introduction for the picture book that Herb was editing and had been working on a play and a series of children's stories. (Written for a celebrations committee in Lexington, the play was about the life of George Rogers Clark, the older brother of William, who had been the original choice to go on the Lewis and Clark Expedition. The plan was to present the play as part of a promotion to make the Clark Memorial in Clarksville a national park.) Bud told Herb that he was going to send the children's stories to him, not for submission but to get his advice on them. He added, "I am about to sign a contract with Houghton Mifflin for a last novel. You reckon I can write it? You reckon I'll live long enough?" (9/15/67). The novel would eventually be called *Arfive* and would not be the last novel in the series after all.

In early November, Bud went to Chicago, ostensibly on book

business with Herb, and stayed several days with the Luthins. Shortly after, he wrote a thank-you letter; this time his letter was addressed to Herb and Carol. Several letters followed that were addressed to the two of them, and then, having taken that step toward his objective, Bud's correspondence as it continued was addressed exclusively to Carol. He began including every now and then notes in his letters addressed to the Luthin children, Amy and Bill.

Among the others Bud was writing to was his daughter, Helen. While his son, Bert, was somewhat estranged from him, he had always been very close Helen. (Bert had drawn away from his father. He was not a letter writer, not interested in literary things, and not fond at all of environmentalists. His main concerns were his immediate family and establishing a working ranch on which he could raise cattle and sheep. Helen, on the other hand, was glad to read her father's manuscripts and make suggestions.) Helen was divorced in September 1966. Both Bud and Chick were worried about her, but she wrote to Bud in October, "Bill [an old friend] has a new hobby, which is called 'Prevent Helen from getting the screamers.' He calls every day, and most every evening. It's no bother. I think it is nice of him to do it—but he is inclined to think that all divorced people are going to fare as badly as he has. And I just can't see that I'll be in very bad shape" (10/28/66).

Some indication of how close Helen and her father were is suggested by her tone in the following letter:

> Enclosed is my check for $50, which you must cash. If you don't, I'll send you a money order. You must remember that you will not be doing me any favor by not cashing it—you will only be encouraging my bad habits. And it is already entirely too easy to ask you for loot. If I get in tough shape some month and find I cannot find $50 to

send to you, I'll let you know but in the meantime please
let me pay a debt I intended all along to pay. It is not your
role to finance my marital disasters. (1/30/67?)

As time went on in the fall of 1967, Bud continued to work on
his children's stories, revising and adding material. He wanted to
introduce each story with a verse. Herb had commented that the
verse Bud had used to introduce Cousin Frog gave away the story.
So he composed a new one and included it in a letter to Carol:

THE UNSUNG SONG OF AMPHIBIOUS
The heart of Mother Earth
Keeps beating with our own,
And no one, feeling it,
Need feel himself alone.

The birds flap-soar above
And cry or sing their feat,
But each and all return
To feel the mother beat.

The sky is made to look at,
For some made to explore,
But foot to earth is homing,
And that's enough and more.

Commenting on his composition, he wrote to Carol, "You will
see, dear, that I'm a versifier and not a poet. The fact is that I am
out of pitch with the poets of today. I don't understand them. I
don't like the ragged lines. I miss rhymes and rhythms. My preferences date me, and my lack of understanding marks me as a slob.
And the hell with that!" (11/15/67).

As his letters to Carol continued, they became more and more intimate rather quickly. He addressed them first with "Carol, dear," then "Carol, dear ONE," and then "Carol, dearest" and "Carol, my dear." Two months after the correspondence began, Bud wrote to her expressing mixed emotions. He warned her, "Sweetheart, never forget your treasures and never risk them. More and more, Herb grows on me. And the kids! I have nothing to offer nearly so precious." Bud had guessed that her marriage was in trouble, but he didn't yet know how bad the trouble was.

He went on to tell her,

> God knows I am not tossing you aside. I am trying to divorce myself from sentiment while sentiment insists. I am a kind of half-assed gentleman. Warning: I may forget myself and chase you through the chokeberry bushes.
>
> You have an inflated image of me, Carol, I am old, too old for you, and am not the man you imagine. Honesty I have, and compassion and maybe a little bit of talent. And surely, with you, desire, for you are both such a lovely and giving girl, the kind that I should have married. Unhappily, I married a frigid woman and am covered with scar tissue. . . .
>
> Damn it, the only time I can mind-see you is late at night. Then I go to sleep with you to comfort me. I want pictures of you. (11/18/67)

She would send photos, but before that a photographer friend provided one he had taken of Carol with Herb. Bud told her, "The picture is here in the study, and you are looking at me now. You, so young and fresh and really little girlish. You take me back to high school days, and I am singing, 'When you and I were seventeen . . .' Surely you are an illusion, one gladly embraced. A guy needs a prime illusion" (12/5/67).

Occasionally, in his letters to Carol, Bud would depart from his courting to get on his soapbox, expressing as he often did to friends and relatives strong political opinions:

> Now I am going to get mad and write a Letter to the Editor. I do not believe the economists, those practitioners of the dismal science, always know what they're talking about. A tax increase is not deflationary. It is the opposite, for the bigger the tax take the more the pressure for advanced prices from both labor and enterprise. If the U.S. treasury needs money—and it does—let the administration remove that fat 27½ per cent depletion allowance that has made so many Texans rich. Let it tax the great and growing commercial involvements of churches. Religion has no business in business anyhow. And let it cut the pork barrel in half. Half of the remaining half might be justified.

Then he added, "Now I know I am boring you" (12/1/67).

He mentioned his daughter to Carol in his letters, and Carol wondered how Helen would react to their relationship. Bud replied, "Please have no worries about my Helen. I haven't told her about you, and I'm sure that Janie hasn't, either. But even if she were informed, I'm sure her response would be: Harrah for Father! We are THAT close. She will love you, and you will love her. This much I can guarantee" (12/1/67).

Whatever he had done earlier with the project that would be called "Arfive" had been cast aside, and he reported in early December that he had "started" on his novel. He told Carol that he was pleased with what he had written, a draft of most of the first chapter. Although, he added, "I have only the vaguest idea of where I'm going."

CHAPTER TWELVE

The Old Man and the Young Woman Wed

Going back to the end of 1967, Bud wrote to complain about the cold in Missoula, quoting lines from Keats's "The Eve of St. Agnes": "Ah, bitter chill it was!" He suspected that this was only "the beginning of a bitch-bastard of a winter." Going out the front door one morning to fetch his little Dachshund, he encountered a silvery lace on the walk, and fell, spinning around and then down onto his back. When Janie, hearing his cry, came out to rescue him, she also slipped and slid, hands waving in the air, and fell. She was all right, only a bit shaken. He told Carol that no, he didn't bust his ass but may have broken a finger, which made it damn hard to type. "Should I attribute my fall to ice or infirmity? I favor the former." And at the end of his letter, "I would write more if not maimed" (12/24/67). On New Year's Eve he resolved, first, to see her again and to write as well and as much as he could, and then to "forego dignity in favor of devotion." Then, as his correspondence continued in the New Year, his letters reflected a growing determination to woo Carol and come to a resolution of the desire they knew they both shared. He wrote,

> My dear one, shall we quit analyzing and accept what is? Cannot the heart beat a truer drum than the brain? In our case I think so.
>
> I am not so strong as you imagine or so honorable as I argue. I am pretending, out of skull rather than heart. Pretense can be indulged only when you are out of reach. And I do feel, despite the ghosts that haunt me, that you could and would exorcise them and restore me.

And then two days later, he continued:

> Sweetheart, I really don't know how to talk to you. I do want you for mine, body and spirit. Against my need for you is—I must say—a faltering honor. I do not choose to hurt you, first of all, or your family. And I would disappoint you, physically I so much fear. It has been so long. My life in that direction has been a life of frustration. Yet, Honey, thought, conversation, gaiety, that lovely feeling of first things forever—?
>
> I hope I am making sense, and I love you, Bud (1/28/68)

As his romance blossomed, he was making progress on his manuscript. It would seem clear that there was a connection between the two. His love and his effort to express conflicted emotions in his letters engendered hope for a new lease on life, something to work for and look forward to. In mid-January he told Carol, "I've been working. Hear? Working! I don't know where I'm going, but I have ten pages in what I believe to be final form. Not much, one would say, unless he knew how slowly I create, how insistent

I am on the right words and rhythms and how much I dislike exposition in fiction" (1/11/68).

As he made progress with the manuscript and the story began to declare itself, he was exultant to be in the middle of a book at last after a long draught, but he began to worry. As he was finishing chapter 3 in late February, he wrote, "[The book] is so different from the other two that I wonder if readers will hold still. Yet I dare to hope it is illuminating, funny, pitiful and right. Within my constricted limits, you understand" (2/21/68).

A week later he wrote that his sister had just left for school: "so here I am alone, but suffering from no more than doubt about how to proceed with chapter 4. I have five pages written, and they suit me, but where do I go from there? An unfortunate man, the writer, reduced to doing the one thing that torments him. He would be glad to be doing anything else—if only he could." He wrote that he was not at all a safe man when involved in writing a book. If he wants to go down to the mailbox, he takes the wrong car keys, sometimes misses stop signs, and finds himself making wrong turns and going up the wrong street. And when he wants to use the double boiler, he forgets to put water in the bottom pan. He continued:

> All the time, you see, I am writing lines for a world imaginary. Sometimes the lines seem to turn out well, but by that time a cop is giving me a ticket or the kitchen's on fire. My response is: Oh, pardon me, I forgot that this was Missoula in the year of our Lord 1968. Honest answers like that, though, don't get me far.
>
> Already it's noon, and I am going to go upstairs and make myself a toasted-cheese sandwich, if only I remember to twist the broiler button. (3/1/68)

Bud sent the chapters of "Arfive" to Helen as he came up with a final draft of each. After reading the first chapter, she wrote to her father, "It's off to a fine start . . . I hadn't known it was going to be so autobiographical—but then why not? . . . I'm curious about some things. Like where did you get 'Arfive'? To which question you will probably answer, 'Out of my head.' I found the name Collingsworth a little hard to swallow—which may be exactly the effect you want. . . . You got one effect you want: Hub [her husband], Jane [a friend] and I all think 'My heavens, what will we do with ourselves until we get Chapter II?' So push ahead" (2/16/68). ("Arfive," not yet at this point a settled title, actually came from the cattle brand—"R5"—used by Tom Larson on his ranch, a brand still used by Bert on the ranch he inherited.)

Early in March of 1968, Carol ended her silence about the extent of the difficulties in her marriage. Bud wrote back, "I am glad you said what you did in your last letter. Though I felt I knew a good deal about you and your situation, the confirmation was needed and welcome. Yes, Honey, we have to have underneath the core of steel" (3/11/68).

On April 22, 1968, Bud wrote to Carol, "Harriet, my divorced wife, died yesterday. A friend who had come to call on her found her prostrate and unconscious in the morning. A few hours later she died at the hospital in Great Falls. The doctor said he found no evidence of drugs or alcohol and is puzzled as to the cause of death." A week later, he wrote,

> I am not so grieved at Harriet's death as I am at her life in the last dozen years or so. She had a rough go, part of it my fault, no doubt. Part of it my selfishness. It was to save myself, I think, that I divorced her. Yet, had I stayed with her, there is no doubt in my mind that both of us would

have gone down the drain. I was able to get on my feet again; she wasn't. It is too easy to say she brought things on herself. A truer assessment is that she could not help herself. I have reached the point at which I dislike to assign faults. All of us are on safer and better grounds if we talk facts. Facts aren't judgments, really, and they avoid the odium of fault-finding. (5/1/68)

Through May and June, he reported regularly on his progress with his manuscript. In June he told Carol,

What can a lone person report, unless he be Thoreau? I sleep, eat, work and take care of the dog, who has become terribly demanding, out of anxiety, I suppose. The work goes haltingly. It requires a hell of a wrench to go from the whorehouse (Chapter Six) to Methodist services (Chapter Seven). Only a fool would tackle such a transition.
I'll proceed with the impossible now. (6/12/68)

Carol, Herb, and the two children, Bill and Amy, came to Twin Lakes two days before the annual family get-together on July 4. He asked Carol to get there early because he felt he needed help in getting the place ready for the many visitors he expected. He promised that if her husband and children wanted to take a pack trip, he could arrange one with horses and a guide with his neighbor Alice Gleason, who owned the Circle 8 ranch. Although Bud was very gratified to see Carol again, the stay of the Luthins at Twin Lakes was difficult. It was clear to all that there was a relationship between Bud and Carol, and they themselves could see that others knew. Carol's stay at Twin Lakes would bring the situation to a head.

At first, in mid-July, Bud simply expressed regret that she was gone: "When I listen, I hear your shoes a-clatter on time. I watch the expression on your face, now shining, now tearful. And, god-dam it, I miss the hell out of you. Come back!" But in terms of his writing, "I have about concluded that, if I am going to get any work done. I must return to Missoula. Too many visitors here (Not you.)" (7/17/68), (7/22/68).

But then on the first of August, Bud got a letter in which Carol told him that she would just have to separate from Herb, at least for a time. She would take the kids to her parents in Davenport. In a crucial letter Bud departed from his previous caution in expressing what he thought she should do:

> I am afraid you will be having a hard time. It would be right if I were there to share the burden with you, though I don't know how I would defend us except to say I love you. Your mother and father probably will think your attitude fantastic, an aberration that time will shortly rectify, a something you will dismiss when you come to your senses. . . .
>
> I feel you must divorce Herb, even if not to marry me. Your marriage was down the drain, I think and hope, long before we met. Your life with him must be insufferable. Even to reflect on it is insufferable to me. It hurts me to think of you as the semi-servile little housewife. Damn it, Carol, you are a good and giving little girl who, for the sake of family and solidity, has put up with too much. Now I ask you to think of yourself, to stand up with the pride you've kept subdued. I am proud of you, so should you be proud of yourself, too damn proud not to exert your fine individuality. Living as you are, you are destroying yourself. Day by day the wealth of you is dissipated. The precious dies.
>
> I cannot believe it is good for the children to live in

that home atmosphere. And, Dear, though Herb may be a bastard, I doubt he's satisfied with the fortune that he has. I feel sorry for him, as one must feel sorry for those who find, somehow, a perverse pleasure in making life unpleasant. . . .

Your parents are going to hate me. I can't fault them. If we marry, then at the very least the children are going to treat me with a reserve they do not now. Though too old, I fear, to be a proper father to them, I love Bill and Amy. (8/2/68)

Having decided that she had to get a divorce, she traveled to Davenport to break the news to her parents, hoping for their support. Actually, she was asking for permission. She recalled,

Things had been getting worse, and I just realized that I wasn't helping my husband and he was sure not helping me and my children . . . and so I went home and I talked to my parents. . . . My mother and father were very big Methodist pillars . . . very conventional, religious people. . . . And [so I asked them], do you think a woman has a right to divorce the father of her children? . . . And that's when a window opened. They were thrilled at the thought I would be divorcing this man.

Her father asked his attorney and through him found an attorney for her, and she came home from Davenport to Lake Bluff and asked her husband for a divorce: "Then began the really terrible time." (The divorce was supposed to take place in the fall of 1968, but Herb delayed it in one way or another and it didn't happen until January of 1969. After the divorce Carol took her children back to her parents' house in Iowa. She couldn't go farther because one of the conditions of the divorce was that she couldn't take the children more than 200 miles from Chicago.)

Even though Bud never formally proposed to her, they just assumed they would marry. But how? Carol's lawyer told her that the 200-mile restriction was so unfair that it could easily be overturned. But he changed his mind as he tried to do so and was unsuccessful. She and Bud began, in her words, a "kind of agitated correspondence" about what they were going to do. It was a correspondence that began as the divorce process began and lasted throughout the fall and into the next year. Bud told her that although he was totally devoted to her, he thought it would be best if they waited to get married until the legal problems of custody were settled. He also thought it might be best if they waited until after he finished the "Arfive" manuscript: "Will you and can you give me a little time? I'd like to finish my book, if only to prove myself. Then, with you and a new heart, I could face the slings and arrows" (9/19/68).

As part of their agitated correspondence, Bud wrote that he was certain that she must not surrender her kids to Herb nor agree to "having them separated in some ruinous fifty-fifty deal." He agonized over his inability to be of more help to her in her time of crisis. And then in a final plea in his letter, he told her, "Please, Jesus Christ, Sweetheart, don't love me out of desperation! I will always know you could have done far better" (9/5/68).

The agony continued as he told Carol, "I wish I knew what to say to you, Sweetheart. My first—and selfish impulse—is to advise you to get your divorce, even at the cost of the children, and come marry me. You can't do that, and I can't tell you to. Your life, and mine, would then be burdened with guilt" (10/11/68). And a few weeks later he thanked her for her phone call the previous evening and her letter that he received that morning—they raised his spirit. He added, however, "the more I hear about Herb, his attitudes and his behavior, the more I'm convinced that you have been married, not to a man, but to a selfish and even vicious child. . . . It seems to me that for sixteen years your marriage has held together only because you always gave in" (11/9/68). In December Bud arranged to meet her, if only briefly. He would fly to Memphis to see Helen and her husband on the twenty-second and then have a two-hour layover at the Chicago airport.

He wanted to visit Helen and talk to her about his plans, plans that he had recently revealed to her for the first time. He was disappointed by her reaction. She had written to him, as he reported to Carol, and "she did not answer quite with the whole heart" he expected, but said, "I would try not to make my opinions another obstacle you and Carol would have to overcome" (11/9/68). Her coldness hurt him. Of all people, he expected support from her.

In the darkness of his life, he had struggled mightily through storm and high water toward what he saw as the light in the distance. Carol was in his mind his salvation—it was his hope, but as events progressed and he got closer to the light, it went beyond a hope to become a fixation, an elemental need. His hope had already paid off in real progress with the novel that had stalled for years. He thought he was alive again.

But none of Bud's family was particularly happy with the idea of his marrying Carol. He put on a happy face for Janie and Peggy, so they had been only dimly aware of his general depression and addiction to drink. In the family there was the feeling that a pretty "girl" had picked off this famous man, that she had turned to him not out of genuine affection but to escape a bad marriage, and that she was simply too young for him. There was also the feeling that Carol might be marrying him for his money. But neither of them had very much, and according to Carol, she had more than he did.

Janie was particularly devastated, although she didn't let on. The last thing she wanted to do was hurt Bud's feelings. She depended on him, for company, for dinner, and for emotional support, and she enjoyed his humor and sense of play—she would miss their weekend cocktail parties. They had fun. Bud wrote, "My midgets [Janie and Peggy] had prepared for my return [from Twin Lakes in the fall of 1968]. On the front door, under a rosette, hung a sign, 'Who's on?' (meaning who's cookin' tonight?) Janie had tied a big bow to a six pack. My bedroom door bore a greeting, 'How's this for courtesy?' and inside was a bouquet. That's not all. In her transport the dog peed on the carpet" (10/11/68). In February of the next year, as his plans for marriage began to jell, Janie asked him, "Has it ever occurred to you, Buddie, that if you don't get married, I am perfectly willing to become your dependent?" (2/12/69).

Despite the two hundred–mile limitation still in effect, Carol and Bud decided to get married. After the ceremony and a honeymoon, Carol would go back to Davenport and Bud to Missoula until the divorce agreement could be changed. Or, if hell froze over, Herb might change his mind. In February, Bud wrote to Carol about the arrangements for the wedding: "About a week ago I called my old friend, Judge Victor H. Fall, to ask if he'd marry us. He was delighted. Wanted us to get married at his domicile in Helena, where I imagine he'll have some rare vintages for the occasion" (2/12/69).

Judge Fall went on to make reservations for a suite with a fireplace, and for dinner with champagne for the wedding night. He was enjoying himself.

Bud met Carol at the Great Falls airport and they drove to Helena, where they were married on the evening of April 3. Carol recalls that she wasn't prepared for the publicity—a note in *Time* magazine and brief articles in the *Lexington Leader* and *Missoulian*. The *Missoulian* wrote, "The 68-year-old Pulitzer Prize winner and his 38-year-old bride were married in a ceremony performed by District Judge Victor H. Fall in the judge's Helena residence."

When asked by a reporter about the difference in age, Bud joked and passed it off, "I'm not going to give up to those characters like Justice Douglas and Strom Thurmond." (Douglas and Thurmond had both married women much younger than them in recent years.)

Commenting on the articles' emphasis on the difference in their ages, Carol has said, "Boy, wasn't this just too cool for me!" She added, "I think it bothered the family a whole lot. . . . Bud knew his family didn't approve of us. They didn't come to the wedding or anything. But he thought it would all go away. Everything would be fine. But it didn't."

Bud had descended into Carol's hell to rescue her, and Carol had descended into his to raise him up and bring him back into this world. One should not underestimate the desperation and need that led to that mutual rescue. Bud continued for the rest of his life to hold tight to that salvation by not only embracing Carol but by endearing himself to her children as well. But the children of his previous marriage, although not cast away, were alienated from him and, particularly, from Carol.

Bud and Carol flew to San Francisco for their honeymoon and then went back to Montana and Twin Lakes for a week (even though there was still snow on the ground). For several months Bud had expressed a concern that he wouldn't be able to "perform" as a husband should. However, a letter written after the honeymoon suggests that everything went well: "It is damn hard to settle down after my days and nights with you. My feet don't know where to walk, my hand is lost and my mind has fled to Iowa . . . Thus disabled, how can I function? Nights are worst. Bed is a prison. When I reach out, my hand encounters the wall of nothing. When I am warm, it is by the vice of artificial heat. Fly back, my love, fly back!" (4/14/69).

A few days later, he made clear that his relationship with Carol had made a dramatic difference in his work and in his confidence in his work: "I must tell you that being married to you has given me more faith and strength in my work. Sweetheart, I am going to have more than just a good book. Never before have I felt that it will be one hell of a book. The thought of you is an immense lift to me—and we did right to be married when we did, though I miss you sorely." He signed off "Your goddam doting husband, Bud" (4/19/69).

Their separation, which lasted for more than a year after the marriage, was a tough time for both of them, but for Bud it was also a rewarding one. In their frustration, both Bud in Montana and Carol in Iowa consulted lawyer after lawyer in order to find a way that would free Carol from the court order. But it was a rewarding time for Bud in that he was inspired by his love for Carol and his desire to make enough money to secure their future to continue to work every day on his novel. Again, he would write her almost every day, and he told her, "I find I do my work better if I type a few lines to you first. That's because, with you, I don't have to cudgel my imagination. Everything exists in reality" (9/12/69). There wasn't a whole lot to tell her in his letters—his progress with the novel, the weather, what Janie and Peggy had been up to and, of course, that he loved and missed her.

Although separated, they were able to see each other on occasion. One trip to meet her at Chicago's Union Station he found particularly frustrating, "Hell! No more rendezvoozes . . . I ask you: is this progress?" They exchanged gifts, Carol sending him a stack of the mysteries he loved to read, and they arranged for her to fly out to Montana in late October. They would drive from Great Falls to Choteau, attend an "old-timers" get-together, and then go on to Twin Lakes. The next two summers Carol would come out to Twin Lakes with her children, Carol for the summer and the children for three weeks, spending the same amount of time with their father in Lake Bluff on the North Shore of Chicago. Carol worried about the family's reaction to her at the annual Fourth of July gatherings, and each time, Bud assured her that everything would be all right, that the family would recognize that she was good for him. But they didn't.

Bert, as the first president Bush would say, was "out of the loop," and there was no problem with him. Helen, however, who had been so close, sharing her father's humor and reading his manuscripts, more and more felt neglected and passed over. Janie, feeling somewhat abandoned, felt she had to go along with whatever her brother wanted to do. However, in the hope that eventually he and Carol might stay with her on occasion, Janie redid his bedroom, painting it, purchasing a mirror, and selecting material for new drapes. In June she wrote her brother, "When you and Carol come over you must do your best to let on it's always looked this way. She'll know better, of course, but, thank God, won't know how awful it has been" (6/18/69). In August, she wrote to him at Twin Lakes to explain that because of his mistake, he had paid his phone bill to her twice. "I'm wondering now how often I can get away with this. It's absolutely the best angle I've come across. Our long-standing consensus that you're brighter than I perhaps needs further study" (8/17/69). Bud would continue to stay with her for almost another year. She was happy with that, although

Bud, separated from Carol, yearned for his wife and was uneasy about the resolution of her situation.

Helen wrote to her father in October from Los Angeles with an amusing experience: "Chet Huntley was in town last week and Hub and I went to a luncheon in his honor. He is retiring next spring from NBC and as you probably know will be engaged in building some kind of vacation facility near Yellowstone. I had to laugh when he told me he had received 'special permission' from the State to use the name BIG SKY" (10/27/69).

In the meantime, Bud had courted Carol's children, Amy and Bill, and they became very fond of him as he became genuinely fond of them. After witnessing their father's tantrums and the way he treated their mother, the children were grateful to be away from him and noted the differences between their father and Bud. Amy recalled, "They [Bud and their mother] had a true love affair, and we all had it. I mean it sounds just dorky as hell, but he was the kindest person I had ever known. . . . They brought out the best in each other and I think all their friends would agree. . . . It was the whole family that got divorced . . . we were frankly quite grateful to not have to see him, to see our dad."

That Christmas season of 1969, Carol flew to Missoula to stay at Janie's with Bud in his redecorated room, and during their time together they decided that their separation had to end, enough was enough. Bud had consulted his friend Randall Swanberg, and the lawyer told him that the only thing they could do was for Carol just to take the children and bring them to Montana. However, Carol felt she had to ask their permission. She didn't want "to drag them around" and felt "they had to realize what was at stake." Right after Carol left, Bud wrote to Bill and Amy:

The time has come now, I believe, that I speak my piece. . . . We married, my Carol and I, because we loved each other and were sure of our love. It is not right, nor does it accord with our desires, that we live apart. And so, come what may, we're not going to beyond the end of your school year.

Thus you youngsters will have to make a choice, a hard one, I know, and one that demands courage and decision from you. I speak particularly here of you, Billie, for of all the independencies, maybe the most difficult is that declared by son to father. I understand and am not unsympathetic. . . .

You know I am fond of you. If I am able, as I have reason to think I may be, I will see you through to educated maturity. It would be good for me to have you around. I want you.

Whatever your decisions, you will have to stand stout. We all do, finally.

Now if one or both of you whippersnappers answers that I'm unworthy of your mother, I'll like you all the better for the recognition of truth. (1/2/70)

During the fall of 1969 and on into the spring, Bud worked steadily on the "Arfive" manuscript. He reported regularly to Carol in his letters on his struggles and progress, or lack of it. He frequently felt lost, wondering where to go next. When he was on the twenty-fourth chapter on November 5, he decided that the chapter had to be written from the point of view of Benton Collingsworth (the primary character, who was patterned after Bud's father), and it had to show at great length the changes in the town (Arfive) and surrounding countryside. Bud despised expositions, so he had to figure out how to show those changes indirectly.

Then, toward the end of the month, he told Carol that he was gratified that his subconscious was still working. While he was half-asleep in bed the night before, he had what seemed to him a really good idea in connection with the chapter he was writing. He told himself that he would have to review it in the clear light of day, and in doing so the next morning, decided that it was still a "capital idea" and that he would use it in the pages he would write that day.

He finished his draft of the novel early the next year and began the drudgery of an overall review of it:

> It is dog's work I'm doing—going over the manuscript page by page, making minute corrections and marking lines that must be revised. I spent six hours at the chore yesterday and blundered upstairs bushed and blind. And at that I had waded through only one specimen copy, list-ing the pages where changes could be and were made by pen and the additional pages what will require typed revi-sions. Today, with that list at hand, I will correct the pub-lisher's copy. There's no joy in this picayune but necessary business. And I'm afraid I can't complete it until tomor-row. (2/19/70)

He had finished this phase of his work by the end of February and sent his manuscript through his agent into Houghton Miff-lin. Guthrie was not the kind of writer who worried about "talk-ing out" his writing before he wrote (one of Hemingway's bug-aboos). He discussed his work and its problems freely with those around him, and he gave copies of his manuscript while it was in progress to several people for comment. Chapters of "Arfive" were sent to Helen and Carol, and to his book agent and his Holly-wood agent. Editors at his publisher also read chapters. He didn't seem to mind criticism or suggestions. And the comments came, one after another; he was grateful for some, refuted some, and ig-nored others. But the process seemed to stimulate him and give him confidence. He differed from most writers in that he loved having others engaged in his work.

In early March he went back to stay a few days with Carol, her children, and her parents in Davenport. After getting back, he regretted he didn't stay longer, but he was worried about communication with his publisher and any further work they might request. (Another) Carol, his agent, wrote him that she thought that he might need a few final paragraphs to end the novel more definitely. But in reporting this to his wife, he said, "I think not. The best way to end a book is to leave the reader wishing for more." He also reported that he had decided to dedicate the book both to her and to Janie and that, when he told Janie, she was delighted.

As March, April, and May went by, he became more and more impatient, waiting for Carol's arrival in June. At the beginning of May he wrote to her, "In little more than a month I shall meet you at the Great Falls airport, and we'll embrace and be happy and have a drink in celebration" (5/5/70). But then he worried about taking her out of the bosom of her (birth) family: "I have thought often about the sadness you will feel in leaving Davenport and those so close to you. To move away by half a continent, to depart from the shelter of that love, will be painful both in fact and by right."

But, he added that they had made the best judgment they could, and said, "If anyone ever can know the right, we know it. So, Sweetheart, acknowledging your loss, be sure still of the golden days we have to spend."

Then he paraphrased Robert Frost, saying, "We have not only many but exciting miles to go before we sleep" (5/27/70).

CHAPTER THIRTEEN

Arfive, and Speaking to
the Young—Earth Day

After Carol landed in Great Falls, Bud met her and drove her directly out through Choteau to Twin Lakes. Twin Lakes was his harbor. However, it was not a place where they could live year-round, and that summer Janie looked for a house in Missoula for them (she, the little sister, would not have trusted his judgment and taste to look for one himself). Amy and Bill went first to their father in Lake Bluff for two weeks and then on to Twin Lakes. At the time, their father did not know that they would not be coming back, but after a while they wrote to tell him that they were staying in Montana.

Early in the summer Janie wrote to "Buddie, Carol, Amy, Bill" at Twin Lakes and said, "My God, but I got a lot of relatives in a hurry. I don't think this relates to the population explosion, but really, Buddie!" She added that she had been looking for a house with the help of a realtor: "I wish to gosh just the right place would show up and you could get over here, Carol. I know you'll feel more secure once you have a place in mind for the winter" (6/15/70). After evaluating a number of possibilities, she was able to find a place to rent on Queen Street that she felt would suit her brother's lifestyle (it had a finished basement where, as at her house, he could write).

That fall Amy entered as a freshman and Bill as a junior in Missoula's Sentinel High School, only a block from their house (which, to quote Carol, "spared Buddy from the thing that he most dreaded— ferrying children"). Also that fall the two teenagers went to the lawyer Swanberg's office in Great Falls to give a deposition stating that they had come to Montana of their own free will and that they desired to stay with their mother.

Since Bud and Carol went to all the PTA meetings, plays, and other school affairs, everyone at the school was aware that Bill and Amy were his children. And there was no resentment or hostility, although Amy felt that some of the English teachers were somewhat intimidated. Bill, who was very bright, was allowed to design a class for himself, reading what he wanted to read, if he could find a teacher to monitor it. It was a privilege he probably would not have had if he were not Guthrie's son. Amy was asked to stay after school on several occasions while one of her teachers read his poetry to her, apparently in the hope that she would, in Amy's words, "go back and tell Bud how great his poetry was. It wasn't." The Guthrie children found it amusing that a couple of their teachers had had Janie as a teacher when they were in elementary school.

Spending the whole summer in Montana, Bill and Amy became as attached to Twin Lakes as Bud was and began to reflect their stepfather's feeling that he was part of nature, rather than separate from it. They came to understand his devotion to conservation and his anger at those who would despoil his (and now their) state out of greed. Over previous years Bud had written a number of articles about his natural surroundings. In such pieces as "The Rockies," "Our Lordly Mountains," and "Montana," he put in a plug for conservation, sometimes subtly—particularly in the earlier published articles—but more and more overtly as time went by. There was a refrain through his articles that reflected what he said was the theme of *The Big Sky*: man tends to destroy the very things he loves. In that novel, Dick Summers tells old Zeb Calloway,

> "Caudill and Deakins, here, aim to be mountain men."
> [Zeb replies], "Huh! They better be borned ag'in."
> "How so?"
> "Ten year too late anyhow." Uncle Zeb's jaw worked on the tobacco. "She's gone, goddam it! Gone!"
> "What's gone?" asked Summers.
> "The whole shitaree. Gone by God, and naught to care savin' some of us who seen 'er new." He took the knife from his belt and started jabbing at the ground with it, as if it eased his feelings. He was silent for awhile.

The whole stream of Guthrie's six literary novels, running from the days of near wilderness in the early nineteenth century to the mid-twentieth century, depicts this loss, a gradual decline in the quality of life in nature through settlement and exploitation. Settlement he understood as something inevitable, although it could have been managed better. But exploitation made him angry. The chief villain here in Montana was the Anaconda Copper Company, which through its wealth was an overwhelming force in politics, a force reinforced by its near monopoly of the Montana media. This power allowed it to mutilate the land and pollute the streams with impunity under the banner of "progress."

As mentioned earlier, in 1959 Guthrie wrote a foreword to a new

edition of *Montana: High, Wide, and Handsome* by his close friend
Joseph Kinsey Howard (a book first published in 1943). In his foreword, in which he revealed many of his own values, Bud wrote,

> When Joseph Kinsey Howard died in August of 1951, I said
> that Montana had lost her conscience. Who but he could
> push and lead us to a recognition of our shortcomings?
> Who would tackle prejudice and privilege and so awaken
> us to them? What voice would speak for the neglected, the
> oppressed, the victimized? Or for our misused inheritance
> of soil and water and timber? . . .
>
> It wasn't Anaconda alone that the book offended. It
> was its friends and business associates. It was some of the
> ranchers, who were not only sympathetic with the com-
> pany but also confirmed in ways of land use that How-
> ard decried. It was the complacent people. It was the peo-
> ple shaped in thought by old circumstances, the people of
> whom Howard spoke when he [wrote] of early get-rich-
> and-run behavior.

And then, quoting Howard, he said, "It was an inauspicious beginning for a Treasure State, for thus was established a social and
economic pattern of spoliation which subsequently was impressed
upon the laws, customs, and even minds of Montanans and their
eastern exploiters."

Outspoken in articles and even in a number of letters to the editor, by 1971 Guthrie had become known locally, and was gradually becoming known nationally, as a champion of conservation.
For that year's celebration of Earth Day, he was invited to write a
piece for the *Sunday Missoulian*, which he titled, "A Message to
the Young":

> The belief that the world was made for man, as the

Scripture[s] have it, threatens to be the end of us. We have had our dominion over the fish of the sea, the birds of the heavens and over the cattle and every creeping thing, and we have been fruitful and multiplied, and we have subdued the earth, all as ordained; and the dread end looms as deprivation if indeed not extinction. . . .

Greed [has been] at work . . . an assured and thoughtless greed hardly faced yet with the grim results of its grasping. As it was at work then, so it is at work now, more nakedly, though, and more egregiously because its aftereffects have become evident everywhere—evident in fouled air, poisoned streams, lakes dead or dying, in perished and perishing species and in the increase in physical, human disorders. (4/18/71)

He wrote this during Amy and Bill's first year in high school in Missoula, and Amy recalled, "He encouraged us to start an environmental group in our high school, and that was one of the first Earth Days, and he wrote a big piece, but we had an environmental group at the high school named Time Limited. We were very issue based, and we cleaned up places, and we did a bunch of stuff quite ahead of the time. He was really excited . . . all of a sudden he realized that he was affecting younger people and that was kind of a neat thing."

At the end of his Earth Day essay, Bud wrote an appeal to these young people:

It is late, just maybe too late, to manage correction, but there is hope in the awakening consciousness and active endeavor of press and public and further hope in the growing awareness and outrage of young people.

I say to them: Be Outraged! Too often you have dissented

and protested without aim, or without an aim worthy of your outward expressions. But here is a cause. Embrace it, all of you! We oldsters will thank you, your generation will thank you, and further generations, if there be any, will be in your debt.

Bud tried hard to bring his new family together, bringing them to him with an extraordinary outpouring of love and engaging them in his writing life. Part of his effort was to support his children in their schooling with an active interest and help when needed. Another part was involving Carol, Amy, and Bill in his writing. Bud would write every day, which he called "good journalism discipline," adding, "if you are waiting for inspiration you are screwed." At Queen Street he would go down to work (he was again consigned to the basement), and then he would come up when he had pages of a draft for Carol to read, and she would pass them on to Bill. Amy recalls, "Mom was an excellent editor, no question in another life she would have been doing that. And my brother . . . was very good because he writes as well. His language sense was always so right and if there were words or twists or something that didn't feel right, he was very good at discussing that with Bud. . . . You know we are talking about kids who were in high school. From the very beginning, he allowed Bill and Mom to contribute. It was just kind of neat."

This family editing, which also involved a lot of discussion among them about the writing, became a routine. But it had only just started during the summer and fall of 1970, when *Arfive* was being edited at the publisher and going into galleys. Amy remembered that she didn't read drafts of the various projects but would just listen to others when they talked about them. Then when the galleys came, she would go through them with a fresh eye (the others had already read so many versions) and try to make sure that everything still made sense. She added, "I always felt so important." In addition to helping edit her husband's writing, Carol took on the job of illustrating Bud's children's book, *Once upon a Pond*, which had been in progress for several years by the time they were married.

Arfive was published by Houghton Mifflin on January 18, 1971. It was a breakthrough in that his last major work, *These Thousand Hills*, was published way back in 1956. Of course, he had published his collection of short stories, *The Big It and Other Stories*, in 1960, and his autobiography, *The Blue Hen's Chick*, in 1965. But most of the stories in the collection had already been published, and although writing the autobiography was also a bit like treading water, it provided the nutrient from which *Arfive* was able to grow. And with the publication of that book, and a new family, he was back on track again and during the next decade and a half published an amazing amount of material, including two more major novels and five mysteries. All this during a period that might be called his old age.

The reviews of the novel were for the most part favorable, with a few reservations here and there. Most of the reservations had to do with Guthrie's use of familiar Western materials; at the same time, none of the reviews in major periodicals mentioned that it was highly unusual in a Western to make the protagonist a male, midwestern schoolteacher. While some of the material in the novel might be familiar, there were no shootouts, posses, or roundups. The novel was set in a different, more recent time than his previous books. Typical of the reviews was this one by Vernon Scannell in the *New Statesman*, where, in part, he wrote,

> *Arfive* is the fourth and last of a sequence of novels which deal with the development of the American West from the early 19th century to the outbreak of the First World War.

It is certainly a less impressive piece of work than the first
. . . of the sequence, *The Big Sky.* . . . It was the strange-
ness, the foreignness of *The Big Sky* that lent it so much of
its power. We are anything but strangers to the setting of
Arfive, the small town in Montana with its chapel, saloon,
store and sheriff's office, the bullying deputy, crooked gambler, and even a whore with a heart of gold. We have seen
it before in scores of Western movies. If Guthrie were not
a very fine writer, this book would be no more than a run-
of-the-mill Western, but the quality of his prose and the
pressure of his passionate concern for his subject, the old
West crushed beneath the steel-shod advance of technol-
ogy are enough to lift it well out of the rut.

More biting was the comment by the *Observer*: "The author wrote
the screenplay for 'Shane' and knows his conventions only too
well."

On the other hand, the *Christian Science Monitor* said, "These
people speak as such people would speak, and they feel as real people feel on the edge of civilization. . . . "Arfive" is a novel about
human people, not about gun-totin' cowboys of impossible virtue,
bravery, accuracy and ferocity." And the *Washington Post* agreed:
"The dialogue is biting and colloquial, and the descriptions are
superb" (2/9/71).

The complaint that Guthrie used materials, particularly characters, that we have seen in Western movies was not new but came
up in reviews of all his novels. His response was that he was selec-
tive, using only those characters that were historically valid, and
individualizing them as much as possible, in addition to bringing
them together with characters who were totally out of the pulp-
Western mold. The problem was that even the pulps and movies
had many characters and conventions that were commonly found

in the historical record. To ignore these might leave the writer of historical novels about the West with little to write about.

One of the aspects of the novel that bothered some readers and a few reviewers was the lesbian episode. Amy recalls one reviewer from a Montana paper who was very hostile about it, not on the basis that Bud should not have written about it, but because, as an early feminist, she felt that the characters' shocked, negative reaction to it wouldn't have happened: "Everybody would have understood and would have been nice." Both Bud's agent and his editor, however, were somewhat dubious about the inclusion of such material, while his family, including Helen, were supportive. Helen wrote,

> At last I got to read all of ARFIVE [she had read several chapters while it was in progress]. Liked it, too [like her father, she wouldn't have hesitated to say that she didn't]. In fact I can't think of a single criticism. One, maybe: damn lucky for you the publishers talked you out of THE STEADFAST BUTTE, which may be a good title, but not for this book. I was not at all distressed by the lesbian episode (you remember Cal [at the agency] had alerted me to it saying she couldn't quite go for it whole hog). (1/4/71)

Bud also got a number of letters of congratulation from fellow writers, including Wallace Stegner. A fellow environmentalist and Bread Loaf staff member (but not at the same time as Bud), Bud and Wally often wrote to each other to ask for blurbs for jackets and advertising of their work. Occasionally, their writings paralleled each other's. We might recall that Wally had sent Bud galleys of, *Wolf Willow*, his memoir of growing up in a small town on the Great Plains in Saskatchewan, at the same time as Bud was planning to write his autobiography of growing up in Choteau. Bud wrote him that he liked the book but that Wally had beaten him to the punch again. Wally replied, "Your punches are so much your own that I doubt I have stolen any, really" (7/14/62).

Several months after *Arfive* was published, Wally wrote him with regret—he had been out of the country when the galleys arrived and couldn't get a blurb to Bud in time for his publishers to use. But he wanted to tell him how much liked he book and that he found himself in it:

> It's a fine, fit capstone—or maybe it isn't a capstone, maybe there's more to come—to your edifice on the Teton. As you can imagine, I recognize and responded to all sorts of things in the developing history of that town. The hopefulness, above all. My God, the hopefulness! It seems centuries since that kind of spirit had any force in the places where I have lived. I wish it was back. But the formation of the school, the petty politicking, the self-aggrandizing deputies, the saloon keeper with more integrity than a lot of the church wardens—that's all familiar, real, and honest. I confess I know the Chinaman well, and have eaten his chop suey and stolen his candy bars. I know the wind that chased Mrs. Ross . . . out of the country; it damn near chased my mother, too, and she was tough as latigo leather. I can't walk across windy grassland even yet without its all coming back. And that's one of the beautiful things about your book. The country is always there just outside, never much dwelt on, never romanticized or written for Holiday, but big and clean and blessedly empty, and smelling right. . . .
>
> The trouble with too much western fiction is that the people in it can't be allowed to be people. They've to be Tom Mix or Willa Cather's Wick Cutter. Yours are people,

a lot of very various people, and it was a stroke of genius to make your principal not Shane but a he-schoolmarm. (4/8/71)

After the publication of *Arfive*, Bud Guthrie entered one of the busiest, most productive periods of his life. The first order of business was book signings, which he did, with Carol, traveling to bookstores in Missoula, Billings, Bozeman, and Havre. The signings usually also involved interviews by the local newspaper. It was not the grand book tour that so many writers take nowadays—Bud no longer enjoyed travel, particularly on airplanes. They did go to Davenport, however, and Amy remembers that she and her brother had to have a babysitter: "We were in high school and we were mortified."

Bud was in demand. Over the next couple of years, he was asked to give speeches to various groups, and he usually talked about conservation. Sometimes, as in a speech to the Bozeman, Montana, Chamber of Commerce, he laid out his convictions in front of an obviously unsympathetic audience. "I am an odd selection to speak at a chamber of commerce meeting," he began, and soldiered on in the face of unsmiling faces. Typical of him in dealing with controversy, he first gave a nod to the other side: "Though I recognize, with sympathy, some of the problems businessmen face today—I can't be uncritical." He was not a barn-burning orator, but he spoke clearly and slowly during his speeches. Carol, who was always in attendance, marveled that he invariably spoke in perfect sentences and formed perfect paragraphs even when speaking off the cuff. Maybe not rousing, but certainly understandable and effective.

Bud and Carol, along with Amy and Bill (except when they were away at college), lived in the house on Queen Street in Missoula from 1971 to 1977. For the first two years, they rented, and then they arranged to purchase. Bud's daily routine began with coffee and the newspaper, and occasionally breakfast, at the kitchen table. He was, in the family's words, a "table sitter." After a skimpy lunch, he would go down to his desk in the basement, write some letters, and go on to spend as much as three hours on his current project. When at home, applying his newspaperman's discipline, he was religious in following his writing routine. Unlike what we know about most recent novelists, who usually start writing the first thing in the morning, he did almost all his work in the afternoon.

While the manuscript of *Arfive* was being processed by the publisher in the fall of 1970, Bud started on the first of five western mysteries, *Wild Pitch*. Why he went back to this form, which had carried his disastrous first novel, *Murders at Moon Dance*, is somewhat of a mystery in itself. Perhaps it was an effort to erase his previous failure and clear his conscience. (Carol recalls that her husband made her promise that she would never read it.) He was a very persistent man who hated to give up on anything. However, it must be noted that he, and both his first wife and Carol, enjoyed reading mysteries. Carol remembers that her husband "loved Nero Wolfe mysteries," which she "always felt was unfortunate" because she found them boring; but she said, "He loved them and he read them all." He read and enjoyed all the classic mystery writers—Father Brown, Agatha Christie, and especially Ellery Queen.

But beyond his reading enjoyment of the form, perhaps the main reason he turned to mysteries in between more serious projects was because writing them was fun. He could relax, still writing as well as he could but without the pressure to write the great American novel. According to his wife, "He decided it would be a kick to do this, and so he did it, and it made quite a bit of money. So he felt 'wow, this is pretty much fun,' and so he wrote five of them. They were never my favorite books." In fact, his stepdaughter

Amy has declared, "I think I can say without hesitation I am the only one [of the family] who ever liked any of them. . . . They are pretty darn amusing."

Bud always wrote on a typewriter, a Smith Corona portable. Carol remembers, "Occasionally, we would have great alarms and excursions when that typewriter wasn't working right. . . . Changing ribbons was not a good thing for him." His frustrations usually came out of his perfectionism—he wanted the process to go as perfectly as possible, and he wanted his revised manuscript to be perfect in every way. That was why he had so many people read his manuscripts (once they had gone through many revisions) and why he wouldn't allow anyone to read a first draft. As he wrote his revisions, he would crumple pages of the first draft, one at time, as he finished work on them, and throw them into the wastebasket.

First in line to do a review was Carol, who recalled, "After it had been completed, the finished draft, he would bring to me, and I would look at it. He wanted to know what I thought of it. And I always said I was Mrs. Middle America, and so if something bothered me in it . . . I usually just thought it was fine and didn't say anything, but if there was something I really thought didn't hit me quite right, or that I didn't quite understand, then I would mention it to him." He would take a look at the passage, think about it, and try other possibilities. Sometimes he would change it and sometimes not. After he had a pile of four chapters or so, Carol would take the pile to the typist. But once the entire manuscript was done, he would go back and read the whole thing again. There would always be passages that he didn't feel were quite right, and he would start cutting and pasting. Then back to the typist the manuscript would go.

Most of his copy editors were fine, but he did have a lot of trouble with one, a contract copy editor who wanted to rewrite the manuscript to her own taste. For example, one time Bud wrote, "the wall flight of the mountains," and she changed it to "the white walls of the mountains." Then, he had a quotation in his manuscript from Badger Clark, and she queried, "Who is this?" He wrote back in care of the publisher's editor, "He was a singing son of a bitch I met on roundup." About halfway through the copy editing process, he had had enough, and, jumping up from his desk, he exclaimed, "No, no, no," and in a fury called his editor. The copy editor was fired. At least from that job.

Badger Clark was a cowboy poet who published a collection, *Sun & Saddle Leather*, in 1915. In *Wild Pitch* Guthrie quotes from Clark "lines contrasting east and west":

> Such as they never could understand
> The way we have loved you, young, young land.

While Bud was working on *Wild Pitch*, Carol spent a year doing the illustrations for his children's book, *Once upon a Pond*. In addition to that job, she had a constant battle to keep Bud's working hours from being interrupted. According to Carol, "He could be easily distracted. He didn't want to be, but he was a very convivial, gregarious guy." Whether in Missoula or later in their home outside of Choteau, they had people who would want to come by in the afternoon to see him. If they called, Carol would try to ward them off until after 4 p.m. Reporters wanted to come by for interviews, fellow authors wanted to meet him, or young writers wanted advice.

Ed McClanahan, along with Wendell Berry, attended a writer's conference at the university and also sought him out. They were "fellow Kentuckians" who admired Bud for his attachment to the land. Bud and Carol saw Ivan Doig frequently. Bud was particularly impressed by Richard Ford, who came by several times. Ford called him "Sir," a Southern thing, and that gave Bud a warm call back to his years in Kentucky. And on several occasions, bearded, hippy-looking men stopped by—they all looked the same—knocked on the door, asked to see Bud, and when Bud came to the door, would ask: "Whatever happened to Boone?" The antihero protagonist of *The Big Sky* had become a countercultural hero.

In addition to the writers who visited from out of the area, the Guthries had a number of more local writer friends who would visit or come to dinner. The poet Richard Hugo (*The Lady in Kicking Horse Reservoir*) moved to Missoula in 1969 to teach at the university. (In the late 1970s Bill Luthin, Bud's stepson, was one of his students, and he recalled that "Dick would rave over poems that he liked, but was never unkind about poems that didn't work for him—even about flat-out crappy poems by people who would never be writers.") Hugo went on to marry Ripley Schemm, also a teacher at the university and the daughter of the novelist Mildred Walker. The Schemms, Mildred Walker and Ferd, had a house in Great Falls, where Bud was acquainted with them, but more importantly, they had a cabin not far from Twin Lakes out on the Eastern Front.

Then there was Jim Welch, noted for his Native American novels (*Fools Crow, Winter in the Blood*), who was married to Lois Welch, a professor at the university, and the essayist and short story writer, Bill Kittredge (*We Are Not in This Together*), who taught at the university. And finally, there was the novelist Dorothy Johnson. These people all knew each other and often got together, although not all of them at the same time. The Hugos and Welchs were often guests at the Schemm cabin so that there was a remarkable locus of literary folk in both Missoula and the Teton Valley that included the Guthries.

Bud was particularly fond of Dick Hugo. Both had been heavy

drinkers until they were married and then reformed. Bud had for the most part given up hard liquor by agreement with Carol and usually drank only wine in Missoula and beer at Twin Lakes. He was limited to two glasses of wine; he often tried to get more but was stopped in reaction to his wife's disapproval. Nevertheless, it was a joke among their friends that Bud would try to make the most of his two glasses, filling them to the brim or even above and then walking carefully to his chair. Although Dick was a city boy from Seattle and Bud was basically country, they had a great rapport. They were both fishermen and planned for years to fish together—it became a routine between them when they met that expressed their mutual love for the rural landscape. But sadly they never did go.

Dorothy Johnson, who had taught journalism at the university, was a prolific writer of novels and short stories; among the latter were "The Man Who Shot Liberty Valance" and "A Man Called Horse," both of which were made into popular movies. Her work was unusually realistic in its depiction of the West and frequently treated the plight of women on the frontier and the lives of Native Americans. She had become a kind of icon among Montana writers, respected and admired—a gracious lady of great accomplishment. She was a bit younger than Bud, but age was catching up to her when the Guthries were living in Missoula, and she had developed Parkinson's, which made her very unsteady. Amy Luthin recalled, "Mother would still use the Wedgwood. She would say, "You know Dorothy Johnson is a lady, and she will eat on those dishes, and if she breaks one . . . she breaks one. Dorothy is a friend."

Mildred Walker was another matter. Again, to quote Amy, "She was just quite full of herself, she was always right, and she was always very proper and highly critical." Like Johnson she frequently turned to the theme of how the women of the West gained or lost their identity, but her work never achieved the popularity that Johnson's did. As haughty and sure of herself as Walker was in public, her daughter Ripley's biography of her reveals in her letters and journals a constant self-doubt and complaint that she is unappreciated. After more than a dozen novels, the best known of which is *Winter Wheat*, she had a difficult time even getting her final novel published.

Once, at a dinner party, Bud and Mildred were having a long, heated discussion about an aspect of her work. Although he never really wrote literary criticism, Bud had taught at a number of writer's conferences and thought he knew a great deal about the basics of fiction. (Indeed, his last book was *A Field Guide to Writing Fiction*.) The discussion was witnessed by Ripley, who felt that her mother was getting her feelings hurt. As Amy puts it, "He was pretty much point blank about things, and Ripley didn't like him for years." But later she realized that Bud was right and that her mother was trying very hard to listen to that advice. Once, when Mildred was invited to teach at a writer's conference, she wrote to Bud for his "rules for good fiction writing" that he had employed in teaching at conferences, and with his recommendation she was invited to teach at Bread Loaf.

The year 1973 was notable for the publication of *Wild Pitch* and his collection of animal fables, *Once upon a Pond*. Bud began writing the last novel in what has been called his "settlement trilogy," *The Last Valley*. During the writing Bud had to take time out to go to Texas to have arterial bypasses in both of his legs, surgeries performed by Dr. Michael DeBakey.

Even though *Wild Pitch* was written out of a need to have some fun, it was an amazing success, which must have completely erased Bud's sense of failure over *Murders at Moon Dance*. And even though no one in his family except Amy cared much for it, all the major periodicals loved it. Many of the reviewers noted that the skill demonstrated in his serious novels had been successfully carried over to this work meant primarily for entertainment. It may have been just a mystery novel, but it was a mystery novel with literary quality.

The *Saturday Review* expressed the hope that it would "see a lot more of Sheriff Chick Charleston and his winning Western Watson, seventeen-year-old Jason Beard." The *Review* continued, "They're the cool combination combating crime in a town numbering 1,500 souls. *Wild Pitch* . . . has an uncanny sense of place that conveys precisely what the small Montana settlement is like through the medium of a murder and the hunt for the murderer. Guthrie's tetralogy [*sic*] about the West—*The Big Sky*, *The Way West*, *These Thousand Hills*, and *Arfive*—is well known and deservedly appreciated. *Wild Pitch* is a change of pace for Guthrie and a bonus for us. It's tough, taut, and terrific."

With somewhat less alliteration, the *New York Times Book Review* also praised the book by calling it a "curiously attractive book" that "also is a tightly plotted beautifully worked out example of the detective story." And the *Sunday World-Herald Magazine* pointed out that "what makes 'Wild Pitch' is what make all good mystery stories, characterizations and atmosphere. Guthrie shines in both departments."

The description, as in this passage, comes in passing as the narrator, Jason, moves from one place to another, pursuing his duties: "Like most thunder showers, this one didn't last long. By the time I braked the car above the picnic grounds, the sky was clear over my head. Everything smelled good to me as I scrambled down the wet ridge. Everything—grass, juniper, scrub pine—breathed revival. The patches of gravel lay polished, each pebble clean and distinct. The sun was low in the west. It had started kindling a cumulus cloud. A good time to fish, to catch that prize cutthroat."

The use of young Jason as narrator of this and the other mysteries was for Guthrie a stroke of genius. As another review pointed out, it is Jason "with his fresh eyes—with his unmuddied response to village and weather and the behavior of people—who gives the novel a sturdy and pleasurable actuality."

Jason is modeled in some respects on Guthrie's own life as a youth in Choteau. The title, *Wild Pitch*, refers to Jason's pitching for the Midbury town baseball team, just as Guthrie pitched for Choteau, and like Guthrie, Jason dreams of graduating to the big leagues. Guthrie's interest in baseball lasted throughout his life. Jason has a mother and father who roughly match Guthrie's. And Jason's town, Midbury, is, like Choteau, the county seat, located on the eastern front of the Rockies. Guthrie fished on the Teton River, a river matched in the novel by the Rose, where Jason fishes.

Also out of personal experience is the fictionalized account of a practical joke, told in the novel by Chick Charleston, which in life involved Bud's close friends George Sexton and George Jackson. Sexton, who was a surgeon in town, had a cabin on the Circle 8 ranch, two miles from Twin Lakes. According to Dr. George Sexton's daughter, Mary, who was eight at the time, the real story begins with her and her father going from their cabin out to the barn in the early morning to care for their horses. They suddenly encountered a skunk and were thoroughly sprayed. Instead of cleaning up, the father and daughter got into their car and drove to Twin Lakes. Sexton knew that George Jackson was there, probably sleeping, and so he and his daughter went quietly into the bedroom where Jackson was in bed. They just stood there, stinking, letting the smell drift over the sleeping man.

George Jackson began to thrash around, waking up, and tried to fumble for his glasses (he couldn't see at all without them). At this point the Sextons tiptoed out. As Amy remembered the story, George Sexton "came over later that day after making sure he didn't smell of skunk any more, and he came in and George Jackson said, 'You know, I don't know what the hell happened last night. I had the most vivid dream I have ever had. Come back here—it still smells like skunk. What is it? Did a skunk just walk into the house and back out?' I think they kept that story. I don't think they ever told him that they had pranked him on that one. Those guys just got each other every time they could."

In *Wild Pitch*, and in his other mysteries, Guthrie takes the opportunity here and there to include, indirectly, an environmentalist message. One of his characters is a former petroleum geologist who tells Jason and the sheriff, "They are on my conscience, my ecological conscience, the oil fields I was instrumental in finding. . . . Sometimes I have the feeling I am living on the proceeds of wrong-doing." The sheriff nods and smiles in understanding and says, "I know a cattle rancher who curses the day oil was found on his land. An ex-rancher, I should say. But I doubt that stockholders and General Motors share your sentiment."

During the first years of his marriage, Bud kept in touch with a number of old friends by correspondence, as well as keeping up by calling on the phone, and the correspondence of the longest duration was probably that which he had with his old neighbor in Kentucky, Tom Clark, the historian. Two or three times a year, Tom would report on his writing projects (he was as long-lived as Bud and, like Bud, continued to work) and on the situation at the university and in Lexington. He talked of seeing old friends and despaired (ever more, year after year) of Kentucky politicians and the growing traffic problems.

He also kept up his banter with Bud, as he displayed in this letter:

This morning Henry Hornsby has a little piece about you [in the Lexington *Herald-Leader*], which I am enclosing. He is a damned liar about your being so squeamish about killing chickens. You murderous bastard, it seems to me you had a bleeding chicken in your hands throughout World War II. . . .

How are Helen and "Nonnie"? People are constantly asking me about you and your children. I can answer vaguely about all of you, but would indeed like to know specifically about what is happening. Tell your wife that she is a good-looking chick married to a damned old stick horse. If you were near enough, I would throw you down on the floor, or slam you against a tree, or do something manful just to prove that the seventy years which have run over me had done nothing but add to my vigor. (12/23/73)

CHAPTER FOURTEEN

The Twin Lakes Imbroglio and Building the "Barn"

When the family gathered for their annual reunion over the Fourth of July at Twin Lakes in 1974, there were fireworks—not in the sky, but between Bud and his daughter, Helen. Bud's son and daughter by his first marriage each inherited a quarter of Twin Lakes and a quarter of the title to the Larson ranch at the death of their mother. Helen had no interest in the ranch and traded with her brother to get a half interest in Twin Lakes. Since all of the ranch would eventually go to Bert, she assumed she would get all of the vacation property; in fact, she thought she had an agreement from her father to that effect.

Two years earlier, Bud had begun a campaign to insure that Carol would have rights to Twin Lakes after he was gone. He sent a letter to his daughter telling her that he wanted her to sign a statement giving Carol "first right of refusal" in case of rental or sale. Helen replied,

> Your letter was distressing to me. I cannot sit tight until

the summer to settle things. I have no intention of spoiling my vacation haggling over why you would consider breaking your promise to me.

I think we can figure things out now, and I choose to do so by mail. I have sent this to Janie only because you asked me not to write, and I thought perhaps you had some reason for not wanting correspondence to come to your home. One thing more, this is a private matter, between you and me. It is impossible to see you alone. As you know, I have not seen you alone since you married, not even for a few minutes. I miss you terribly and cannot help feeling shoved aside. Your letter confirms my feeling. But so be it. If I cannot talk privately to you on private matters, and if I can no longer visit with you alone, I can by God write you privately. . . .

Your personal remarks insinuating that I have been less than friendly to Carol are a particular annoyance. I cannot see how my behavior can be faulted. I come to see you every year. I remember her and her kids at Christmas. What more do you want of me? You should recognize we have only you in common. I'm sure I am no more her kind of persona than she is mine. I find it ironic that Carol is everything you taught me not to be. She has submerged her identity in yours, she has no profession, and she is not independent. While this may be exactly what you need, and while I can appreciate Carol for her good care of you, you must not be critical of me because I grew up the way you wanted me to, and you must not try to force us to pretend a closeness neither of us feels. (12/7/72)

Three months later, she added, "I will not sign any statement giving Carol first right of refusal in case of rental or sale because certainly I would not sign such a statement on the half that is already mine. You are asking me to put Carol ahead of everyone else in the family. . . . You may not *force* me into putting Carol in the position of being my first consideration. I cannot put her before the rest of my family. She would not put me first in her considerations" (2/26/73).

Then, that summer of 1974, when Helen found out from her father that he was planning to leave his half of the property to Carol, she exploded—she certainly did not want to share it with Carol. The very thought of that made her angry. If her brother Bert would get full title to the Larson ranch, Twin Lakes should be hers. It was only fair. She had already felt cheated once. Her father had a library of Western literature and history, collected over a period of years, that he kept in a concrete blockhouse at Twin Lakes. Helen understood that she would get the library. But then Bud needed money and sold the collection without telling her about it.

Bud thought, of course, that it was up to him to decide who would get his property, and he wanted Carol to have a place in Montana on his beloved Eastern Front after he was gone. In battling Helen, he felt he was protecting Carol's interest; she was the love of his life, who in his view had brought him back to life. Both Helen and her father were outspoken and stubborn, and the argument was vociferous, upsetting the reunion of the family and their guests—thirty people in all.

Bud wrote to his brother and described the uproar and the pain it had caused him. Chick, who now was a retired newspaperman in Minneapolis, had always been a supporter, even a cheerleader for his brother. Chick had published a column over the years (sometimes syndicated), had placed articles and stories in several national publications, but had never reached the level of his brother's success and had every reason to be jealous. (Both he and their sister,

Janie, had written book manuscripts never published.) Still, whenever he was able to get the assignment, he had written favorable reviews of Bud's books, had checked to make sure that the local bookstores ordered copies, and time after time encouraged Bud and expressed his admiration for his books and articles.

So it was natural, then, that, as fond as he was of Helen, he would take his brother's side in his reply to news of the dispute: "I wasn't too surprised to hear about the Twin Lakes imbroglio. Helen is a capable and talented gal but she comes on awfully damned strong, is a take-charge person and—with no offense intended—is inclined to think more about herself than anyone else" (8/4/74).

Helen recalled,

> The campaign started that he was going to leave his half of Twin Lakes to Carol. And I was going to get suckered out of that. Then the fight was on. And it got real mean and real nasty because I saw no way I could possibly share Twin Lakes with Carol. So it became mean in the extreme, and before it was over I had to ask my brother for his help. . . . And I had to hire a lawyer . . . my father hired a lawyer. The correspondence between my father and myself became bitter and acrimonious in the extreme. We never quite got over it. Finally, it culminated in his giving me a quick claim deed on his half of Twin Lakes.

As gut-wrenching as the battle had been for all concerned, it turned out rather well for both Bud and Carol in the long run. However, first—not only did Carol feel partly responsible for dividing the family, she also faced the blow of the death of both parents, her father in November of 1973 and her mother in June of the following year. But she did receive a large inheritance that summer, and that changed her and Bud's outlook for the future. With the impending possible loss of Twin Lakes, they began to plan to build a place of their own on the Front near the Teton River. Bud had previously purchased a parcel separate from Twin Lakes, on the south side of the river. It was not a piece of land that was much good for anything, ranching or farming—a flat, barren, rocky area with little growth beyond an occasional tortured jack pine; and except at the height of summer, a chill wind could sweep across it, a reminder that the mountains were near. But what made it worthwhile for Bud was that the parcel had an unimpeded view of the Rockies, one that featured, front and center, Ear Mountain, an odd-shaped purple cutout against a light-blue sky.

Staying at Twin Lakes until late October in 1974, Bud wrote to his stepdaughter, Amy:

> Today (I may have the date wrong above) is the opening of the hunting season, and Helen Harris hardly dares venture out her door for fear of being mistaken for wildlife. We have heard no shots in the neighborhood yet this morning and so conclude she has not been added to a marksman's bag.
>
> Almost the last leaf has fallen hereabouts, and the country would look drear were the weather not so balmy. The "melancholy" days are marked by their own rewards. One of them is that the bird feeder, loaded, now, is attracting the sprightly chickadee. Another is that the rabbits have grown tamer. Daily a big one feeds on the lawn, almost ignoring our presence. He has a broad roach on his back, and we call him Bigwig after a character in "Watership Down." (10/20/74)

From the beginning the new house was Carol's project. Keeping in mind the age difference between her and Bud, it would be a house for her, one that would be left to her after Bud was gone. As early as September, after the fateful summer, she began drawing up plans for the house. Later, she brought in an architect who approved of her plans, only modifying them to make the structure larger. It would be called "The Barn," since outside it had something like the shape of a barn and inside it was open throughout with a loft. The loft at one end would be Bud's office, with a window looking out at Ear Mountain. For the first time in many years, he would be out of the basement and have a view to the outside from his office. Even at Twin Lakes he did his writing in the concrete "block house" where he had his library, and that was about the same as writing in a basement. At the center of the barn on the ground floor was the kitchen, with an island and table and chairs, and the kitchen would be the center of activity. Beyond the kitchen and under the loft was a sunroom that also had a view of the Rockies.

Even while they were still living on Queen Street in Missoula, Bud did much of the cooking. Carol learned his favorites and became "the assistant cook." They had a pasta machine and a sausage machine. "I would grind it," Carol remembers, "and Bud would stand there and lift them as they came off. We did it always together." He loved bangers and mash. Carol recalled that "Bud had a special thing about his mother's cooking. She came from southern Indiana, and it is really quite a Southern cuisine—they cook green beans all day long and things like that. He tried to reproduce the dishes that she had done."

He was still devoted to corn dodger, and according to Carol, it was always a recipe in progress—he could never quite get it to taste like his mother's. She noted, "There was one really important thing—it had to be made with white cornmeal because where

Bud's parents came from yellow cornmeal was for the stock . . . I have spent hours looking for white cornmeal."

But Bud went beyond his mother's cooking. He had a large recipe collection and often experimented with the recipes. As Carol puts it, "He freely just threw things in the pot," whereas she found it hard to deviate from the written directions. Another activity that Bud and Carol shared was refinishing furniture (or finishing furniture that had to be assembled from a kit). Refinishing had been a hobby of Bud's ever since his years in Kentucky, when he acquired and restored a number of old pieces of furniture that were near-antiques. He had the tools and materials and showed Carol how he did it, and she went on to finish a number of unfinished furniture pieces for the barn.

In the meantime, Bud was busy writing, working on *The Last Valley*. Depending how you group his literary novels, this was either the sequel to *Arfive* or the third novel in his "Settlement Trilogy" (following *These Thousand Hills* and *Arfive*). But it might be best to think of the novel as a sequel, since many of the same characters are carried over from *Arfive* to *The Last Valley*, and many of the same themes are central to both. The critic Thomas Ford has said that "*Arfive* may be viewed as representing one of those social stages occurring shortly after the disappearance of free land, and from this angle Guthrie is dramatizing those social changes and their meanings." *The Last Valley* continues this focus on changes in the West and their meanings, and continuing, as well as concluding, Guthrie's "difficult task of composing a sustained historical series, 'of trying to interpret American life to the American people.'" It was an extremely ambitious task that was carried out with a lifetime of perseverance—a perseverance sustained at the end by a happy marriage.

Both novels take place looking back at a time period when

Guthrie was alive and in several ways reflect his own life and experiences. Thus, as Ford notes, these novels lose the distancing, which in the earlier novels enhanced a "past which is just out of reach." Among the autobiographical elements is Guthrie's use of his father and mother as models for the central characters of Benton Collingsworth and his wife, May. Collingsworth's rigid religiosity and Victorianism, especially in his view of sex, become important ingredients in the conflicts of both novels. His rigidity is balanced by his wife's gentleness and kindness; and, like Guthrie's mother, May suffers a series of miscarriages and dies before her husband.

Other autobiographical ingredients in *The Last Valley* are the small town, Arfive, patterned after Choteau; its newspaper; and its new owner-editor, Ben Tate, who is the novel's protagonist. Guthrie, of course, worked on the *Acantha* in Choteau when his father owned it, and his twenty years on a paper in Lexington, many of them as editor, gave him intimate knowledge of the pressures and conflicts encountered by the newspaper editor. Like Jason Beard, the baseball player in *Wild Pitch*, Ben Tate is not modeled directly on the author but created out of the author's experiences. One of the themes of *The Last Valley* is the role of a newspaper in a small town, its responsibilities and difficulties. Bud thought that good newspapers were essential to good democracy, whether in county, state, or nation.

With so much personal experience and memory as a basis for these novels, several reviewers charged that they were dominated by nostalgia, a sentimental revival of the past. The *Virginia Quarterly Review* wrote, "The setting is Arfive, Montana, in an America as we would like to remember it: a place of good intentions and lasting friendships, a place where evil deeds are punished as swiftly as good works are praised, a place where the town doctor makes house calls and dispenses folksy wisdom, a place where an idealistic young man can buy the town newspaper, support progressive causes and learn from his mistakes." However, the review concludes by saying, "*The Last Valley* may be nine-tenths nostalgia, but it is, at least, first-rate nostalgia."

The protagonist, Ben Tate, is the scale by which change is weighed and measured throughout the novel. As editor of the local newspaper, he feels, at least at first, obliged to support progress, which is represented in the novel by a proposal to build a dam. The construction of the dam will mean jobs, irrigation water for surrounding agriculture, and flood control. But what the issue of the dam represents in the context of the novel is a central issue of modern life—the difficult choices we are forced to make every day between keeping what we have as opposed to allowing change and what can be called "progress." What Ben comes to realize is that with progress and its benefits, there are penalties in losses to lifestyle and degradation of the environment.

In 1975, the year after the summer of dispute and the split of the family, and the start of construction on the barn, *The Last Valley* was published. For the first time since his first novel, *Murders at Moon Dance*, the response by reviewers was tepid. As always, the novel was compared to *The Big Sky*, and settlement and the complications of advancing civilization didn't have nearly the power of the adventures of the mountain men on the raw frontier or even the wagon train trip to Oregon. The reviewers usually praised Guthrie's extraordinary ability to sketch in the qualities of the environment and to make readers feel that they were in the landscape. For example, the *Christian Science Monitor* said, "What one feels most of all is the part which the actual land and the spirit of place play in it all. . . . The familiar rhapsodic descriptions of landscape which one associates with most westerns are rendered with special beauty here."

But many reviewers didn't like what they called the melodrama, domestic conflict rather than conflict on a more heroic scale. The irony of this was that if there were complaints about his earlier work, it was that there was too much dependence on the Western myth. Now that he had largely abandoned that myth to deal with more contemporary problems, reviewers didn't like that either.

Almost all reviewers ignored the important theme in the novel, that of the challenges of change in an increasingly complex world. In the novel Benton Collingsworth recalls what a friend said after dinner one night: "Change is the order of nature. It is in our nature somehow to resist while forwarding it. What comes, comes, to our dismay or delight or more likely both, and both diminished."

Thomas Ford comments on this, "The key word . . . is the word *diminished*. The exuberant energy of *The Big Sky*—whether that energy was used to save life or destroy it—that *anima*, that life force, which was felt by identification with unspoiled land and space, is *diminished*. The big sky contracts with the advance of civilization." With sad resignation, Guthrie accepts change as inevitable, not entirely good or bad, but it worries him, and he can only hope for the best as we work out compromises between what we value of our past and what we hope for in the future.

The Last Valley is the most directly environmentally conscious of all of Guthrie's novels. Toward the end of the novel, speaking to his son, who expresses a desire to also become a newspaperman, Ben Tate says,

> We can't keep digging and cutting and polluting. We can't keep poisoning and exhausting our topsoil or giving it to the wind. We can't if we want to survive. . . . Just remember

that the earth is all we have. Her riches are limited. When she goes, we go. That's plain to see, or should be. But in the name of progress we keep drawing on an account that can be overdrawn. Progress. Progress be damned! Progress leaves us no retreat. . . . So here's the positive. Here's a coming great role of a good and free press. Here's what you can do and all I can try to do as long as I last. . . . Educate and inform. Look to the years ahead. Make people think. Speak from knowledge and concern for the future. That's not all you can do, but it's one hell of a challenge, and you'll have to fight. . . . If only we can get people to love the earth.

In a way this speech, with its firm declaration of awareness on the part of Tate, is the culmination of the novel—what it is really about. It says some things that some people didn't want to hear. The *National Observer*, published for a decade and a half by the *Wall Street Journal*, published one of the most virulent reviews received by any author for any book:

> *The Last Valley* . . . is a near-total disaster as a work of fiction. . . . One can scarcely believe that the man who wrote *The Big Sky* and *The Way West* is responsible for it.
>
> Guthrie seems to have forgotten everything he once so splendidly knew about craft, form, function, and the vagaries of the human heart; every page, every line, almost every sentence treats us to an unhappy spectacle of ineptitude, not unlike watching a man attempting to hack a tree stump into a piano with a dull ax.

One might suspect that the writer here, L. J. Davis, admired and would endorse the complete entrepreneurial freedom pictured in

The Big Sky and misses it dearly in the social complexity, with its restraints, in *The Last Valley*. Anything but tough individualism—such as community concern and involvement—is weak and sentimental.

Not every reviewer was so hostile. The *New York Times Book Review* complimented the author by saying that "Arfive, Mont. is a town where the most exciting thing to do is, as the saying goes, watch the grass grow. In the hands of A. B. Guthrie, Jr. even this phenomenon is laced with more than ordinary human interest."

And a few reviewers even seemed to get the point of the novel: "*The Last Valley* is more insistently political than the others in that the small town becomes a microcosm of our contemporary problems: freedom of the press, the influence of large corporations, appropriate and inappropriate modes of patriotism, the need for progress versus the demands of ecology."

During the construction season of summer 1975, the Barn was built, and Bud's stepson, Bill, was on the crew, helping with the electrical wiring. With a lot of beams over open spaces inside, and a number of custom touches in the flooring, paneling, railings, closets, and cabinets, building the barn was not an easy job. It was amazing, really, that so much was accomplished in one season. The Guthrie budget was tight, and they made all their own lamps. According to Bill, they made them "out of weird stuff, you know— milk bottles and milk strainers and all kinds of strange things that my mother found to make lamps out of." The following year, 1976, the Guthries divided their time between the Missoula house and the Barn, which had been winterized for year-round occupancy. In 1977 they sold the Missoula house and moved into the Barn full-time.

While they were at the Barn, the presents that Bud gave Carol, for Christmas, birthdays, and on their anniversary, were often reflective of his sense of humor. Early in their occupancy of the Barn, on their anniversary he gave her a load of gravel to pave their driveway. Once on their anniversary Carol wanted to get Bud a dozen roses. However, the only florist for a hundred miles was a man who was also the surveyor who had botched the job on their property so badly they had taken him to court. Amy recalled, "So she just panicked. She went to town, and she got twelve bottles of Rosé and put them in a basket."

During this period Bud was following in the newspapers the progress of the Bolle Committee, which had been appointed by the Montana senator Lee Metcalf to investigate public land management practices. Bolle was a professional forester and former dean of the University of Montana's School of Forestry. When Bud read that an excursion was planned to go to the Bitterroot National Forest to investigate the clear-cutting there and that three senators would be going along, he called up a friend, the reporter Dale Burk, and asked if it could be arranged for him to go.

Fifteen Forest Service vehicles were assigned to the caravan. Burk recalls that they started from Missoula at daybreak "and then . . . had field trips where they would get out and talk." He said, "Then they treated us to dinner where they had a table set up and showed us what a great job they had been doing. After that it was two-and-a-half to three hours back to Missoula." The trip took fourteen hours. It was a long, long trip. Bud was in the van with Burk, along with Senator Metcalf (later, the area near the Bitterroot became the Lee Metcalf National Wildlife Refuge). He and Senator Gale W. McGee from Wyoming were on the trip to convince Senator Floyd K. Haskell of Colorado to support the Bolle Report and the effort to pass the National Forest Management Act.

On the Bolle Committee, and in the van with the senators and Bud, was a professor from the University of Montana, Dr. Les

Pengelly, one of the three most eminent wildlife biologists in the United States. Burk continues to describe the trip:

> We came to a canyon up on the Bitterroot River and into a forest, but it had been heavily clear cut, and here over the river right along the bank was this big, big solitary tree. Les Pengelly had been talking philosophically about the values of protecting watershed, protecting the land and forest for future generations. And then [pointing at the solitary tree amid the clear cut], Pengelly asked the question, "I wonder what that proves here?" And the Forest Service person who was with us, a district ranger said, "About $350." Bud Guthrie just lit into him. He said, "Young man, you just told me more about the Forest Service than anybody else today."

Pengelly later used that dialogue to illustrate to the committee how the Forest Service had gone astray—they could deal with trees only in terms of monetary value. A few months after the Bolle Committee Report was submitted to Congress in 1976, the National Forest Management Act was passed by both houses.

On another trip to the Bitterroot Forest that Bud took with Burk and others, the Forest Service was talking to the passengers in a van about the great opportunities for tourism that they were preserving. Also along was Gui Brandborg from the university, who, at one point in the spiel, took the microphone from the ranger and asked that they go up the road a half mile. When they got there, the ranger looked around and exclaimed, "Oh my God, a clear cut!" The area was known for years as the "Oh my God clear cut."

Burk recalled, "I am just glad that Bud was in Missoula then. He was kind of a constant phone caller—'What are you going to do about this?'" But Burk was working for a newspaper and felt that it was his job to be as objective as possible and that Bud, on the other hand, had the freedom and leverage to expose those who were exploiting the land. And this he did, in frequent letters to the editor and in articles—and even in his novels.

In 1977 Bud was asked by the State Department, as part of the American Specialist program, to go around Germany to give lectures and seminars on western American literature. In April, Bud and Carol, along with Bud's stepdaughter, Amy, traveled to Europe. (Amy would tour England and Europe separately.) Carol had been to Europe before, but this would be the first time for Bud. When notice of his trip was sent out to American embassies and consulates in Europe, a number of them requested that he come there also, so that his itinerary spread out for a six-week period as they traveled from England to France, Germany, Spain, Italy, Switzerland, and Portugal. Quite a schedule—they were not just touring, but working.

It was fun, but it was also hectic. And it was often hard on Bud—he was seventy-seven years old, and Carol had to take care of the travel logistics. One problem that made it hectic was that they didn't receive the letter from the State Department with a vital authorization number before they left. At each stop Carol had to go to the embassy or consulate and fight her way through the bureaucracy in order to get authorization. When they got back to Montana, there was the authorizing letter.

Another thing that made it tough was a schedule so tight that they hardly had any time for sightseeing. A day here, a day traveling by train, another two days elsewhere, and so on. At the same time, what the hosts wanted from Bud seemed to change from place to place. When they would get to a city and discover what the hosts wanted from him, as tired as they might be from their trip, they would have to sit down in the hotel room and prepare for the next day. They found that his material was more formal than was needed. Carol remembers, "Sometimes we'd have to really put together something in a hurry." Bud would compose aloud and Carol would write it down.

Their first stop was in England, where there was very little for him to do—a taped interview at the University of East Anglia at Norwich. The next stop was France, which was difficult for Bud because he was not an academic, and what they wanted to know had to do with esoteric literary theory. The real tour began after they flew to Germany. As Carol recalled, "His programs varied. Sometimes he spoke at an evening thing and gave a formal speech, sometimes he would go up to a classroom and talk, and sometimes he would do a reading." In his appearances Bud talked mostly about the West and growing up in the West. Sometimes he talked about the writing process, sometimes about one of his books or stories, and sometimes he would read from something of his own.

His appearances were under the auspices of the American Studies Program, sponsored in part by the State Department, and so the students in the program, who made up the audiences, usually had some proficiency in English. The professors who were shepherding Bud and Carol thought that because Bud was from the West that they had to take him out in the country. "So," Carol remembered, "we spent a day finding out what this crop was and that crop was." In Germany, when they went into a classroom and Bud talked or read, the students didn't applaud—they knocked on their desks. One rainy afternoon at a school in Hamburg, Bud read "April in Montana" (from the autobiography), and the appreciative students began to knock mightily, which startled Bud, who at first didn't know what was going on—perhaps this was a sign of disapproval or even the prelude to an attack.

In Hamburg they had a lot of parties and receptions with teachers and writers. At one, Bud was paired off with a prominent local writer, and everyone began to worry about how the two would get along, since the German writer spoke very little English. "The man who had arranged the party," as Carol remembers, "said, 'What do you think they are talking about?' and I said, 'Well, I will find out.' And so I walked over and said something to Bud, and Bud said, 'This fellow is just getting screwed on his royalties.' So I went back and I said, 'Don't worry.'"

They went down to Munich, to Friedberg, Lucerne, and then Innsbruck. At a college in Innsbruck, Bud had a meeting with graduate students and talked to them informally about his books—which they had read. Somebody asked him how he got his characters, and Bud said, "Well, they just walk onto the page." This caused quite a stir. They thought he was joking or just being sarcastic, and the student who asked the question was a little angry and looked downcast. "[Thinking] we were supposed to be Americans doing good abroad," Carol said, "if I could just interrupt a minute . . . you might think that was a facetious comment, but my husband meant that, that is how his characters come into being as he is working, and all of a sudden they are on the page, and he can't tell you how that happens." Her explanation smoothed things over, and the meeting ended with good feelings all around.

(In an interview in 1974, Guthrie said, "Sometimes an author, despite himself, introduces characters he hadn't foreseen. . . . Until I met Jim Deakins, I didn't know what a character he was. He had a certain vitality of his own, a way of looking at things, and I followed it along. I know that sounds mystical, doesn't it?")

From Innsbruck the Guthries took the train to Vienna. There they went to a cocktail buffet with people from the arts in a large drawing room, and the man who arranged the event had arranged for a showing of *Shane*. After the showing was over, Bud talked about the making of the movie and answered questions. A young woman was assigned to them as a driver that evening, and as they were getting into the car to go back to the hotel, she asked, "Tell me about Alan Ladd." Carol recalled, "The thing is that movie is a very fresh looking piece, the colors are pretty, and it doesn't look as old as it is. She was all ready to go to Hollywood and meet Alan Ladd. I didn't know if he was still alive. It was just the cutest thing. Buddy was very sweet—he didn't care for Alan Ladd, but he didn't say that."

After Vienna they flew to Rome, where there was a gathering of children in American Studies from all over Italy for a spring festival. They were going to show *The Big Sky* in a Roman palace, and Bud was asked to talk about it after the showing. The night before, according to Carol,

> We were fudging up something for him to do for this in the hotel room, and I said, "Buddy, these kids are going to have seen that movie, and they are probably going to like it. They are probably going to think it is good, and so don't be too terrible about it, because they would feel crushed if they had indeed enjoyed it." And so we got there, dutifully, because he was trusting my instincts very much at that point. And he said, "Well, there are some very nice things about this movie"—or something like that—and the kids said, "That was a terrible movie." My instincts took a back seat after that. . . . It kind of broke everyone up—it broke Bud up. He looked at me, laughing. It was pretty funny.

They went on to Madrid where Bud gave a formal presentation from a platform—a professor translated and the audience wore headphones. From there Bud went on to give another formal presentation at a Barcelona estate. In Portugal he was to address a class in American Studies, and, again, the night before, they sat in their hotel room thinking of what he might talk about to this audience. Bud came up with the idea of telling the story of John "Portuguese" Phillips. A Wyoming frontier hero, he rode through hostile Indian country 236 miles from Fort Phil Kearny to Fort Laramie with news of the disaster involving the annihilation of Captain William J. Fetterman and his men. It was a story out of western history, not something Bud had written about. After the questions and discussion was over, the teacher said to Bud that there was something that the children would like to give him. One of the children got up and gave him a French comic book, and on the cover was a Western bad man drawn from Jack Palance, who famously played the cold-blooded gunfighter, Stark Wilson, in *Shane*. There he was, looking menacing from under his cowboy hat and wearing the black leather glove.

(Palance had never played a gunfighter before and this was one of his earliest roles, so he was very nervous about it. He spent days practicing a fast draw and he practiced until his hand got raw. So during his practice he started wearing a black glove on his gun hand. The director, George Stevens, had watched him, and when they started shooting the movie, he told Palance, "Wear that glove.")

At the end of their European tour, the Guthries flew to Washington, DC, and went to the Harry S. Truman Building to be debriefed by the State Department. After entering the imposing entrance and being guided through security, they were taken to a room where several people in the overseas American Studies Program were seated around a polished mahogany table. Each of the people who were in charge of the program in various countries had reported back, and the people around the table asked the Guthries about their experiences in light of the reports. One woman had written to say that Bud's presentation for her was very unsuccessful, which made the Guthries furious.

In Switzerland, Bud had given a successful reading and discussion session at the university in Lucerne, but their caretaker had insisted that he also go to a small school out in the country, even though that was not on the schedule. Bud didn't want to go, but at last agreed. As Carol recalled, "So an extra day, and we went to this thing, and it didn't go over very well. Those kids didn't understand English, and it was just a bust. And that was too bad, because that was the one performance that I didn't think worked very well." That the woman who had insisted on the event blamed the failure on Bud was, for the Guthries, almost enough to spoil the memory of the whole trip.

They were supposed to go on to Innsbruck, but since they were off their schedule, the official wasn't able to put them on the train until 5 o'clock in the afternoon. Carol remembered, "We were to get there about 10 o'clock that night, and there was no dining. And that wasn't funny. Bud had been putting out, and he needed his food. . . . So I ended up hanging out the window at a stop and getting one of those fellows who sells food at the side of the train. We got a big sausage and I think I even got some beer. Anyway . . . we were furious because we had done that [event] for her."

From Washington, they flew to Missoula and then drove to Twin Lakes. When they got back they called Helen to tell her that they had brought a present home for her daughter, Eden. Helen recalled,

> I drove the 74 miles or whatever it is one way, and I had no
> money for gas . . . and their present for Eden was a bar of
> hotel soap, one of those tiny bars of hotel soap. So I drove
> almost 150 miles to get a bar of hotel soap. And Carol would

never let father answer the phone. She always answered the phone, so all my phone calls were strained and I couldn't talk to him. And he told me at one point not to send him any personal letters. If I had to write to him, please send the letters to my Aunt Janie and . . . he could go over to her house to read my correspondence—this is when they had a house in Missoula. Like a fine cutting horse, she had just cut him out of the herd. . . . I never did hate him except when he took up with Carol. And it was, do I hate him or do I hate her? And finally I decided, well, he's letting it happen. So I tried not to focus on her.

Bud and his sister, Jane.
Courtesy of Peggy
Bloom.

Bud's niece Peggy and
his sister, Jane. Courtesy
of Peggy Bloom.

Bud at Twin Lakes, 1969. Courtesy of
Amy Sakariassen.

(*Opposite top*) Carol's children, Bill and
Amy Luthin, Bud, and Carol in the Twin
Lakes cabin, 1969. Courtesy of Amy
Sakariassen.

(*Opposite bottom*) In the dining room
at Twin Lakes in the summer of 1979.
From left, Carol, Bud, Lois Welch, Ripley
Hugo, Richard Hugo (foreground), and
Matt Hansen. Courtesy of Lois Welch.

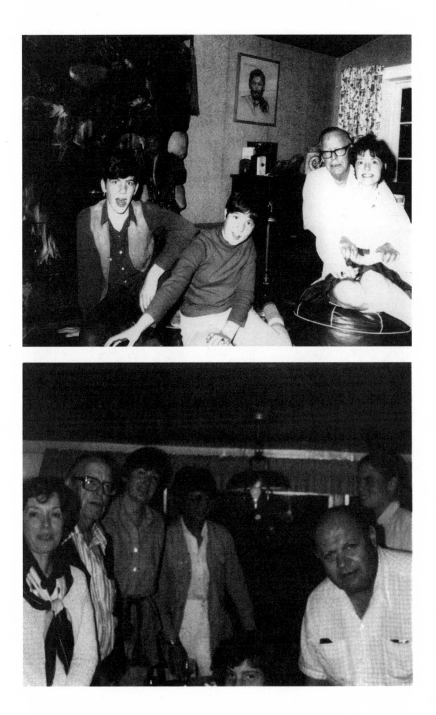

(*Opposite top*) Dr. Tom Clark and Bud at the Kentucky Book Fair, 1985. Courtesy of Amy Sakariassen.

(*Opposite bottom*) Bud and Carol at Twin Lakes the summer after their April marriage, 1969. Courtesy of Amy Sakariassen.

Jim and Lois Welch. Courtesy of Lois Welch.

(*Opposite top*) Richard Hugo. Courtesy of Ripley Hugo.

(*Opposite bottom*) Bud looking out on the Rocky
Mountain Front from his office at the Barn, ca. 1984.
Courtesy of Amy Sakariassen.

Bud in his Barn office with the photographer's son,
Miles Gaede, 1988. Photo by Marc Gaede.

Carol, Bud, and a Forest Service filmmaker at Schafer Meadow.
Courtesy of Amy Sakariassen.

CHAPTER FIFTEEN

"What Happened to Boone?"

There is no doubt that Carol was protective of her husband and at the same time protective of her husband's relationships to her own family. While she did not push Bud's attentions toward her children, she was gratified that he developed a great affection for them. That doesn't mean that she actively campaigned to separate him from Helen, Bert, and Janie. On his own volition Bud drifted more and more into the sphere of his new family, which was probably only natural. Like Bud, Carol wanted everyone to get along but hoped that Bud's focus would continue to be on her, Bill, and Amy. Helen separated from her father because of her antagonism for Carol and her feeling that her father was not treating her fairly. Bert, on the other hand, had more antagonism for his own father than for Carol. And Janie accepted Carol but gave her a hard time.

Recently divorced when the Luthins came on the scene, Janie found it hard to have Bud move away from her and change his life again. They had had a very compatible relationship, a comfortable routine, and Janie was very much like her brother—assertive, outspoken, determined, with a ready sense of humor. They balanced each other very well, with a lot of give and take. Amy has described Janie as "kind of a vinegary lady": "She'd constantly get on Mom [Carol]. She was not terribly nice to Mom, but Mom never was disturbed about it, because she said that Janie always felt bad about it. She said she knew when Janie said something kind of nasty that Janie felt worse [than she did] about it. And she said there is something about those Guthries. They just can't resist a clever comment even if it stings." On the other hand, Amy recalled that Janie "was unfailingly fun." She added, "She and Peggy [Janie's daughter] used to take me out—they thought that I would be lonely after my brother went off to college. So they would come and get me, and then we would go drive out in the country. Or, Janie had this car, and I had to go and drive with her so that she could blow the carbon out and keep her company."

In the summer of 1976, just after Amy graduated from the university, she went to work as an anthropologist with a Princeton team, headed by Jack Horner, doing a dig on the Peebles ranch just east of the Barn. At the same time, Bill went to work with a seismographic survey team employed by Shell Oil, which was operating in much the same area as the anthropologists. The survey team was scheduled to go near to where the dig was, according to Bill, and there was some fear that the two teams would come into conflict. The survey gang had gained a reputation for being tough and intimidating. Bud and Carol, fearing the worst for their children, took colored tape and on two T-shirts formed the words "FOSSILS" on the front and on the back of Bud's, "THE OLD MAN." And on the appointed day, they went out to the ranch to try to

defuse the situation with humor. They were apparently successful—nothing happened except some banter.

In the spring of 1979, Chick was diagnosed with a recurrence of
his prostate cancer. After another operation that August, he died.
He was seventy-four; Bud was seventy-six. Even though Bud and
his brother had not seen each other often in recent years, they were
very close and corresponded frequently. Bud admired his brother,
admired him so much that he always felt that he had not lived up
to his potential, even though he became a respected newspaper
editor and columnist. When a new high school was built in Choteau in 1968, Chick, son of the original principle, was invited to
come from Minneapolis to give the dedicatory speech. Bud wrote
to Carol, "Did I tell you that brother Chickie, a much better man
than I, is going to be here the last of the month to make the address at the New Choteau High School?" (9/9/68). Chick had
the same sense of humor as his brother but was a more temperate
man, quieter and in some ways gentler. His humor and sensibility
was expressed in his columns. In the memorial address, Richard
Mathison described Charles M. Guthrie as "a man who could write
like Norman Rockwell could paint." He observed, "He watched
our great moments and our disastrous ones, our hilarious times
and our clumsy ones, our presumptuous days and our humble
ones—and then let his typewriter tell the world about us." Bud
had loved him dearly, and his death was a shock, particularly since
he was the younger.

In the spring of 1977, the Guthries sold the Missoula house, and
in the fall, after a summer at Twin Lakes, they moved to the Barn
full-time. Their routine was similar to that on Queen Street, except
when Bud went to write, he did not slink down into the basement
but rose up to the glory of his view of Elephant Ear Mountain in

the center of his window. Later, having lived with this view for several years, Bud would write:

> I doubt the practical sense of claiming kinship to a mountain, but sometimes it seems to me that Ear Mountain and I are on a common journey, made relatives by times and vicissitudes. Of course its life will outlast mine, but I'd rather it missed me than that I grieved for it.
>
> I'm not alone in my feelings for what was originally called Elephant Ear Butte. Neighbors share my sentiments and look often to it for reassurance in their unassured lives.

To get down to business, however, he faced his chair to his desk, looking out in the other direction, across the beams on the barn ceiling. If they had visitors, they tried to have them in the late afternoon, and after visitors were gone and dinner over, they would settle down, each with a glass of wine and a mystery. Reading mysteries was their recreation, and they read until late at night and then got up late the next morning. Once you started a mystery, you were driven to finish it. Over time Carol gradually took over the cooking chores, especially when they had company for dinner.

Although during these years Bud occasionally drank hard liquor, Carol limited him to two glasses of wine a day. He sometimes tried to go for three, and she would stop him—which he accepted gracefully, knowing that she did it for his own good. Visitors, as always, marveled at Bud's ability to fill his wine glass to the brim, and then above the brim. Then, at Easter it became traditional for someone to hide bottles of beer, rather than eggs. So alcohol was not banished, only somewhat limited.

If he drank whiskey, it was usually at parties and large gatherings of friends. After several drinks it was common for him to sing—he loved the old ballads, particularly "Sam Hall"—and sang in what has been described as "an old cowhand voice." And he was a great storyteller—he was, as several have described him, a happy drunk. He could be very funny, and people loved to be with him. But Carol tried to limit his drinking occasions and protect him from what she called his "drinking buddies." Maybe, as some thought, she was trying also to keep him for herself.

At one point Bud decided he wanted to get the family and close friends together at a dinner party, and Carol agreed to it. It was held at a restaurant called The Cow Track, which was not far from Twin Lakes. They had George Sexton, the family doctor, and his wife, Helen; Bud's daughter, Helen, and her husband; Bud's son, Bert, and his wife; and Bill and Amy Luthin. According to his daughter, Helen,

> Father was going to have this nice, like we-all-get-along, dinner party. Of course, we all went. My Aunt Alva was still alive then and she went—a pretty sizable table of us. You know how sometimes just a hush can come over a dinner table for no reason. This great hush came over, and then George, who had this booming voice, said, "Good God, Bud, why have you abandoned us?" And we all— Oh shit, what are we going to do now? We all just started chit chatting away, you know like nothing had happened. But father said, "I haven't abandoned anybody." Well, that was not true.

Bud had finished the manuscript for the second in his string of mysteries, *The Genuine Article*, in the fall of 1976, and it was published the following year. (Three others followed—*No Second Wind* in 1980, *Playing Catch-Up* in 1985, and *Murder in the Cotswolds* in 1990). As in *Wild Pitch*, the novel featured the sheriff, Chick Charleston, and his deputy, Jason Beard. The sheriff, named after

Bud's brother, would seem to express many of the brother's qualities: a calm rationality, a quiet competence, and a good sense of humor. Like Chick the columnist, the sheriff has a fondness for telling yarns, stories told to illustrate a point.

Once again the sly Guthrie slips in a few ethical or political points, made in passing by the narrator, Jason, or the sheriff. As he had before, Guthrie attacks rigid religious fundamentalism, satirizing the traveling evangelist, Brother Sam, "an auctioneer, auctioning salvation with an auctioneer's jabber." And once again he shows, through the actions of a disciple of the preacher, the hypocrisy of the true believer's Puritanism. And then in a swipe at the macho spirit of the West, Jason notes on a trip to interview a suspect that the sheriff tries to avoid running over a migration of picket pin gophers on the road. When, despite all of his efforts, he flattens one, Jason sees Chick shake his head and comments, "Another rider would have thought he was too softhearted for the office of sheriff."

But perhaps the most telling new aspect of *The Genuine Article* is Guthrie's including Indians as major characters in one of his mysteries and making their encampment a key location. The Indians are treated as people, multifaceted, not all of them admirable. Yet, through Jason, the author shows the Indians collectively a good deal of sympathy: "I turned my eyes to the intent, watching faces. They tended to be high in the cheekbones. Some were dark, some half-dark, some copper-tinted, some barely suggestive of Indian blood. They were good faces, I thought, good faces almost all, better than the circumstances of their lives. Call them breeds, call them war-whoops, treat them that way, and so put an end to hopes not ended already." The encampment is Breedtown, which, as we have already noted, was modeled on an actual location outside of Choteau. When Bud was a youngster and the town had crime or disorder, it had a tendency to look toward Breedtown as somehow responsible, whereas the whites gathered together to think of themselves as beyond suspicion.

Even while he was finishing the revisions of his latest mystery in late 1976, Bud was already thinking about what his next project would be. Complicating the decision was Houghton Mifflin's recent failure to communicate with him, and he was beginning to wonder if he had been discarded. He was inclined to change publishers, although his agent, Carol Brandt, counseled against that. She suggested that the reason for the lapse was that the publisher had changed his editor, the previous one having retired, and that he should write the new editor with his ideas about possible projects.

One idea that he had was to extend his autobiography with a sequel, an idea he kept in the back of his mind for most of the rest of his life, even periodically taking notes toward writing it. However, Houghton Mifflin was not interested, and so he tried on his own to sell it to others, but without success. This disappointment was another grudge that he held against Houghton Mifflin, along with his resentment that they not only refused to publish his children's book but refused to distribute it after he got a private publisher. Still, he went along with Carol's suggestion of contacting his new editor about his ideas for the future.

Writing to the editor, Grant Ujifusa, Bud laid out several possible projects. Two of them reflected his increasing involvement in environmental causes. The first was something that had evolved out of his idea for extending his autobiography, a book of essays and reflections with the title "Old Man, Young Wife and Other Hurrahs." He was not good with titles. After a section about his marriage, he would go on "to discuss the environment and [his] efforts to help the West preserve itself." He went on to note, "I have initiated a suit against the state board of health, the local county commissioners and a trio of developers who propose to create a shanty town hard by my holdings. . . . The troubled business of strip mining and forest destruction are on my mind, too. I know something about both and will learn more."

Then he told Grant that he could write a novel about strip mining, although he was "loath to do it." He would focus on "the overbearing arrogance of the mining companies." He thought such a project, however, would require travel, research, and a lot of time, and he didn't know if he was up to it. Also, he could do another mystery, but maybe it would be too close on the heels of the one that was just published. More to his immediate liking was a story about Mort Ewing, which would start long before he is introduced in *Arfive*. Ewing, as we might recall, was patterned in part after Tom Larson, and Bud said, "[Ewing was] to me . . . a sort of alter ego, the kind of man I wish I could be, a person of rather frolicsome good sense, compassion, and courage" (6/14/77).

It is clear from the letter that lack of money was a factor in driving him to find something to go forward with. He even included in his letter to Grant the thought that he might go back to screen writing, not in Hollywood but at home. There would be, he wrote, more money in that than in any of the other ideas he had suggested (6/14/77). There is no doubt that he had been generous with his money, occasionally sending money to Chick but more often to Janie. On one occasion when he had sent her money to help her go to Minneapolis to see Chick and his family, she told him that she was grateful but that he shouldn't send money unless she sent him a distress call: "Again, Brother dear, my thanks. There's never been a time when I needed you that you weren't there. Sometimes you're even there when I don't need you! But it's nice" (6/18/77).

In October 1977 Carol Brandt wrote Bud to find out what decision he had made and what he was working on. Bud replied,
"I haven't been doing any [writing] except fiddling at the typewriter with some ideas, making a speech now and then and touring Montana to sign books. It is high time I really got to work"
(10/11/77). But he was sidelined that winter by a long bout with
pneumonia, which lasted through February of the following year.
In March he wrote to Carol Brandt that he hadn't been able to
do much, although he had written some personal essays that he
hoped he would be able to eventually pull together into a book.
Then he told her, "The time has come for me to get busy. After
long consideration, I've decided my immediate project should be
another mystery, again involving Jason Beard and Chick Charleston. Much of it is already in my mind" (3/22/78).

Bud may not have deliberately "abandoned" anyone, but he
had given himself up entirely to Carol, and his relationships with
others had changed over the years. As he grew older, particularly
during the last few years of his life, he became more and more
housebound, less willing to travel—the only exceptions were occasional trips to attend conferences or make speeches, almost always in Montana. As articles about him came out showing him
at his desk with a view of the Front in the background, those irritated with his environmental stance in nearby Choteau called him
a "window environmentalist." Some environmentalists who frequently hiked in the mountains behind the Front also resented this
eighty-year-old man for much the same reason.

The "window environmentalist" label was unfair. His view of
Ear Mountain was the prayer stone of his old age, something solid
and ageless in an inconstant world, a world he knew he would be
leaving all too soon. In 1922 he wrote an article, "Trail Riding,"
for the college magazine *Frontier*. Aside from his excursions into

the mountains in his youth and his work for the Forest Service, he had made a number of pack trips into the Bob Marshall Wilderness after leaving Kentucky for Montana in 1953. A man who took such joy in his natural surroundings could in no way be characterized as an "indoor man." He took advantage of his trips into the wilderness to gather material for articles such as "The Rockies" and "Our Lordly Mountains," both published in *Holiday*.

In the first of these, he wrote,

> But I remember pack trips in the mountains and a stream talking near my bed and the all-well tolling of the bell mare's bell and the moon like a ripe fish egg where the high hills shored the sky. . . . It had been a good day. We had caught fish and seen the utter purity of sego lilies and the sprayed pride of beargrass and, in a burn, the flame of fireweed. High on a shelf a wild goat floated like a piece of cloud. We had come back to camp tired with a good tiredness and had scorched the supper trout and offered the platter with apologies to Ray Gibler, our guide and friend, and he had answered characteristically, "I'm like a graveyard; I'm atakin' anything."

Bud had quite a correspondence with Tom Edwards of the White Tail Ranch who led excursions into the wilderness every summer (the Helena Wilderness Ride). Edwards, who called himself "Hobnail Tom," was pleased to have Bud along on at least two occasions in the late 1950s and early 1960s. He looked forward to Bud's storytelling around the campfire—"your yarns and robust tales of the old west as I knew it as a kid surely [would be] a contribution to the jollification of everyone" (1/28/59). He told Bud that he could come along free of charge—he would even mend his saddle for him. Bud replied that he would, for such consideration, also regale the company with renditions of the many Methodist hymns that he knew. Hobnail Tom replied, "Good! Now I know 'Jesus Wants Me for a Sunbeam' will be given its proper place on the Agenda of *Rocky*, Rocky Mt. Music. We're waitin' fer yer saddle" (5/1/59).

The editor of the Choteau *Acantha* noted in a column written after Bud's death that "while Guthrie gained national fame and praise for his writing, he developed an uneasy relationship with his hometown, a conservative agricultural-based community." Another longtime resident, Mabel Crane, put her neighbors' feelings more bluntly: "I think the feeling in Choteau was they didn't like him." Much of the antagonism came from the area ranchers, and they, in turn, tended to infect the attitudes of the townsfolk. Feeling the dislike, even, in some instances, hatred, around him, Guthrie returned the insults with one of his own, referring to the more outspoken and usually well-to-do critics as "the pig shit aristocracy"—stirring up even more antagonism.

In his late seventies and eighties, Bud began to worry about Carol's situation after he might die and, like most, began to hate growing old and to resent his increased fragility. He would frequently comment that "the only good thing about getting old is that you get to see so many sons of bitches bite the dust." While maintaining friendships with his neighbors on the Front, Alice and Ken Gleason of the Circle 8 and Dr. George and Helen Sexton, Bud and Carol tended to turn more in these years toward the companionship provided by literary friends, getting together with them as summer neighbors on the Front but also sometimes in Missoula or Bozeman at conferences. These were two couples, Ripley and Dick Hugo and Lois and Jim Welch.

Dick Hugo, a bear of a man and a brilliant poet, became a particularly good friend of Bud's. According Lois Welch, "They were just psychologically attuned to each other." Hugo had grown up in a working-class suburb of Seattle with his grandparents and had volunteered during World War II and served as a bombardier in the Mediterranean, flying thirty-five combat missions. After the war, he went to the University of Washington, majoring in creative writing and studying under Theodore Roethke. After graduation he went to work at Boeing, where he was a technical writer for nearly thirteen years and wrote poetry on his own time.

His first book of poetry was published in 1961, when he was thirty-seven, and then in 1964 he was hired to teach English and creative writing at the University of Montana. His wife, not happy with life in Missoula, left him shortly after they arrived; they were divorced, and he entered a decade of loneliness and heavy drinking. He was in Missoula when Bud was living there with his sister, but they didn't meet until much later. In *The Triggering Town*, a book on creative writing, Dick advised that a poet should "never write a poem about anything that ought to have a poem written about it." In his poems he wrote about abandoned towns, ragged landscapes, and the working people of the Northwest.

Bud met Dick at a conference at the university; at another conference he was talking to Ripley Schemm and started to introduce her to Dick but found that they already knew each other and were in fact dating. Dick and Ripley were married in 1974, and thereafter Bud and Carol would see them several times during the summer. Ripley recalls, "[They] used to come up to our little cabin, and the Welchs often came up to stay for a long weekend. We talked about everything." Lois Welch has observed that Dick "always felt he was fat and unlovable. Certainly Ripley did for Hugo what Carol did for Bud, that's for sure."

A big man, but a gentle and sensitive man and needy himself, Dick Hugo spread affection and good will in whatever ways he could. Ripley recalled a time when Bud and his longtime friend and neighbor in the canyon Ken Gleason were at loggerheads and stopped talking to each other. When Dick heard about it, he told his wife that there are so few people up here, they have to be friends. He decided that they should go over and talk to the Gleasons. As Ripley remembered the incident, "He said, Kenneth, you can't stay mad over a fence and gate, and then we went down to see Bud and Carol, and Dick said the same thing to Bud. And he felt that he had prevailed upon both of them." She added, "Dick was like that. He was a lovely man to live with."

Bud's stepson, Bill Luthin, has said that Bud met many of the people at the university, beyond those he knew from the Front, because he, Bill, had transferred from Reed College to the university in Missoula in 1974 and had become involved in the creative writing program. It was then, according to friends, that Bud became a part of the "writers community." Strangely enough, he had spent several years living with his sister in Missoula without any contact with that community. After he came to know these writers and teachers, he was often invited to speak at conferences and give readings, invitations he accepted, although less and less as he grew older.

A decade earlier, Jim Welch took creative writing from Dick Hugo, who was teaching his first class at the university. After Jim sat in the class not doing much for several weeks, Dick invited him to come in for a talk in his office. Jim remembered the session, with Dick first asking him, "You don't know anything about poems, do you?" Jim said, "I sat for a moment trying to think up a defense for my sorry attempts in class, but nothing came to me, so I said, 'No.' To my surprise, Hugo said, 'That's OK. What do you know about?' When I couldn't answer that question, he said, 'Where did you grow up?' I could at least answer that and I did.

Hugo, in his infinite wisdom and generosity, said, 'Go ahead, write about the reservation, the landscape, the people.'" Welch went on to write about the Blackfeet Indian experience in a series of novels. Michael Moore has said, "As much as anything, Welch's books—'Fools Crow' and 'Killing Custer' in particular—have scuttled the stereotypes that whites have erected around Indians."

Tall and solidly built, Jim was usually quiet and reserved, somewhat studious-looking, with glasses and a smile that endeared him to almost everyone, in addition to disarming them. For he could also be tough—tough-minded and steadfast in his values and opinions. Jim and Lois met Bud and Carol for the first time at a party at Bill Kittredge's house during a literary festival, "Who Owns the West," in Missoula. Jim recalled, "There must have been two hundred people there, and so we were squashed against a wall in the living room, contemplating going getting a drink, if we could find our way to the kitchen and beer. And there was this little old guy right next to me and his wife, and we just got to talking. I had no idea who that was. He introduced himself as Bud Guthrie, and I introduced myself and then we all met."

During the years that followed, the Welches, Hugos, and Guthries would periodically get together. They would talk about the poets they admired, the writers they liked, and the writers they didn't like. Dick and Bud were particularly compatible, since two of their favorite subjects were poetry and baseball. At the Barn, Carol would have a cocktail hour with wine, cheese, and Vidalia onions. Dick and Bud would like to joke with each other, and as Lois recalled, "With Dick and Bud it was kind of a show that you wanted to watch, not participate in." Jim added, "I'd usually listen. I am not very forceful, and those were two very forceful personalities—they were enormously forceful. . . . There is a kind of camaraderie in that sort of joking, bullying that you can only do with people that are very much your peers."

What often started them off was Bud's habit of making pronouncements. On one occasion at dinner, Bud had been reading Dick's poetry, and he questioned his use of a word at the end of one of the poems. He asked Dick if he had thought about the word in the context of the ending, and suggested another word. The table was frozen. Here was Bud, who was no shakes as a poet, criticizing a professional poet, the editor of the Yale Younger Poets Review and twice finalist for the Pulitzer. Amy, who was at the table, tells the story: "Richard looked over and said, you know I did, Bud, but you know I like the sound, I like the first letter in this word better—especially when you think about it with the line in front of it. And Bud said okay. All the rest of us were just mortified." One poem of Dick's that Bud liked was "Driving Montana" because there was music in it and the music made up for the lack of rhyme.

Although Bud and Jim enjoyed giving readings together in Missoula, Bud tended to treat the much younger Jim as a student— an attitude that led to a lot of joking and sparring between them. In Missoula in those days, the writers all supported each other. As Bill Kittredge has noted, "We all read each other's books, we all got along, we'd ask each other to parties." Jim would send all his novels to Bud, who in turn would give them a grade on a postcard with a wry comment. When Bud read *Winter in the Blood*, a postmodern triumph, Bud sent Jim a postcard, grading it "A-" because "it has no plot." And Jim smiled, commenting to his wife, "That's true." Dick sent some of Bill Kittredge's stories to Bud, who decided, "This guy doesn't know how to write an ending." He was, as Kittredge has reflected, very traditional in his views of literature.

Bud occasionally talked to Jim about Native American history and culture, something he became more intensely interested in during the late 1970s and 1980s because he was planning a novel in which they played an important part. For Bud the Indians were an essential part of western history, but he did not think of them in contemporary terms. Ripley has said that Bud "belonged to the old school of thinking . . . [and] thought of Indians as a people kind of going out of style." Ripley and Dick had the Welches and Guthries over to dinner at their house in Missoula, and after several drinks Bud said, "Well, I think the Indians should all assimilate." Ripley recalled, "We all looked at him in shock, and I said, 'That will never happen, Bud,' and he gave me that slightly aloof look of the older person because he had known me since I was so high. But then they talked, and Bud listened to Jim, and I admired that."

The novel Bud was planning would become *Fair Land, Fair Land*, and he told Jim about it and asked him if he thought he should write it. He was in doubt, since it would be a final, sixth novel in his historical series, the third of those that featured Dick Summers, and he wasn't sure if he shouldn't just leave the series as it was. He was afraid he might spoil things by adding to the story. He told Jim he planned on using the Marias Massacre to end his story. Jim recalls, "I told him I thought that would be great because I was working on the same thing [in *Fools Crow*]. I thought it would be great to see what we both came up with." Lois added, "I remember when you were talking, talking about that, and at one point he got absolutely teary about Teal Eye, he loved that character so much."

Teal Eye was the Indian woman that Boone, in *The Big Sky*, had abandoned, along with his son. In the new book Bud would have Dick Summers find her, and with her son form a family that lived with the Indians. The book, with its tragic ending, would be written largely from the Indian standpoint, particularly in the ending. Even though its central character was white, it was clear that Jim's input had made a deep impression on Guthrie.

One of the things, perhaps the main thing, that led Bud to write his final historical novel was the persistent question that seemed to haunt him, "What happened to Boone?" Bill Luthin recalled that at least a couple of times every summer, there would be someone who would show up "want[ing] the old man and talk about Boone." He added, "And they, of course, thought that Boone was the hero. . . . They would want to talk about how he tanned hides, techniques of rifle bores. And he [Bud] was always very gracious to them. That's really why he had to write *Fair Land, Fair Land*." There was the historical gap, he said, "but I think the big impulse was to resolve Boone who was out there crying in the wilderness after *The Big Sky*."

In an interview with Professor Bill Bevis, Bud said, "I get long distance calls as a result of arguments. One from Miami, Florida. What happened to Boone? Well, no answer. The reader writes his own end. My first impulse was to get the whole thing tied up, boxed with a fancy ribbon on it, everything, but I think that was a bad impulse. Let the reader write his own end." Later, Bud added, "I have said to beginning authors, the reader is smarter than you think, so you don't have to spell out everything for him. Don't do it. You don't have to be so absolute. The function of fiction is to free the imagination, not to imprison it."

Jim Welch was a student in Bill Bevis's course on Montana writers (about 1983 or 1984, before Welch wrote *Fools Crow*) when Bevis asked the students what they thought of *The Big Sky*. From the back of the class came a shout, "*Treasure Island!*" Bevis opens his book, *Ten Tough Trips*, by referring to this incident but refers to an anonymous "Blackfeet student"; in fact, it was Jim. Bevis couldn't get an explanation from him at the time but talked to him about his outburst later. Guthrie was still alive, of course, and Jim said, "I'll tell you what I meant, but don't tell anyone. . . . You know it is just a fantasy of going out West to live like an Indian, same old shit, escaping to some paradise island." Bevis has felt that Guthrie was very realistic for his time, taking the image of the mountain man, which at that point was more like Roy Rogers and Tom Mix, and presenting a character who was "a swearing, filthy, violent sonofabitch loner." But Jim, from an Indian point of view, saw it as the same old romantic fantasy.

Bevis interviewed Guthrie several times, and off mike, after an interview, he would like to have said, "Bud, you pay no attention to the tribalism in the Indian camp in *The Big Sky*. You present it as if the loner Boone just joined a bunch of other loners. There is not a single paragraph from Teal Eye's point of view. While Boone is sitting there, happy, the drums are beating for the death of everybody in the tribe from smallpox. And we never get any scene or chapter where the Indians' view of themselves as a communal people comes to the foreground, rather than living wild and free like [the white idea of] Indians." He has added that "it would be wonderful if some woman would write a great novel totally within Teal Eye, using Guthrie's material."

The critic Bevis has a more up-to-date revisionism than the revisionist Guthrie. His requirement for more inclusiveness in the novel reflects the points he, himself, as author would like to make— writing from an Indian and feminist point of view. But that was neither Guthrie's aim nor his theme. Requiring such is a bit like criticizing Steinbeck for writing about the white Okies and not dealing with the Mexicans and Filipinos who were also in the fields. Steinbeck wrote a lot about Mexicans and Mexican Americans, but *The Grapes of Wrath* was not about them. And the author gets to choose.

Bevis has felt that Guthrie was in love with "the outlaw West," an escape to a wild, free place, with a free individualism. His is an idea that might lead us to understand the popularity of *The Big Sky* and the enduring appeal of Boone. We have always romanticized, even idealized, our bad men, whether Jesse James, the Daltons, Butch Cassidy and the Sundance Kid, or even Liver Eating Johnson. But does Guthrie idealize Boone? The idea of a lost paradise, of a time and place without limits, would seem to have had more appeal to Bud than the outlaw Boone, who abuses his freedom and would have been to the writer an unsavory although dynamic character. What we have lost by that abuse would seem to have been the key question for him. "We destroy the things we love," and Boone is the archetypal destroyer, not only of the environment but of his best friend and, although he doesn't destroy them, he abandons his wife and their son, and certainly destroys their lives together. Destroyer he may be, yet there seems to be little doubt that with all his misgivings about him, Guthrie could still identify with Boone. Maybe it was, for Guthrie, living "Treasure Island," the same old shit.

Perhaps there are many pieces of history that in retrospect turn into a dream, a fantasy, no matter how realistically they are treated. Dreams, of course, have value, even though they may well be nullified by the reality of human nature and experience. The mountain man West, like Huck Finn's lighting out for the territory or the Joads' vision of California, is an expression of what we have so often called the American dream, a dream that frequently involves going west to find prosperity, freedom, and independence.

Just before he died in 1982, Dick Hugo wrote a poem dedicated to Bud Guthrie. The poem puts the spirit of *The Big Sky* into a larger perspective than that in which Bevis seems to see it. Often, when they saw each other, Dick and Bud, both fishermen, would talk about going on a fishing trip together, a trip to Pishkun Reservoir. It was a dream they both held on to and cherished because it brought them together in spirit. They defied reality.

PISHKUN RESERVOIR (for Bud Guthrie)
Think of those big trout, Bud, fifty years
back and more and no limit then, no game regulations
and no sonic booms cracking the dam
or the dam tender's house, mortar and stone,
How those big rainbows danced
on their tails. How fishermen believed skies
full of willing women. This land spreads big
as the big sky and there's plenty of room
for the dead, for enemies who died and dead friends.
I know what poets I'd bury here and everyone's
a king. I'd ring the reservoir with their stones
and all night their spirits would dance over
the waters. All day trout would dance on our leaders.
We imagine a man in the dam tender's house
stationed there decades ago and forgotten,
beginning to crack like the house. If he came
to us asking the year we'd say "welcome,"
we'd say we too forget the President's name.
Here the hard wind blows all hurt away:
the maimed bison moaning at the bottom
of the jump, Indians starving that year
no bison were seen, the sadness of children
and the sadness of none. We would be

hard as that wind. We're lucky enough to cast down it
and just as we guess the high white jet trail
a major run, say Chicago-Seattle, your bobber
moves some right slightly wrong way and we know
no matter how faint that nibble seems
it could be fifty years old, something real big.
Still no limit, Bud. No limit that counts.

CHAPTER SIXTEEN

Fair Land, Fair Land
The End of the Trail

R ichard Hugo died of leukemia in October of 1982. He was only fifty-eight. Deeply affected by his untimely death, Bud Guthrie wrote a poem of his own dedicated to Richard, a poem never sent to his widow or published.

> DAYS AND RAINBOWS (for Richard Hugo)
> I said to the poet in bed,
> "Endurance is the name of the game,
> And hope is the bow on the cloud."
> "Bull," he said. "Speak loud. Speak brave,
> and cheer the invalid. How's fishin'?
> Trout are what to talk about."
> "My bones are brittle, my eyes bum,
> I'm skittish all alone. I haven't gone.
> Sure, I remember that we talked
> Of fishing in the Pishkun, of rainbows
> yanking line, dancing on their tails.

But the afternoon turned hot, fishing
Would be slow. We didn't go."

I remembered the grey lake, treeless,
unpromising from surface view,
so wind-whipped that an angler cast to lee
or got the hook back in his face.
Old times then, the lake just filled
as storage for an irrigation ditch.
Rich food, fresh-water shrimp,
for rainbows of five pounds and more.
A tumult in the waters. "Hey, look!
I've hooked onto a lunker. See."
An old companion, dead now, shouting,
Kept there and loud in my recall.

"Next season then we've got to go,"
the poet said. "No damned hallucination—
out there a wowser waits to dance for me."
I left him, thinking of restoratives,
Thinking of big trout.

Despite his family's disparagement of Bud's poetic abilities, this is a moving and beautifully worded poem. Appropriately, it shows Hugo's influence on him over the last few years, displaying it both in the poem's form and language. Guthrie was influenced by his friends—he listened to them, whether Jim Welch or Dick Hugo. No longer were Tennyson and E. A. Robinson his guides.

More than two years before Dick Hugo's death, the Guthries had another visitor at the Barn. A student from an eastern university showed up at their door and asked to see Mr. Guthrie. Carol could hardly deny Bud was there, since he was in plain view of the doorway. Inside, the student blurted out the usual question, and Bud calmly gave his usual answer, "What do you think happened to him?" Then he went on to explain that he was "finished with that book." But he wasn't. It may be that this clean-cut Ivy League young man who cared enough about Boone to seek out the author clear across the country tipped the balance, and the idea of continuing the story grew until he began to ask his friends and family if they thought it was, indeed, something he should do.

All during the late 1970s, however, he continued trying to push his plan with agent and publisher for a collection of personal essays. He sent several of these essays to Carol Brandt, but Houghton Mifflin did not think such a collection would sell. The only fruit of this effort was that Carol sold some of the essays to magazines. Then, in early June of 1980, Bud wrote to Carol with a new proposal:

> I have long been aware of a gap in my western panel—between the fading out of Dick Summers at the end of *The Way West* and the appearance of Lat Evans in *These Thousand Hills*. The gap covers 30 years, in that time many things happened in the interior northwest and Montana—the thinning of the buffalo, the signing of Indian treaties, the formulation and implementation of the reservation system, Texas cattle drives, the increasing plight of the Indians, the beginnings of white settlements and finally the massacre on the Marias in 1870. Inserted in this list should be the Montana gold strikes and the road bandits under the direction of the infamous Sheriff Plummer.
>
> I do not know that I would touch on all these subjects, but they provide an idea of the opportunities.
>
> The protagonist would be Dick summers, old Dick

Summers finally, with no right home in the universe, because he and his kind had destroyed it unwittingly. That theme, of course, is not new, and I believe I could make it fresh and poignant. (6/5/80)

A month later he reported to Carol, his agent, that he had finished the first chapter, and a month after that, in August of 1980, he received a contract for the book from Houghton Mifflin. Returning the signed contract to his agent, he wrote in an accompanying letter, "I will put all I have into this manuscript, hoping it will be a worthy successor—I mean addition—to the western panel" (8/15/80). July of the following year he wrote to tell Carol Brandt that he was enclosing part one of the manuscript and was well into part two and predicted he would finish the manuscript by the first of the year. As he wrote and then revised, he gave the pages, chapter by chapter, to his wife Carol to read, and she in turn passed them on to Bud's stepson Bill. Then in December of 1981 he wrote Carol Brandt that he was mailing her the completed manuscript in time to make the fall publication list.

Fair Land, Fair Land was published in 1982 (in the meantime, the third Chick Charleston mystery, *No Second Wind*, was published in 1980). In the fall of 1982, Bud wrote his publisher: "The autograph sessions, TV appearances and speeches are enough to wear a young man down, not to mention me and my age. Yet the reviewers all do it, starting out, 'At the age of 81 . . .'" (10/28/82).

Carol recalled that when she discussed the book with her husband, she felt that "it was really quite wonderful, the personae that he gave Boone when he reappeared." She added, "I said something to Bud about that and he said, 'That's the only way it could have been.' And he was right. Which is something he felt—you should never give anybody something in a book that you had not prepared him for. You had to lay the ground work for any kind of thing—in some subtle way you had to do that."

The reception of *Fair Land* was mixed but largely positive. Typical was the conclusion of the article in *Kirkus Review*, which stated, "Despite the simplistic themes and lots of idyllic dawdling along the way: a welcome addition to a much-loved series." A more negative appraisal was in *Publisher's Weekly*: "The author captures well the space and grandeur of the West, but unfortunately his hero leads a basically dull and undramatic life." And on the positive side was this notice in *Booklist*: "*Fair Land, Fair Land* [is] a sublime, multilayered story that is sixth in a series that began 23 years ago with Guthrie's now-classic *The Way West*."

Bud claimed that he didn't pay much attention to the reviews, but he did—which is not an unusual denial for an author. Evidence that he did pay attention came out of a flap that developed in the English department at Eastern Montana College. The Montana Writers course had become a tradition, but several professors had voted to drop it because they said that Guthrie's *Big Sky* and Dorothy Johnson's works were written for adolescents.

> A member of the department, Sue Hart, remembered that Bud was called by a reporter, you know, about "What do you think about this?" Well, he thought it was absolute nonsense. He said, "Most of the time they say that they don't want teenagers to read my work because it is too adult." And then he said, "Some people think it is dirty." But then what happened was that somehow or other a book reviewer for the *New York Times* picked up that story, and when *Fair Land, Fair Land* came out, he devoted a good share of his article ("Montana's Novelists") to this controversy in Billings, and Carol said that as a result of that Bud never felt that that book got a fair review in the *Times*.

Finally, they [the English department] reconsidered because it was just getting so much bad publicity. There were editorials in some of the papers saying we can't believe that they offer a course on Tagore [Indian writer who won the Nobel Prize in 1913], for example, and they refused to offer a Montana Writers class in a Montana institution.

Bud did attend literary conferences occasionally and always went with Carol. There was a conference in the early 1980s before Richard Hugo died that was sponsored by the Montana Historical Society and held in downtown Billings. The conference was created to celebrate the achievements of contemporary Montana writing and speakers, including Bud, Norman Maclean, Ivan Doig, Jim Welch, Dick Hugo, and Spike Van Cleve (who had written a ranching memoir). Bud had just written an article, "On Marrying a Younger Woman," and he spent his allotted time talking about writing the article and paying tribute to Carol at some length. That set off everyone else on the program, who had to tell the audience how much their wives had done for them.

Again in the 1980s he and Jim Welch went to Missoula to give readings of chapters that showed how they had separately dealt with the Marias massacre, Bud in *Fair Land, Fair Land* and Jim in *Fools Crow*. During these same years Bud participated in a festival sponsored by the English department in Missoula, "A Sense of Place," with Ed McClanahan, Wendell Berry, and Ken Kesey. All gave readings, and then Bud was on a panel with Wendell. Sue Hart, a professor at Billings, remembers a conference at the state university at Bozeman where she was asked to serve as moderator of a panel. With some anxiety, since she had never performed that function in front of a large audience, she went to an opening reception the first evening. She recalled, "Here were all these people who had known each other for years and years and . . . I did not know anyone. No one talked to me, and I was too shy to approach anybody that I didn't know and start a conversation. And then Bud and Carol arrived. The very first thing that happened was that they both came over and gave me a hug and a kiss and after that everybody talked to me."

Back when *The Genuine Article* came out, Bud's old friend Dorothy Johnson, whom he often saw at conferences, wrote a very flattering review of his book, and Bud wrote her a thank-you letter:

> What a love of a review you gave my book! Both Carol and I treasure it, and both of us thank you.
>
> More, it's time I told you I envied you. You write—I speak not just of the review—with a charming simplicity and directness without loss of subtlety. Simplicity and subtlety. The hoped-for combination! It was said of Frost that he achieved it, and I say it of you. (7/12/77)

A few years later at a conference he encountered Dorothy, who was very elderly at this point. He said to her, "Dorothy, that was awfully good last night," and Dorothy came right back, "Oh, was that you Bud?"

Not that he had ever been recalcitrant in expressing his opinions, but as he grew older he became a more emphatic conservationist, more pronounced in his political opinions. He was drawn to reporters and editors, not just because of his own background, but because they could help give him a voice.

One among several reporters that Bud became acquainted with in the late 1970s and the 1980s was Bert Lindler, a bespectacled, wiry young man with a prickly journalistic conscience. He had spent a lot of time in the outdoors and worked for the Great Falls *Tribune*, giving Bud a sympathetic local news connection. However, Lindler, like Dale Burk before him, was devoted to objectivity and accuracy, regardless of his environmentalist sympathies, and because of that he and Bud occasionally crossed swords. Not that Bud was against accuracy, quite the contrary, but he was bothered about giving the other side what he thought was too much emphasis. He wanted the facts to persuade to his point of view.

The two got together when Lindler called Bud and asked to interview him, and thereafter Lindler cultivated Bud as a source. He would stop by the Barn whenever he would be in the mountains, and although he always came to see Bud, it was Bud and Carol together that he saw. Carol would answer the door, and Lindler recollected, "Bud might be upstairs [in his office], and she would get him, and then we would all sit out there in their glassed-in sunroom. So she appeared to play, you know, a very key role in his life at that time." Lindler recalled, "[They had] just incredible hours— I would not call out there before 1 p.m. You did not call before 1 p.m. I don't know when exactly they went to bed, but it was not at the time a lot of people go to sleep."

Lindler thought that Carol was concerned about Bud's health, particularly since they lived so far from the hospital, but said, "I think her chief concern was Bud's reputation, Bud's ability to continue working." Lindler decided that

> Bud's ideas seemed sharper than my own, and often when I would go out there I would notice that, and reflect on it, and I assumed after several visits out there that my sharp ideas got rounded because I had to call all sides of every argument. And my sharp ideas didn't stay sharp the way his did. He stayed there and thought and thought and thought, and he came to very clear conclusions, and I don't think he cared to have those challenged directly at that stage in his life. . . . He didn't mince words and try to smooth things over, ever.

Shortly after their first meeting, Bud called Bert to tell him that a dinosaur egg had been discovered at the Princeton archaeological dig on the Peeples' ranch, a few miles from the Barn. The egg was the first intact egg found in North America (found by an intern, Fran Tannenbaum, in 1979) and was startling news. The day after Bud called to tell Bert, he heard that people from a rock shop in Bynum had shown up at the site causing quite a stir. Enraged, Bud thought that Bert had violated a confidence, and chewed him out.

Bert told Bud, "I'm sorry if anything I did caused any problems, but I certainly didn't feel I was under any confidence." He went on to tell him that he was just then ready to leave to go out to the dig and was "certainly going to write a story for the newspaper" when he got back. He had not communicated with the rock shop. "At any rate," Bert recalled, "he was pretty tifted, and I don't think we met for a year or so after that. So I am confident that reporters who wrote certain stories would not have found themselves welcomed back."

But not all the contacts between the two turned out so badly. When Amy was working for the Nature Conservancy at the Pine Butte Guest Ranch (formerly Alice and Ken Gleason's Circle 8 Guest Ranch), there was an uncapped dry test well that was leaking into the swamp. Bud asked her to call Bert and tell him about it. Amy recalled, "It was just stinking up the place and oozing stuff, and Bert made a little bit of trouble over that, which was quite pleasant. Bert recalled that there was a story in the *Tribune* that discussed the problems you have when the father has one set of views and the son has another set of views, and that was not an area that I suspected Bud really wanted to discuss at any length. So I certainly didn't discuss it with him, in the interests of getting a newspaper story, because I knew if I did that type of story, that

I won't be getting any more." What Bert was referring to was a conflict, which became very public, between the conservationist Bud and his rancher son over the protection of the grizzlies on the Eastern Front of the Rockies.

The public face of the wrangling lasted through much of 1985 and 1986. During this period Lindler interviewed Bud twice on his views on what the community had come to consider "the grizzly problem." But he did not touch the controversy between father and son. He quoted Bud in one of his articles as feeling that the level of concern in Teton County was a "sort of hysteria, promoted by extremists." In another article, Lindler wrote, "The grizzly has reappeared on the plains in recent years for the first time in the memory of the oldest inhabitants. But have you considered the reasons? Guthrie said, 'Have you considered the careless disposal of dead livestock by ranchers and, especially, feed lots? Feed lots are a rather recent entry on the front. The coincidence of feed lots and the reappearance of the bears cannot be overlooked,' he said."

The survival of the grizzly in Montana became a cause célèbre for Bud during the 1980s. The grizzly was a token of a lost past and an icon that represented the loss of wilderness. Its near disappearance in this country personified for him the tragic results of our exploitation of nature. In a way the grizzly represented everything that Bud had been writing about all those years.

In his novel *Fair Land, Fair Land* (1982), Dick Summers discovers, lying on the trail, "the biggest bear he had ever seen." It was barely conscious and bleeding, having lost a foreleg above the second joint from a gunshot wound. Summers gets down on one knee and sighs, "Ephraim, Old Ephraim." Then, "he called to mind old days with the beaver traps, and young men, the traps lifted, sitting around campfires, and they would speak of Old Ephraim, the great white bear, and their tones held respect and awe and a sort of love, as if Ephraim somehow was a part of them, a living marker of the wild life they lived. Old Ephraim."

His companion Higgins objects, "I never heard you take on over a critter, and him nigh onto dead." And in a reply that comes right out of Bud Guthrie's heart, Summers says, "It's not just the one I'm thinkin' on. It's the whole breed, the whole goddamn family. What can you say later on? 'Yep, there was grizzles in those days? There was Ephraim. You should have seen him.'"

Summers gives water to the prostrate bear and leaves him meat, hoping he might somehow be able to survive. Then, back on the trail, they run into the man who had shot the bear and who has been tracking him. Summers asks,

> "So you aim to finish him off?"
> "Course."
> "Why?"
> "So I can say I kilt him, the biggest grizzly any man ever seen."

While Bert Lindler did not write about the conflict between Bud and his son, another staff writer on the *Tribune*, Mike Dennison, did. During the height of the dispute in 1986, the paper published "Two Guthries Disagree Pointedly on Grizzly Management," datelined from Choteau:

> There's no better way to heat up a conversation in this farm and ranch town along the Rocky Mountain Front than to mention a particular local inhabitant: the grizzly bear.
>
> "The ranchers can't see anything but killing the bear. You can't suggest any modification in their view," says an outspoken defender of bears, native son and Pulitzer Prize-winning novelist A. B. "Bud" Guthrie, Jr.
>
> Ironically, one rancher who wants the right to shoot

grizzlies if they threaten his livestock is A. B. "Bert" Guthrie III, the author's son.

"The grizzly bear is depriving me of my livelihood," he says. If you were a store owner, would you allow a shoplifter to come into your shop every day? That's what people are asking the stockmen to put up with."

That one issue can foster harsh disagreement between father and son is indicative of its divisiveness here, pitting neighbor against neighbor.

Looking back on this period, Bert Guthrie has said that on one occasion he lost half his flock of ewes (about one hundred at that time, down from a high of eighteen hundred) to grizzlies, and he got no sympathy from the fish and game people or any from his father. It was frustrating. He would report his losses to animal damage control, and they would tell him that they would try to solve his problem. So they put out some snares, and they snared two of the bears, relocated them over on the North Fork of the Flathead, and three days later they were back. Bert recalled that he "finally realized that the only way that you are going to correct the problem is to be a vigilante." "God, I didn't want to exterminate the species," he said, "but I don't want them down here on private land."

Bud's stepson Bill recalled that Bud and Bert would see each other at least three or four times a year, and "Bert would always be out on the Fourth of July and a few other times he would come out, and they usually got into an argument over something. Bert's politics were one way and Bud's were another, and neither one of them was much inclined to compromise. Neither one of them was inclined to keep quiet about it. So if Bert wasn't baiting Buddy, Buddy was baiting Bert."

Adding to the strain between father and son was Bud's support of the Nature Conservancy, which eventually took over the Gleason's Circle 8 Guest Ranch and to which Bud would give 80 acres of his land. The Conservancy had been buying up property on the Front in order to preserve the land from development and to protect wildlife, including the bears. Bert's view was that such groups, with the backing of government officials, were in effect "raising bears," and had a responsibility to keep them off ranchland. Bert has said, "They are a bunch of freeloaders—501C3 of the IRS code ought to be repealed. It was originally established to protect religious organizations, and now this umbrella is expanded to where you can have an outfit like this Nature Conservancy that's got almost a billion dollar a year budget and is non-profit. And all those yo-yos up there that are working for them—they aren't non-profit, they are getting damn well paid." They may have differed, they may have fought, but that may be because Bert and Helen had a good deal of Bud in them—independent, opinionated, tough, and outspoken.

Bill had a guitar and often sang alone or joined by the family at get-togethers. His had been a beautiful voice, but Bud detected in recent months a raspy quality that must have come from smoking. Bud said, "Boy, it is time for you to quit." And Bill said, "Oh no, I can't do that." Then Bud told him, "Well, if I quit, will you quit?" So they quit together. A friend brought them a big two-pound jar of hard candy, and Bud and Bill sat together on the couch in the Barn and ate candy or chewed gum. Bill recalled the experience: "Just sitting on the couch. I will never forget that. We quit, and he would be on one end of the couch and I would be on the other, and we would be sitting there, twiddling our thumbs usually, chewing our gum and looking at the ceiling. And then about every three minutes either I would look over at Buddy or he would look over at me and say, "How long has it been?" Bert Lindler remembered that he stopped by the Barn because he had been up in the mountains and was told that Bud just stopped smoking. "Immediately I would do a news story about somebody 87 years old stopping smoking. . . . That is pretty remarkable." Commenting on the later consequences, Amy said, "My poor damn brother is in a pact with a dead man. He is totally trapped—he can't smoke again."

Late September the following year Helen was called down from Butte to help take care of Janie who, as it turned out, was on her deathbed. Bud had been alerted, but, as Helen recalled, "He was in deep denial. It was I who said to him that if he intended to see her before she died, he had better get on with it. Quick. I was harsh about it because Janie kept asking me where was Buddy?"

Bud and Carol drove to Missoula, and Peggy, Janie's daughter, let them in. She and Carol sat in the living room while Bud went into the bedroom to talk with his sister. She was bedridden but alert. Peggy recalled, "He came out of the bedroom looking sad and shaken. He wanted to leave quickly and said little—but he knew Mom had little time to live." Helen called him the next day tell him that Janie had died. His little sister. That left only Bud of the three siblings.

Helen volunteered to take the ashes and scatter them around the original Guthrie place in Choteau and along the Teton River. Peggy recalls, "I thought Mom would like the idea . . . so I agreed to the plan and remained in Missoula while Helen drove to Twin Lakes with the box. Later—totally to my surprise and dismay—she said she gave Buddie half the ashes and told him to scatter them. This was hard for Bud, Carol told me later. But he did it and made a kind of ceremony out of scattering them off the Teton Bridge." When she found out about it, Helen was not happy. The ashes, she reflected, would go down the Teton, down the Missouri, and then to the Mississippi, and "now she's floating in the gulf. Not what she had in mind."

A broad view of Bud's environmental writings over the years came in 1988 with the publication of *Big Sky, Fair Land: The Environmental Essays of A. B. Guthrie, Jr.* Bud and Carol helped David Peterson, who interviewed them and edited the volume. The essays ran from the early "A Death of an Eagle" (1939), written while Bud was still in Kentucky, to "The Rocky Mountain Front," which appeared in *Montana Magazine* in 1987. Then going back in time, the collection ended with the meditative "An April in Montana," the last chapter in *The Blue Hen's Chick* (1965), Bud's autobiography.

In his introduction to one of Bud's essays, "Here and Hereafter" (1983), Peterson noted that it was originally delivered as a speech in Bozeman as the capstone in a lecture series. He describes the occasion: "Guthrie had undergone surgery for a skin cancer, leaving one arm temporarily in a sling. In spite of his 82 years, the physical drain of recent surgery and 17 days of hospitalization, plus the discomfort and inconvenience of the sling, Guthrie stood for 40 minutes to deliver this talk—which he and Carol Guthrie promptly dubbed his "'one-armed speech.'" He had been in the hospital, released, and then the stitches came out, and so he had to go back. During the whole ordeal the thing that bothered him the most, he told his agent, was that he couldn't type.

A few months later, he was having trouble working. He just didn't seem to have the energy, and as he got older and weaker he worried more and more about whether there would be enough money for Carol to carry on at the Barn. Carol finally got him to go to the doctor, who examined him and told him that he had such a decreased ability to breathe that it was if he were living at 16,000 feet. The doctor put him on oxygen, and he began to haul a little tank around behind him with tubing attached to his nose.

Ever since his discussions with Jim Welch about the Marias Massacre and his using the massacre to end *Fair Land, Fair Land*, Bud had wanted to visit the site. The photographer Marc Gaede, who was a frequent visitor to the Barn, had discovered the location from Jim (who had lost several relatives in the massacre), and he offered to take Bud and Carol there. They met with Gaede outside Choteau, and he drove them in his new four-wheel-drive Ford pickup, carrying an extra bottle of oxygen for Bud and a bottle of champagne to toast Meriwether Lewis and Heavy Runner on the banks of the Marias River.

They stopped in Shelby for lunch and afterward drove several miles east and then south on an infrequently used road. They passed several Minuteman missile silos and at last turned on to a nearly obscured dirt road that went around fields and over ridges, until they reached the edge of a steep canyon. Below was the Marias River. The road down was only a track with a number of washouts and dirt slides. As they slip-slid and thumped over rocks down the steep canyon wall, there were times when Gaede worried that the wheels on the cliff-side might slide over the edge.

All the way down, Bud hung on for dear life and Carol kept saying, "Marc, I don't think . . ." But at the bottom, on the flat, they all breathed a sigh of relief, although the brush was so high they couldn't see much beyond the hood of the truck. Gradually, as they pressed forward the brush became lower, visibility good, and from his research, Bud was able to point out the location of the camp and the strategy of the attack. They went forward again toward the river and had to stop at the delta of a creek that separated them from the gravel of the river's edge. Marc wanted Bud to be able to step out and stand by the river and told them that with his four-wheel-drive he could make it across the mud flat.

Stepping up to the window, Carol said, "Marc, I don't know. Montana mud is different from what you are used to." But Marc replied, "Carol, I grew up in four-wheel-drives. Leave it to me." Determined and convinced he could make it, he floored the gas, trusting in the 351-horsepower engine and radical cross-country tires. In his words, "We hit the delta at least thirty miles an hour backed by four thousand pounds of kinetic energy—and immediately sink to the frame in the bottomless Montana mud."

After trying the usual remedies—rocking the truck back and forth, jacking up the rear, putting a small fallen tree under the drive wheel—all came to naught. The only thing that could save them was a tow truck. Cursing the mud and cursing himself for taking such a chance, Marc told the Guthries to stay put while he went for help. An ex-Marine and frequent hiker in the backcountry, Marc was in good shape and trotted to the top of the canyon and on across a field, trying to get to a paved road. His worry increased as it began to get late and as he thought about the drain on Bud's second oxygen bottle.

All of a sudden, out in the middle of a field, he ran into a missile site, where there was an Air Force unit running a mock antinuclear demonstration exercise. With all of his bad luck, this was incredible good luck. Over a barbed-wire fence he explained his situation to the officer in charge, who tried to connect by radio to someone who could get a tow truck, but the transmission was directed through Malmstrom Air Force Base at Great Falls, and after an hour the officer had no luck. Now it was really getting late, and as the troops began to load up to depart, Marc began to panic.

He ran up to the lieutenant, who was in his jeep, and told him, "I have an eighty-six-year-old man stuck in that river bottom. It is getting dark and cold and he is on oxygen that must be running out by now. I need help and I need it now!" The lieutenant said, "Why didn't you say so? Let's go get him." They learned when they got down in the canyon that Carol has been rationing the oxygen by turning it off and on every fifteen minutes, and needless to say, Bud and Carol were overjoyed at the jeep's appearance. Reflecting on the incident, Marc has said, "One minute we are cursing the U.S. military for the Piegan massacre; the next we are enthusiastically embracing them for saving us."

The officer took Bud and Carol back to Choteau, while Marc arranged for a tow truck, the only one in northern Montana that could get his Ford out of its mess. When the tow truck operator saw the slope, he yelled at Marc, "Good God, look at this road. . . . What in the hell prompted you to come down here?" Later, Marc apologized to Bud for what he got them into, but Bud wrote back,

Dear Marc—

What goes with you, boy? Are you letting the memory of the Marias fester you? For shame. With me it was settled into my bank of pleasant memories. Indeed, I never did think our adventure as terrible as you seemed to. . . .

Bud

Bud had never been particularly handsome, but as he got older many thought that he had become distinguished looking. Now, at eighty-eight, he was frail and shrunken, but his spirit still came out at you through his glasses in a direct and unflinching gaze. He continued to write. He had vague plans of trying to do one more historical novel in his series, but settled once again on a mystery. *Murder in the Cotswolds* was published in 1990, and that same year a mysterious pain in his legs was diagnosed as the beginnings of prostate cancer. He wrote to David Peterson, who had edited the collection of his environmental essays, "The experts weren't much worried about the cancer, saying I was so old something else would kill me before it ever could."

In the fall of 1990 he was occupied with writing his last book, *A Field Guide to Writing Fiction*. It was a project that he had had in mind for many years, but at that late date, Carol recalled, the process was very difficult for him: "I think it was awfully hard on Bud, getting old. He wouldn't give up, and he had more alarms and excursion and more surgeries. And in the hospital, every time he would say, 'You don't think this is it, do you, honey?' He was hanging around for me. Finally, I said to him that things are getting pretty bad—he was getting awfully weak, and I said, Buddy, you have hung on for me for so long and I don't . . . when you are ready to go, you go."

Fishing the Pishkun

That fall he was finishing *A Field Guide to Writing Fiction* and going over the galleys, and for first time in his life he had decided not to look forward to starting another big project. This decision plus the letdown of finishing his book and the approach of winter put him into a depression, very unusual for him. He went for a doctor's appointment in Great Falls, and when the doctor asked him what was wrong, he told him, "Well, I don't know—I'm feeling kind of punk," and the doctor gave him Prozac. He took one of the pills, and the next morning he didn't want to get out of bed. Carol reported to her daughter that he was almost suicidal. The doctor came all the way over from Great Falls to the Barn. Carol asked him, "What did Bud say to you? Why did you give him that medicine?" The doctor said, "He told me he was depressed." Bud interrupted from his bed, "I have never been depressed in my life! I just told you I was blue."

He continued to be very lethargic, almost catatonic at times, in a trance. Amy and her husband, Erik, flew out from North Dakota to help take care of him, along with their stepson, Bill, and his wife, Kay. One day Amy took her baby, Emily, and put her into a springboard baby watcher beside him; all of a sudden, according to Amy, "he starts being alert and paying attention to her, and you know, trying to play patty cake with her, a three month old." Later, Bud wrote a letter to a friend telling him that he had been brought back from the jaws of death by a baby.

A couple of weeks later, there was a writers' conference at the Pine Butte Guest Ranch, which had been organized as a tribute to Bud. Richard Ford came, Mary Clearman Blew, Bill Kittredge and Annick Smith, Jim and Lois Welch, and Ripley Hugo. In addition, there were many locals, including Alice Gleason, Mary Sexton, and several young people who were would-be writers. Ripley read from her poetry and from Dick's poetry, and some of the participants did readings in Choteau for the schoolchildren. Kay Luthin, Bill's wife, and Erik Sakarassin, Amy's husband, both writers, took over Bud's classroom appearances.

In an essay, Bill Kittredge recalled the occasion at the conservancy:

> The first snow of winter had come sweeping over the Rockies Front a night or so before. The great white mountains were vividly distinct against the gray sky. Bud was articulate, his eyes bright with good humor and a no-doubt abiding sense that these were last times.
>
> Bud was dying; he knew it. But he was carrying on right out to the edge, telling us, by the sound of his old ruined voice and the direct way he was staring down the devil, things he always told us: Love what you love, fiercely as you can, and never lose heart. Play your cards.

Jim Welch recalled his impressions of him at such get-togethers: "He liked to be taken care of. He loved women. Kissed Lois's hand all the time and called her honey. He just always paid a lot of attention to women. Here is this frail little man who still had a bit of the rake in him." Lois Welch added her picture of Bud, very frail, hauling his oxygen tank behind him and accompanied always by Carol: "He would shuffle up there when he wanted, but they would work it out, proceed slowly, the two of them." Others recalled him shuffling across the floor, with tank behind and Carol alongside, and as usual carrying a glass of wine filled to the brim and, of course, not spilling a drop.

As winter approached, the Guthries decided to leave the Barn and join Carol's daughter Amy in Bismarck, North Dakota. A winter out in the country, considering Bud's continuing weakness, would be too much for them, and Carol needed to go to a hospital for an operation. There, Bud took up again with his grandchildren, little Emily and five-year-old Alexander. Bud wanted bring Alex up on his lap and tell him stories, but Alex always insisted on finishing Bud's stories for him. "Now, whose story is this, anyway?" Bud would grumble. As Alex remembered, Bud always wore red suspenders, and he had given him a pet nickname: Sandy Scoop Zaperson, Cub Reporter.

In his rented house in Bismarck, Bud had a television for the first time and watched the first Gulf War with fascination. Amy recalled, he "watched them bomb the hell out of everything, and when they said it was over, he said, 'Oh, don't you believe it.'" Amy and Bud talked quite a bit during this period, and on one occasion he told her that there was one thing that he would have done differently: "He would have encouraged Mom to make more friends of her own." Most of their friends had been his friends, and almost all of them were gone.

During his stay in Bismarck he gave his last interview, and the last photograph was taken of him. The photographer told Bud that he had been looking around outside (it was 25 below zero) for a place to photograph him and that he saw an old pump handle out in the backyard. "Would you go out there, Mr. Guthrie," the man asked him, "and I could take your picture there?" Bud looked at him steadily and then said, "No." And then he proceeded to tell the fellow in no uncertain terms that far better and more noted photographers than he had been unable to get him to pose in stupid positions.

In the spring of the following year, in April of 1991, Bud and Carol drove all the way back from Bismarck to the Barn. Shortly after arriving, Bud collapsed. In the hospital Bud sensed what was coming and asked to be taken back to the Barn. Only a few days later, Alfred Bertram Guthrie Jr. was dead at the age of ninety. His body was simply worn out. He was cremated and a service was held in the Choteau cemetery, a park that his father had been responsible for creating and, during its early years, maintaining. He had planted cottonwood trees to shade the graves of his six children who had died in infancy or childhood. In his own childhood, Bud had the chore during the summers to carry pails around and water the trees.

Carol's son Bill wrote a tribute to Bud that he read at the service; the eulogy was delivered by Rick Graetz, of *Montana Magazine*; Mike Malone, who was an eminent historian and the president of Montana State University; and Jim Welch. It had been very fair and sunny when several hundred arrived for the service, but a half hour later it turned cold and started to rain, hard. Jim recalled, "We all thought that was pretty significant." George Schemm, a neighbor and close friend, took Carol and her son Bill up in his plane so they could fly over Ear Mountain and spread Bud's ashes.

Bud Guthrie was one of the few major artists of our time able to bring his beliefs into the totality of his art. He believed that if we had to have progress, it should be a progress in quality rather than quantity—not more people, but more informed and responsible people; not more development and increasing use of resources, but wiser use of resources, taking the long view. In a speech to the League of Women Voters, he said, "The brute fact is that there are too many people on earth and still more on the way to being. . . . Only by recognizing that our planet has limited resources and can support only so many people do we get to the root of the problem."

In another speech he reviewed the history of the West by saying, "We mined the land, felled the timber and dug the metals, all with extravagance, knowing that over the next hills were virgin acres, stands of timber and likely strikes. And so it was that we pillaged a continent and thrived in the process, forgetting that earth is exhaustible."

And in his League of Women Voters speech he outlined his own history when he said,

> Years ago, long before the energy crises, I heard an aged and retired university president worrying about how long the world's oil would last. Later, in a conversation with others, I laughed and asked why, at his age, he should worry. He wouldn't last as long as the oil.
>
> I blush when I think about me in those days. A slob, a dumb kid smarting off. What did I care then, why should anyone care about events after death?
>
> Now I care. I care immensely. That's why I'm here. I think of posterity. I want a decent world left behind me. Thomas Jefferson once swore enmity against any tyranny

over the mind of man. I have sworn opposition to abusers of the land.

It was a statement that might well have served as his epitaph.

One morning before the Guthries left for North Dakota, Bud, Bill, and Erik (Amy's husband) were sitting around the Barn when Bud got the idea that they should go fishing and they should go to Pishkun Reservoir (southwest of Choteau, near the Front). So they got into the car, drove to Choteau to get their fishing licenses and buy bait, and then drove toward the reservoir. Or so they thought. They drove on and on, first one way and then another, but couldn't find it. Bud was sure he knew the way. But Erik finally asked him, "When was the last time you were there?" "Oh," Bud answered, "Chickie and I went fishing there just a few years ago." Erik and Bill groaned. Chick had been dead for a decade, and Bud was probably thinking of a time when he and his brother were young, a half century or more earlier.

After many wrong turns and dead-end roads, they finally found the reservoir. It was windy and cold, and they sat on the treeless bank of the reservoir casting out into the gray water. They were thinking of packing it in when Erik got a strike and pulled in a big pike, which, as he lifted it out of the water, flopped and danced at the end of his line, a wowser. That spurred them on, and they ate their sandwiches and went on fishing, which they did until it started to get dark. Feeling a little pressed by time, Bud suggested they take a shortcut he knew that went back along the Front. Whatever he remembered was no longer there. So their return was even more frustrating in the darkness than their search for the reservoir in the first place. They would turn down a road, go several miles, get to a ranch house with lights on, and the road would end.

In the meantime, Carol, Amy, and Kay were worried—Carol, in fact, was becoming frantic. Bud was on oxygen and his tank would be close to running out. She called the sheriff, and he went out on a search. All the deputies were alerted. Late in the evening, the fishing party did at last get home, hangdog and with apologies. Bud turned to Carol, sighed, and said, "Well, anyway, baby, I fished the Pishkun."

Still no limit, Bud. No limit that counts.

NOTES AND DOCUMENTATION

On the following pages, sources and notes for each chapter are listed under the following categories (when applicable): (1) Interviews, (2) Published Material by A. B. Guthrie Jr., (3) Unpublished Material by A. B. Guthrie Jr., (4) Published Material and Unpublished Material about A. B. Guthrie Jr. and Related Topics, (5) Notes and Sources for Quotations. Items in sections (2), (3), and (4) are listed in order of their appearance in the text of the chapter. No notes are provided for the quoted letters; instead, the source for letters and the recipient are indicated in the text, and the date of the letter is given in parentheses at the end of the quotation. The dates for the letters are given to provide a further guide to the chronology of the life.

1. "By George, I'm Free!"

1. *Interviews.* My thanks to:
Alfred Bertram "Bert" Guthrie III

2. *Published Material by A. B. Guthrie Jr.*
The Blue Hen's Chick: A Life in Context (New York: McGraw-Hill, 1965). Hereafter referred to as *BHC*.

4. *Published and Unpublished Material about A. B. Guthrie Jr. and Related Topics*
Joseph Kinsey Howard, *Montana: High, Wide, and Handsome* (New Haven CT: Yale University Press, 1959).
Montana! A Photographic Celebration, vol. 2, with text by A. B. Guthrie Jr., ed. Rick Graetz (Helena MT: *Montana Magazine*, 1989).
A. C. Spectorsky, "In New York," *Chicago Sun Book Week*, April ? 1947, clipping, n.p.

Charles E. Hood, "Hard Work and Tough Dreaming: A Biography of
A. B. Guthrie, Jr." Master's thesis, University of Montana, 1969.
Charles "Chick" Guthrie, "Mom, the Boys and the Great Majestic," un-
published manuscript.
Charles "Chick" Guthrie, untitled manuscript, outline for a memoir.

5. *Notes and Sources for Quotations*

3	*"a flat gray-blue,"*	Howard, 287.
3	*"the nation got,"*	*Montana!*, 15
4	*"They had never,"*	BHC, 2.
4	*"Overhead,"*	BHC, 2.
5	*"It is a feeling,"*	Spectorsky.
5	*he was challenged,*	Hood, 5.
5	*pointing a pistol,*	BHC, 6.
5	*"Latin, English,"*	Hood, 4.
6	*"he was a very fine,"*	Hood, 4.
6	*"Outside the local,"*	BHC, 35.
6	*"Bud always was,"*	Hood, 3
7	*"the stimulus,"*	BHC, 35.
7	*His father's tales,*	Hood, 7.
7	*"They would gather,"*	BHC, 5
7	*"When he spoke,"*	BHC, 6.
8	*"He loved us,"*	BHC, 36
8	*"a different kind,"*	Hood, 9.
9	*"in his mind,"*	BHC, 36.
9	*"Buddy was quite,"*	Hood, 168.
9	*"quick to mend,"*	Hood, 8.
9	*"Whatever hate,"*	BHC, 38–39.
10	*"Curtis Mack,"*	Hood, 72.
10	*"I was reading,"*	Hood, 9.
11	*"She might have,"*	Chick, 2
11	*"You boys had fun,"*	Chick, 3.
11	*"She made the house,"*	Chick, 3.
12	*"On the day of rest,"*	Chick, 4–5.
13	*Bud has said,*	BHC, 7.
13	*"Washing, Ironing,"*	BHC, 7.
14	*"Twenty years and more,"*	BHC, 7–8.
14	*"Too many deaths,"*	Chick, memoir.

14   *"My memory,"* *BHC,* 14.

14   *"Sometimes I wonder,"* *BHC,* 11.

15   *"I'm glad I grew,"* *Montana!,* 2, 18.

15   *"instead of being green,"* *BHC,* 5.

16   *"I would save,"* *Montana!,* 2, 18.

2. A Smart Aleck and a Wise Guy

2. *Published Material by A. B. Guthrie Jr.*
The Blue Hen's Chick: A Life in Context (New York: McGraw-Hill, 1965). Hereafter referred to as *BHC.*

4. *Published Material and Unpublished Material about A. B. Guthrie Jr. and Related Topics*
Charles "Chick" Guthrie, untitled manuscript, outline for a memoir.
Charles E. Hood, "Hard Work and Tough Dreaming: A Biography of A. B. Guthrie, Jr." Master's thesis, University of Montana, 1969.

5. *Notes and Sources for Quotations*
18   *"joy of hunting,"* *BHC,* 15.

18   *"No longer,"* *BHC,* 17.

18   *"Give 'em hell!"* Chick, memoir.

18   *"The Hound,"* Chick, memoir.

19   *"far greater hell,"* Chick, memoir.

19   *piano lessons,* Chick, memoir.

20   *"I built,"* *BHC,* 21–22.

21   *"Well, in later years,"* *BHC,* 23.

21   *son's resentment,* *BHC,* 47–48.

21   *"the city was too big,"* *BHC,* 49.

22   *Arthur L. Stone,* *BHC,* 49.

23   *"I had been a believer,"* *BHC,* 52–53.

24   *"I had asked,"* Hood, 13.

25   *"in class,"* Hood, 15.

25   *"Bud was the sort,"* Hood, 15–16.

25   *"It wasn't a stuttering,"* Hood, 17.

25   *"Called on to read,"* *BHC,* 54–55.

26   *Model T Ford,* *BHC,* 57–59.

27   *Cajeme, Sonora,* *BHC,* 61–62.

28   *The job was only temporary,* *BHC,* 65.

28   *The ranchers,* BHC, 65.

28   *"Hard times in Montana,"* BHC, 66.

29   *"My position,"* BHC, 68.

3. Alone in a Small and Self-Contained City

2. *Published Material by A. B. Guthrie Jr.*
The Blue Hen's Chick: A Life in Context (New York: McGraw-Hill, 1965). Hereafter referred to as *BHC.*

3. *Unpublished Material by A. B. Guthrie Jr.*
Interview by William Cooper, Kentucky History Oral History Project, June 16, 1979. Referred to hereafter as *KY.*

4. *Published Material and Unpublished Material about A. B. Guthrie Jr. and Related Topics*
Charles E. Hood, "Hard Work and Tough Dreaming: A Biography of A. B. Guthrie, Jr." Master's thesis, University of Montana, 1969.

5. *Notes and Sources for Quotations*

33   *"She was a lady,"* BHC, 95.

34   *"looked impossibly,"* BHC, 77.

35   *"the girl I had wanted,"* BHC, 83.

36   *"Buddy, Oh, Buddy,"* BHC, 83.

37   *aware of a dichotomy,* KY, 2.

38   *"But for Mary Lizzie,"* BHC, 97.

40   *attracted to snakes,* KY, 37.

41   *"We used to bait Dud,"* BHC, 79.

41   *"on the detective force,"* KY, 35.

41   *"the heydays,"* BHC, 94.

42   *"Dan, here's some,"* BHC, 78.

42   *"By 1927 I was,"* BHC, 91–92.

43   *"people have the habit,"* KY, 33.

43   *"strange assemblege,"* KY, 5.

43   *"All right, come on,"* KY, 11.

43   *"Everyone was hiding,"* KY, 11.

43   *"Ladies and Gentlemen,"* KY, 14.

44   *"last night I drank,"* KY, 15.

44   *"It was strictly,"* KY, 4.

44   *"He was nothing,"* KY, 5.

45 *"deep fried cornball,"* KY, 16.
45 *"a new governor today,"* Hood, 201–2.
47 *The President,* KY, 21.
47 *"the swimming pool,"* KY, 23.
47 *"He never said a word,"* KY, 23.
48 *"strange assemblage,"* KY, 5.

4. Marriage, Family, and Separation

1. *Interviews.* My thanks to:
   Thomas D. Clark, Alfred Bertram "Bert" Guthrie, Helen Guthrie Miller

2. *Published Material by A. B. Guthrie Jr.*
   The Blue Hen's Chick: A Life in Context (New York: McGraw-Hill,
   1965). Hereafter referred to as *BHC.*

4. *Published Material and Unpublished Material about A. B. Guthrie Jr.*
   and Related Topics
   Charles E. Hood, "Hard Work and Tough Dreaming: A Biography of
   A. B. Guthrie, Jr." Master's thesis, University of Montana, 1969.

5. *Notes and Sources for Quotations*
   51   *"Incessantly over,"* BHC, 115.
   53   *"rich evenings,"* BHC, 75.
   53   *"I lived a neighbor,"* Hood, 20.
   55   *"The hours,"* BHC, 129.
   55   *"In that time of waiting,"* BHC, 130.
   55   *"Within a month,"* BHC, 131.
   57   *"The mere request,"* BHC, 121.
   58   *"The boys were mannerly,"* BHC, 127.
   59   *The result of the article,* BHC, 126.
   61   *"No one who has not,"* BHC, 139.
   62   *"Once you can bring,"* BHC, 140.
   62   *"My newspaper stories,"* Hood, 205.
   63   *"I felt the need of exposure,"* BHC, 145.

5. The First Novel and Plans for the Big One

1. *Interviews.* My thanks to:
   Helen Guthrie Miller, Thomas D. Clark, William Kittredge, Alfred
   Bertram "Bert" Guthrie

2. *Published Material by A. B. Guthrie Jr.*
Big Sky, Fair Land: The Environmental Essays of A. B. Guthrie, Jr. ed.
David Peterson (Flagstaff AZ: Northland Press, 1988).
The Blue Hen's Chick (New York: McGraw-Hill, 1965). Hereafter
referred to as *BHC*.

4. *Published Material and Unpublished Material about A. B. Guthrie Jr.*
and Related Topics
Bert Lindler, "Guthrie's Thoughts on the West as Clear as His View of
the Front," *Great Falls Tribune*, July 3, 1988: 1E, 3E.
William Kittredge, introduction to reissue of A. B. Guthrie Jr., *Murders
at Moon Dance* (Lincoln: University of Nebraska Press, 1993).
Charles E. Hood, "Hard Work and Tough Dreaming: A Biography of
A. B. Guthrie, Jr." Master's thesis, University of Montana, 1969.

5. *Notes and Sources for Quotations*
    66   *"The idea occurred,"* Hood, 33.
    66   *"All night the great bird,"* Peterson, 71.
    67   *"They both got,"* Lindler, 1E.
    73   *"Though this book,"* Hood, 23.
    73   *"My first book,"* *BHC*, 128.
    74   *"a combination,"* Hood 24.
    74   *"if it had been written,"* Kittredge, xi, xiii, xiv.
    75   *"is an unhappy combination,"* Hood, 25.
    75   *"they are being provided,"* Hood, 29.
    75   *Its inhabitants,* Hood, 30.
    78   *"to assignments,"* *BHC*, 148.
    78   *"about the mountain man,"* *BHC*, 148.
    80   *"After writing three,"* *BHC*, 150.
    80   *"opportunity for a man,"* *BHC*, 151.
    81   *"It was the big break,"* Hood, 38.
    81   *"I remember so well,"* Hood, 38.

6. The Big Break—the Nieman Fellowship

2. *Published Material by A. B. Guthrie Jr.*
The Big Sky (New York: William Sloane Associates, 1947).
The Blue Hen's Chick (New York: McGraw-Hill, 1965). Hereafter
referred to as *BHC*.

4. *Published Material and Unpublished Material about A. B. Guthrie Jr.*
   and Related Topics

"A Reader Unburdens and Comes Up with Some Sound Criticism,"
Nieman Reports, April 1950, 3, as quoted in Thomas W. Ford, *A. B.
Guthrie, Jr.* (Boston: Twayne Publishers, 1981).

Theodore Morrison, *Bread Loaf Writers' Conference: The First Thirty
Years* (Middlebury VT: Middlebury College Press, 1976).

A. C. Spectorsky, "In New York," *Chicago Sun Book Week*, April 1947,
clipping, n.p.

Charles E. Hood, "Hard Work and Tough Dreaming: A Biography
of A. B. Guthrie, Jr." Master's thesis, University of Montana,
1969.

5. *Notes and Sources for Quotations*

83	*"so far to the left,"*	BHC, 161.
84	*"unlike some,"*	BHC, 162.
84	*"Then 43,"*	Hood, 39.
85	*"The best part,"*	BHC, 169–70.
86	*"I would go home,"*	BHC, 170.
86	*"a difficult achievement,"*	BHC, 171.
86	*"As has happened,"*	Hood, 42.
87	*"When I re-wrote,"*	Hood, 44.
87	*"Morrison would,"*	BHC, 173.
88	*"Undeniably the lucky,"*	Ford, 40.
88	*"I work painfully,"*	Ford, 40.
88	*"Word by word,"*	BHC, 185–86.
88	*"in my first chapter,"*	Hood, 44.
89	*"The two months,"*	BHC, 185.
89	*"his contribution,"*	Morrison, 57.
91	*"Except for a couple,"*	BHC, 189–90.
91	*"could be and often was,"*	BHC, 191.
92	*"about and was wont,"*	BHC, 193.
92	*"Swinging on a star,"*	BHC, 194.
94	*"When he came home,"*	Hood, 49.
95	*"Hours and weeks,"*	BHC, 199–200.
98	*"I was in the hospital,"*	Hood, 52.
99	*"The West has always,"*	Spectorsky, n.p.

7. *The Big Sky* Triumph and Tracking *The Way West*

1. *Interviews.* My thanks to:
Thomas D. Clark, Helen Guthrie Miller, Peggy Bloom

2. *Published Material by A. B. Guthrie Jr.*
The Big Sky (New York: William Sloane Associates, 1947).
The Blue Hen's Chick (New York: McGraw-Hill, 1965). Hereafter referred to as *BHC*.

4. *Published Material and Unpublished Material About A. B. Guthrie Jr. and Related Topics*
Charles E. Hood, "Hard Work and Tough Dreaming: A Biography of A. B. Guthrie, Jr." Master's thesis, University of Montana, 1969.
Joseph Kinsey Howard, "A Fine Novel of the Mountain Men," *New York Times Book Review*, May 4, 1947: 1.
Dorothy Canfield Fisher, "Monumental Novel of a 'Mountain Man,'" *New York Herald Tribune Book Review*, May 4, 1947: 1.
"The Big Sky," *The Atlantic*, June 1947: 131.
"Mountain Men," *Time*, May 12, 1947: 108.
Margaret Marshall, "The Big Sky," *The Nation*, May 24, 1947: 362.
J. M. Lalley, "Young Man of the Mountains," *The New Yorker*, May 3, 1947: 98.
"The Big Sky," *Booklist*, June 15, 1947: 330.
"The Big Sky," *Library Journal*, April 15, 1947: 638.
"The Big Sky," *Lexington Herald-Leader*, clipping, n.d.: n.p.
Ed Edstrom, interview of A. B. Guthrie Jr., no title, *The Courier Journal Magazine*, April 27, 1947: clipping n.p.
Joe Jordon, "Publishers Release Guthrie's Historical Novel, 'The Big Sky,'" *Sunday Lexington Herald-Leader*, April 27, 1947: 39. Wayne Chatterton, "A. B. Guthrie, Jr.," *A Literary History of the American West* (Fort Worth: Texas Christian University Press, 1987).
Edward Weeks, "Yonder Was Home," *The Atlantic*, December 1949: 88.
Walter Van Tilburg Clark, "Emigrants on the Oregon Trail," *Saturday Review of Literature*, October 8, 1949: 21.
Robert Gorham Davis, "In the Western Mountain Country," *New York Times Book Review*, October 9, 1949: 5.
"The Way West," *Catholic World*, December 1949: 234.

Brendan Gill, "The Way West," *The New Yorker*, October 15, 1949: 128–29.

George Miles, "The Way West," *Commonweal*, December 16, 1949: 300.

Elrick B. Davis, "Off to Oregon in a Fine New Novel," *New York Herald Tribune Book Review*, October 9, 1949: 3.

5. *Notes and Sources for Quotations*

100	*"I wasn't prepared,"* BHC, 200.
101	*"Until and unless,"* Howard, *Times*, 1.
101	*"A monument of a book!"* Fisher, *Herald*, 1.
101	*"There are passages,"* *Atlantic*, 131–32.
101	*"Author Guthrie's,"* *Time*, 108.
101	*"mountain men,"* Marshall, *Nation*, May 24, 1947, 362.
102	*"His purpose is,"* Lalley, *New Yorker*, May 3, 1947, 98.
102	*"We were so proud,"* Hood, 53.
102	*"It will be hard,"* Hood, 63.
102	*"The best compliment,"* Hood, 74.
102	*"Bud's good Indiana,"* Hood, 53.
103	*"It is a lusty,"* *Booklist*, 330.
103	*"A story rough,"* *Library*, 638.
103	*"There is much drama,"* *Lexington*, clipping, n.p.
103	*"Guthrie is of average,"* *Courier*, clipping, n.p.
104	*"Today it is a worn thing,"* Chatterton, 921.
104	*"More than any other,"* Chatterton, 928–29.
106	*"One hot day,"* Jordon, *Lexington*, 39.
107	*"While I prospered,"* BHC, 201.
108	*"He must know,"* Hood, 79–80.
108	*"The day by day,"* Hood, 80.
109	*"Rained today,"* Hood, 81.
109	*"deliberately made,"* Hood, 81.
109	*"I would call,"* Hood, 85.
111	*"if Bud writes,"* Hood, 86.
111	*"It is in my notes,"* 86.
112	*In an interview,* Hood, 86.
112	*"We watched Bud,"* Hood, 90.
112	*"the buds of the opposite sex,"* Hood, 89; BHC, 202.
113	*"Here he was,"* BHC, 203.

113   *"Penniless,"* BHC, 202.

113   *"Thursday, we traveled,"* Hood, 83–84.

114   *Several of the items,* Hood 84.

115   *where a telegram,* BHC, 203–4.

115   *"The second novel,"* Weeks, 88.

115   *"We say not only,"* Clark, 21.

115   *"Even more successfully,"* Davis, 5.

116   *"If there had never,"* Catholic, 234.

116   *"Lije is Henry Fonda,"* Gill, 128–29.

116   *"all the elements,"* Miles, 300.

116   *"In all the body-torturing,"* Time, n.p.

116   *"The On-to-Oregon company,"* Davis, 3.

117   *"My degree,"* BHC, 201.

117   *"Congratulation, Bud,"* BHC, 204.

117   *"How elated,"* Hood, 103.

118   *"The two novels,"* Hood, 105–6.

118   "The Big Sky *was properly,"* Hood, 111.

118   *"As purely a personal,"* Hood, 103.

8. To Hollywood and *Shane* and the Move to Montana

1. *Interviews.* My thanks to:
Ripley Hugo, Peggy Bloom, Helen Guthrie Miller

2. *Published Material by A. B. Guthrie Jr.*
The Big Sky (New York: William Sloane Associates, 1947).
The Way West (New York: William Sloane Associates, 1949).
The Blue Hen's Chick (New York: McGraw-Hill, 1965). Hereafter
referred to as *BHC*.

4. *Published Material and Unpublished Material about A. B. Guthrie Jr.*
and Related Topics
Thomas W. Ford, *A. B. Guthrie, Jr.* (Boston: Twayne Publishers, 1981).
Charles E. Hood, "Hard Work and Tough Dreaming: A Biography of
A. B. Guthrie, Jr." Master's thesis, University of Montana, 1969.
Jack Schaefer, *Shane* (Critical Edition), ed. James C. Work (Lincoln:
University of Nebraska Press, 1984).
Ann Ronald, *Reader of the Purple Sage: Essays on Western Writers*

and *Environmental Literature* (Reno: University of Nevada Press, 2003).

Matthew J. Costello, "I Didn't Expect to Find Any Fences Around Here," *Journal of American Culture*, September 2004:261–70.

Mary Clearman Blew, "Shane Rides into the Millennium," in *Fifty Years after* The Big Sky, ed. William E. Farr and William W. Bevis (Helena: Montana Historical Society Press, 2001).

Ripley Hugo, *Writing for Her Life: The Novelist Mildred Walker* (Lincoln: University of Nebraska Press, 2003).

5. *Notes and Sources for Quotations*

121	*"I want to write,"*	Hood, 113.
121	*"an outing with us,"*	BHC, 205.
121	*the three writers would travel,*	Ford Chronology.
122	*"looking down,"*	BHC, 207.
122	*"known places again,"*	BHC, 209, 213.
122	*"Like proof of our antiquity,"*	BHC, 212.
123	*"By plane and flatboat,"*	BHC, 215.
123	*"The studio and the director,"*	Hood, 268.
124	*"there was no complete,"*	BHC, 217.
124	*"you would hardly,"*	BHC, 217.
125	*"I taught nights,"*	Schafer, 278–79.
126	*"From its inception,"*	Ronald, 122.
126	*"George Stevens saw."*	Costello, 262.
126	*"One of Schaefer's most,"*	Schaefer, 29.
126	*"The environment itself,"*	Schaefer, 29.
127	*"Not for more than a year,"*	BHC, 216–19.
128	*"its glorious Wyoming,"*	Blew, 205.
131	*"We didn't get together,"*	Hugo, 180.
131	*"In* If a Lion Could Talk,"	Hugo, 210.
131	*"DAMNING,"*	Hugo, 252.
132	*"looked to the cow counties,"*	BHC, 225.
133	*"In those early years,"*	BHC, 234–35.
134	*"a poor politician,"*	BHC, 235.
134	*"Some quality,"*	BHC, 236.
134	*"In his spur-of-the-moment,"*	BHC, 237.
134	*"Pretty rugged,"*	BHC, 237.
135	*"Often as I like,"*	BHC, 236–37.

9. Bucking the Myth

1. *Interviews.* My thanks to:
   Helen Guthrie Miller, Amy Sakariassen, Mary Sexton

2. *Published Material by A. B. Guthrie Jr.*
   The Blue Hen's Chick (New York: McGraw-Hill, 1965). Hereafter
   referred to as *BHC.*
   These Thousand Hills (Boston: Houghton Mifflin, 1956).
   "Dear Joe," *Big Sky, Fair Land,* ed. David Peterson (Flagstaff AZ:
   Northland Press, 1988), 97–101.
   "DeVoto—A Memoir," *Neiman Reports,* January 1956: 3–6.

4. *Published Material and Unpublished Material about A. B. Guthrie Jr.
   and Related Topics*
   "Interview: A. B. Guthrie, Jr.," *The Writer's Mind: Interviews with
   American Authors* Vol. 1, ed. Irv Broughton (Fayetteville: University
   of Arkansas Press, 1989).
   Charles E. Hood, "Hard Work and Tough Dreaming: A Biography of
   A. B. Guthrie, Jr." Master's thesis, University of Montana, 1969.
   "Pioneer of Teton County Free High School," (obituary of Guthrie Sr.)
   Choteau Acantha, September 2, 1954: clipping, n.p.
   Sue Hart, "Some Recollections of and Reflections on A. B. Guthrie, Jr.,
   and His Work," in *Fifty Years after "The Big Sky",* ed. William E. Farr
   and William W. Bevis (Helena: Montana Historical Society Press,
   2001), 157–73.
   Thomas W. Ford, *A. B. Guthrie, Jr.* (Boston: Twayne Publishers, 1981).
   Walter Van Tilburg Clark, "When Settlers Began to Take Over," *New
   York Times Book Review,* November 18, 1956: 1, 54.
   James V. D'Arc, "A. B. Guthrie, Jr., in Hollywood: Variations on the
   Writing Experience," in *Fifty Years after "The Big Sky",* ed. William
   E. Farr and William W. Bevis (Helena: Montana Historical Society
   Press, 2001), 73–105.

5. *Notes and Sources for Quotations*
   138   "I may rewrite,"   Broughton, 100.
   138   "I'll never be prolific,"   Hood, 314.
   138   "God knows how,"   Hood, 131–32.
   139   "Bud is afflicted,"   Hood, 139.
   141   "They take me,"   *BHC,* 255–56.

143 "For sixty days," Hood, 119.

143 *These Thousand Hills,* Hood, 130.

144 After the book, Hart, 173.

145 "Eleven Men made," Hood, 116.

145 "From a rise," Hood, 117.

146 "an excursion," Hood, 129.

146 But these relationships, Ford, 95.

146 "rebel against convention," Hood, 190.

147 *"to be right"* Thousand, 345.

148 *However, even his friend, Dan Cushman,* Hood, 266.

148 *"Bud's style grows,"* Hood, 132.

148 *"drew heavily,"* Hood, 133.

149 *"It would appear,"* Clark, 54.

149 *"Below him lay,"* Thousand, 312.

149 *The passage came,* Hood, 120.

150 *Fox sent story editor,* D'Arc, 88.

150 *"George clapped,"* BHC, 48–49.

152 *"Joe and I,"* Hood, 289.

152 *"Joe Howard meant more,"* Hood, 289.

153 *"Dear Joe,"* Peterson, 97, 99.

154 *obituary editorial,* Times, November 15, 1955, n.p.

154 *"If you were to ask,"* DeVoto—A Memoir, n.p.

10. Down in the Dumps—Drink and Divorce

1. *Interviews.* My thanks to:
Helen Guthrie Miller, Alfred Bertram "Bert" Guthrie III

2. *Published Material by A. B. Guthrie Jr.*
The Blue Hen's Chick (New York: McGraw-Hill, 1965). Hereafter referred to as *BHC.*
The Big It and Other Stories (Boston: Houghton Mifflin, 1960). Hereafter referred to as *TBI.*

4. *Published Material and Unpublished Material about A. B. Guthrie Jr. and Related Topics*
James V. D'Arc, "A. B. Guthrie, Jr., in Hollywood: Variations on the Writing Experience," in *Fifty Years after "The Big Sky,"* ed. William E. Farr and William W. Bevis (Helena: Montana Historical Society Press, 2001), 73–105.

Charles E. Hood, "Hard Work and Tough Dreaming: A Biography of
A. B. Guthrie, Jr." Master's thesis, University of Montana, 1969.

Thomas W. Ford, *A. B. Guthrie, Jr.* (Boston: Twayne Publishers, 1981).

"The Big It," *San Francisco Chronicle*, March 27, 1960: 25.

Fred Erisman, "Early Western Literary Scholars," *A Literary History of
the American West* (Fort Worth: Texas Christian University Press,
1987).

James V. D'Arc, "A. B. Guthrie, Jr., in Hollywood: Variations on the
Writing Experience," in *Fifty Years after "The Big Sky*," ed. William
E. Farr and William W. Bevis (Helena: Montana Historical Society
Press, 2001), 73–105.

R. L. Perkin, "Big Sky Smiled," *Saturday Review*, June 5, 1965: 28.

5. *Notes and Sources for Quotations*

    155   *"In the first half,"* D'Arc, 89–90.

    156   *"Friends ask me,"* BHC, 137.

    156   *"We didn't collaborate,"* Hood, 137.

    157   *"Though I went,"* D'Arc, 91.

    157   *"the film version,"* BHC, 220.

    157   *"Though neither my books,"* BHC, 222.

    157   *"budgeted as an 'A' movie,"* D'Arc, 91.

    159   *"Lives without context,"* BHC, 226–27.

    159   *"I wrote* The Blue Hen's Chick,*"* Hood, 157.

    160   *"It's true that many,"* Hood, 141.

    160   *"a tall time,"* TBI, vi.

    161   *"buck-jumping around,"* TBI, 12.

    161   *The narrator asks,* Ford, 13.

    161   *"because he didn't,"* TBI, 150.

    162   *"With great sensitivity,"* Hood, 148.

    162   *"It is to the publisher's,"* Chronicle, 25.

    162   *"Two stories in the book,"* Hood, 153–54.

    163   *Smith was the author,* Erisman, 313.

    165   *"Harriet didn't know,"* Hood, 319.

    165   *"Jackson was having eye trouble,"* Hood, 317–18.

    166   *sometimes Bud got, "I don't often re-read,"* Hood, 323.

    166   *"When they moved to Great Falls,"* Hood, 322.

    166   *As his sister, Jane, pointed out,* Hood, 322.

167 *"a slavish devotion,"* Hood, 323–24.

169 *Among Bud's many projects,* D'Arc, 93–94.

11. Living with Janie and Courting Carol

1. *Interviews.* My thanks to:

Helen Guthrie Miller, Alfred Bertram "Bert" Guthrie III, Peggy Bloom, William Kittredge, Carol Guthrie

2. *Published Material by A. B. Guthrie Jr.*

The Blue Hen's Chick (New York: McGraw-Hill, 1965).

5. *Notes and Sources for Quotations*

171 "Suddenly the yard," *BHC*, 261.

12. The Old Man and the Young Woman Wed

1. *Interviews.* My thanks to:

Peggy Bloom, Carol Guthrie, Helen Guthrie Miller, Amy Sakariassen

4. *Published Material and Unpublished Material about A. B. Guthrie Jr. and Related Topics*

"Noted Author Weds Iowan in Helena," *Missoulian*, April 5, 1969, clipping, n.p.

5. *Notes and Sources for Quotations*

198 *"The 68-year-old,"* *Missoulian*, clipping, n.p.

13. *Arfive,* and Speaking to the Young—Earth Day

1. *Interviews.* My thanks to:

Carol Guthrie, Amy Sakariassen, Mary Sexton

2. *Published Material by A. B. Guthrie Jr.*

The Big Sky (New York: William Sloane Associates, 1947).

"Preface," *Montana: High, Wide, and Handsome,* by Joseph Kinsey Howard. (New Haven CT: Yale University Press, 1959), ix–xiv. Referred to here in its reprinting as "Dear Joe" in *Big Sky, Fair Land,* ed. David Peterson (Flagstaff AZ: Northland Press, 1988), 97–101.

"A Message to the Young," *Sunday Missoulian,* April 18, 1971, n.p. Referred to here in its reprinting in *Big Sky, Fair Land,* 107–8.

Arfive (Boston: Houghton Mifflin, 1977).

"A Voice of Anger and Thunder," *Big Sky, Fair Land*, 115–20.

Wild Pitch (Boston: Houghton Mifflin, 1973).

Once Upon a Pond (Missoula MT: Mountain Press Publishing, 1973).

4. *Published Material and Unpublished Material about A. B. Guthrie Jr. and Related Topics*

Vernon Scannell, "Western Man," *New Statesman*, February 4, 1972: 151.

"In Brief," *The Observer*, February 20, 1972: 28.

"On the Edge of Civilization," *Christian Science Monitor*, February 11, 1971: 7.

Donald Dresden, "Civilizing the Frontier," *Washington Post*, February 9, 1971: B6.

Review of *Wild Pitch*, *Saturday Review*, March 1973: 72–73.

Newgate Callendar, "Criminals at Large," *New York Times Book Review*, February 11, 1973: 30.

Review of *Wild Pitch*, "A. B. Guthrie Shines Again," *Sunday World-Herald Magazine*, January 21, 1973: 26.

Review of *Wild Pitch*, *New Yorker*, February 24, 1973: 130.

5. *Notes and Sources for Quotations*

207	*"Caudill and Deakins,"*	*The Big Sky*, 150.
208	*"When Joseph Kinsey Howard,"*	"Dear Joe," 99.
208	*"A Message,"*	*Big Sky, Fair Land*, 107.
211	*"Arfive is the fourth,"*	Scannell, 151.
212	*More biting was,*	"In Brief," 28.
212	*"These people speak,"*	Millar, 7.
212	*"The dialogue is biting,"*	Dresden, B6.
215	*"I am an odd selection,"*	"A Voice of Anger," 115.
222	*"see a lot more,"*	*Saturday Review*, 72–73.
222	*"curiously attractive,"*	Callendar, 30.
222	*"what makes 'Wild Pitch,'"*	*World-Herald*, 26.
222	*"Like most thunder showers,"*	*Wild Pitch*, 59.
223	*"with his fresh eyes,"*	*New Yorker*, 130.
224	*"They are on my conscience,"*	*Wild Pitch*, 77.
224	*"I know a cattle rancher,"*	78.

14. The Twin Lakes Imbroglio and Building the "Barn"

1. *Interviews.* My thanks to:

Helen Guthrie Miller, Carol Guthrie, Bill Luthin, Dale Burk

2. *Published Material by A. B. Guthrie Jr.*
   The Last Valley (Boston: Houghton Mifflin, 1975).
   Arfive (Boston: Houghton Mifflin, 1971).

4. *Published Material and Unpublished Material about A. B. Guthrie Jr.*
   and Related Topics
   Thomas W. Ford, *A. B. Guthrie, Jr.* (Boston: Twayne Publishers, 1981).
   "*The Last Valley* by A. B. Guthrie, Jr.," *Virginia Quarterly Review* (Winter 1976): 10–11.
   L. J. Davis, "When the Legend Dies, What of the Balladeer?" *National Observer*, September 13, 1975: 26.
   Martin Levin, "New and Novel," *New York Times Book Review*, October 12, 1975: 49.
   "*The Last Valley*," *Choice* (January 1976): 1444.
   Transcript of an interview of A. B. Guthrie Jr. by Bill Bevis, 1974, presented on KUFM, sponsored by the University of Montana Center for Continuing Education.

5. *Notes and Sources for Quotations*
   232 *"Arfive may be,"* Ford, 111.
   232 *"difficult task,"* Ford, 108.
   233 *"past which is just,"* Ford, 109.
   233 *"The setting is Arfive,"* *Virginia Quarterly*, 10–11.
   234 *"What one feels,"* Gish, 39.
   235 *"Change is the order,"* *The Last Valley*, 100–101.
   235 *"The key word,"* Ford, 113.
   235 *"We can't keep digging,"* 284.
   236 "The Last Valley . . . *is,*" Davis, 26.
   237 *"Arfive, Mont. is a town,"* Levin, 49.
   237 "The Last Valley *is more,*" *Choice*, 1444.
   242 *"Sometimes an author,"* Bevis, 13.

15. "What Happened to Boone?"

1. *Interviews.* My thanks to:
   Helen Guthrie Miller, Amy Sakariassen, Bill Luthin, William Kittredge, Ripley Hugo, Lois Welch, Jim Welch, William Bevis

2. *Published Material by A. B. Guthrie Jr.*

The Genuine Article (Boston: Houghton Mifflin, 1982).

"The Rockies," *Holiday* (July 1955): 98–101, 121–24, 128. Referred to here in its reprinting in *Big Sky, Fair Land.*

4. *Published Material and Unpublished Material about A. B. Guthrie Jr. and Related Topics*

Obituary for Charles Guthrie, *Great Falls Tribune*, August 25, 1977: clipping, n.p.

Rick Graetz, *Montana! A Photographic Celebration* vol. 2 (Helena MT: Rick Graetz with *Montana Magazine*, 1989).

Richard Hugo, *The Real West Marginal Way: A Poet's Autobiography*, ed. Ripley S. Hugo, Lois Welch, and James Welch, intro. by William Matthews (New York: W. W. Norton, 1986).

"Richard Hugo," *The Academy of American Poets*, online, poetry exhibits, April 25, 2005.

Michael Moore, #57 "James Welch: 100 Most Influential Montanans of the Century," *Special for Missoulian Online,,* 1999.

"A. B. Guthrie Jr.," interview by William Bevis presented by KUFM through the University of Montana Center for Continuing Education.

William W. Bevis, *Ten Tough Trips: Montana Writers and the West* (Norman: University of Oklahoma Press, 2003).

Richard Hugo, "Pishkun Reservoir (for Bud Guthrie)," *Making Certain It Goes On: The Collected Poems of Richard Hugo* (New York: W. W. Norton, 1984), 443–44.

5. *Notes and Sources for Quotations*

249   *"a man who could write,"*   *Tribune*, n.p.

250   *"I doubt the practical,"*   Graetz, 63.

252   *"an auctioneer,"*   *The Genuine Article*, 26.

252   *"another rider,"*   37.

252   *"I turned my eyes,"*   98.

256   *"But I remember,"*   "Rockies," 87.

257–58   *Dick Hugo, xv–xxv*; poetry exhibits, 1–2.

259   *"You don't know anything,"*   Moore, 2.

260   *"As much as anything,"*   Moore, 2.

263   *"I get long distance,"*   Bevis, n.p.

266   *"Think of those big trout,"*   Hugo (*Collected Poems*), 443–44.

16. Fair Land, Fair Land

1. *Interviews.* My thanks to:

    Ripley Hugo, Sue Hart, Mary Sexton, William Kittredge, Bill Luthin,
    Amy Sakariassen, Alexander Sakariassen, Carol Guthrie, James Welch,
    Bert Lindler, Alfred Bertram "Bert" Guthrie III, Helen Guthrie
    Miller, Peggy Bloom, Lois Welch, Marc and Marnie Gaede

2. *Published Material by A. B. Guthrie Jr.*

    Fair Land, Fair Land (Boston: Houghton Mifflin, 1982)

    Big Sky, Fair Land: The Environmental Essays of A. B. Guthrie, Jr., ed.
    David Peterson (Flagstaff AZ: Northland Press, 1988).

    A Field Guide to Writing Fiction (New York: Harper Collins, 1991).

3. *Unpublished Material by A. B. Guthrie Jr.*

    "Days and Rainbow (for Richard Hugo)"

    Speech at the Montana Land Use Conference, Billings, Montana, No-
    vember 1973.

    Address to the League of Women Voters at Hamilton's Woodside
    Grange Hall, December 1974.

4. *Published Material and Unpublished Material about A. B. Guthrie Jr.
    and Related Topics*

    Sue Hart, "Some Recollections of and Reflections on A. B. Guthrie,
    Jr. and His Work," in *Fifty Years after "The Big Sky": New Perspectives*,
    ed. William E. Farr and William W. Bevis (Helena: Montana Histori-
    cal Society Press, 2001).

    "Guthrie, A. B., Jr. *Fair Land, Fair Land*," *Kirkus Review*, July 1, 1982:
    750.

    "*Fair Land, Fair Land*," *Publisher's Weekly*, July 2, 1982: 45.

    Bert Lindler, "Guthrie Defends Bears," *Great Falls Tribune*, clipping,
    n.d., n.p.

    Mike Dennison, "Two Guthries Disagree Pointedly on Grizzly Manage-
    ment," *Great Falls Tribune*, January 19, 1986: n.p.

    David Peterson, "Afterword" to A. B. Guthrie Jr., *The Blue Hen's Chick*
    (New York: McGraw-Hill, 1965), 271–79.

    Marc Gaede, "A Visit to the Marias Massacre Site," *Images from the
    Great West*, photographs by Marc Gaede and essay and quotations by
    A. B. Guthrie Jr. (La Canada CA: Chaco Press, 1990), 121–27.

5. *Notes and Sources for Quotations*

268   *"I said to the poet,"* "Days."

270   *"What do you think,"* Hart, 163.

272   *"Despite the simplistic,"* *Kirkus*, 750.

272   *"The author captures,"* *Publisher's Weekly*, 45.

272   *"a sublime, multilayered,"* *Booklist*, 1393–94.

277   *"The Grizzly Has Reappeared,"* Bert Lindler, n.p.

277   *"He called to mind,"* *Fair Land*, 53, 58.

278   *"There's no better way,"* Dennison, clipping, n.p.

280   *"raising bears,"* Dennison, n.p.

282   *"Guthrie had undergone,"* Peterson, 153.

283   *Ever since his discussions*   paraphrase and quotations from Gaede, 121–27.

286   *"The experts weren't,"* "Afterword," 277.

17. Afterword

1. *Interviews.* My thanks to:
Amy Sakariassen, Eric Sakariassen, William Kittredge

4. *Published Material and Unpublished Material about A. B. Guthrie Jr. and Related Topics*
William Kittredge, "Remembering Guthrie, 'King of the Prairies,'" *Great Falls Tribune*, April 28, 1991: n.p.

5. *Notes and Sources for Quotations*

288   *"The first snow of winter,"* Kittredge, n.p.

290   *In the hospital,* "Afterword," 278.

291   *"We mined the land,"* Land Use Conference, speech.

291   *"Years ago, long before,"* League of Women Voters, speech.

INDEX

Page references in *italics* indicate a photograph; the first part of the reference indicates the page of text the photograph section follows; the second part of the reference indicates the page within the photograph section.

Abbott, Teddy Blue, 144, 145
Acheson, Barclay, 57
Across the Wide Missouri (DeVoto), 121, 123
Alger, Horatio, 45
American Boy, 6, 19
American Fur Company of St. Louis, 3
American Fur Trade of the Far West, The (Chittenden), 6, 7, 73
American Studies Program, 241, 244
Anaconda, 132, 207, 208
Anderson, Isaac, 73–74
Argosy, 125
Army Corps of Engineers, 121, 122
Arthur, Jean, 127
Atlantic, 101, 115

Barkley, Alben, 46, 47
baseball, 18–19, 45
Baseball Magazine, 19
Beckham, J. C. W., 44
Benjamin, Ben, 169
Bent's Fort (Lavender), 169
Berry, Wendell, 218, 273
Bevis, William: *Ten Tough Trips: Montana Writers and the West*, 263–66
Big Sky, The (1952), 123–24, 243
Big Sky, The (Guthrie): inspiration for, 1, 7, 78–80; lecture circuit of, 119–20; movie

rights to, 123–24; reviews and success of, 100–107, 112, 115, 118
Bipartisan Combine, 44
Bitterroot National Forest, 238, 239
Blackfeet Indians, 3, 260
Blew, Mary Clearman, 128, 288
Bloom, Peggy, *246/1*; on Bud's cowboy ethic, 132; on Bud's marriage to Carol, 196, 248; as Bud's niece, 107, 172, 173, 281; education of, 177
Bob Marshall Wilderness, 3, 77, 256
Bolle Committee, 238, 239
Booklist, 103, 272
Boone, *The Big Sky* character, 263–66, 270
Boston Globe, 84
Bowmar, Dan, 34, 42, 44, 106, 167
Brandborg, Gui, 239
Brandt, Carol, 253, 255, 270, 271
Bread Loaf Writers' Conference, 89, 90–92, 93, 121, *136/1*
Brown, John Y., 43, 47
Brown Schools, 120
Bud. *See* Guthrie, Alfred Bertram "Bud," Jr.
Buddie's Corn Dodger, 176
buffalo, 99, 148
Burk, Dale, 238, 239, 274
Burroughs, John: *Summit of the Years*, 24

Carradine, John, 129
Cassidy, Butch, 265
Cather, Willa, 2
Catholic World, 116
Cawelti, John, 126
Chandler, Albert Benjamin, 45–46, 47, 167

Chatterton, Wayne: *A Literary History of the American West*, 104
Chittenden, Hiram Martin: *The American Fur Trade of the Far West*, 73
Choteau, Montana, 3
Choteau Acantha, 19–20, 26, 35, 142, 257
Chouteau, Pierre, Jr., 3
Christian Science Monitor, 212, 234
Circle 8 Ranch, *136/4*; guests at, 141, 152, 223; near Bud's cabin, 130; owners of, 173, 192, 257, 276, 280; as Pine Butte Guest Ranch, 276, 280
Clark, Badger: *Sun & Saddle Leather*, 218
Clark, George Rogers, 183
Clark, Thomas D., *246/4*; on Bud's novels, 118; on Bud's success, 102–3; on Bud's teaching, 105; on Bud's writing, 61, 62, 63, 79–80, 81, 94, 112; correspondence with Bud, 148–49, 224–25; friendship with Bud, 224–25; as neighbor of Bud and Harriet, 53, 54, 56, 69–70, 167; on Pulitzer Prize awarded to Bud, 117; *Southern Country Editor*, 56
Clark, Walter Van Tilburg, 2, 72, 74, 115, 149, 177; *The Ox-Bow Incident*, 72, 74
Clark, William, 84, 183
Coffey, Bill, 19
Coffey, Clark, 12
Coffey, George: friendship with Guthrie children, 75–76; on Mr. Guthrie as principal and teacher, 5, 6; on Mr. Guthrie's temperament, 8–9
Collins, Caspar, 112
Colter, John, 161
Commonweal, 116
Cooper, John Sherman, 48
Costello, Matthew J., 126
Course of Empire, The (DeVoto), 121
Cowgill, Fatty, 12
Cow Track, The, 251
Crane, Mabel, 257
Cushman, Dan, 118, 131, 138, 139, 148, 152

Dalby, Al, 26
D'Arc, James V., 155, 157
Davis, L. J., 236
Day, John F., 80
DeBakey, Michael, 221
DeHaas, Judge, 76
Dennison, Mike, 278

Depression, the, 38, 41, 50
Deserts on the March (Sears), 67
DeVoto, Avis, 153
DeVoto, Bernard: *Across the Wide Missouri*, 121, 123; at Bread Loaf conferences, *136/1*, 152, 153; correspondence with Bud, 98, 107–8; *Course of Empire*, 121; drinking habits of, 139; "Due Notice to the F.B.I.," 154; *The Easy Chair*, 154; friendship with Bud, 81, 89, 90–91, 93; retracing Oregon Trail, *136/3*; travels with Bud, 7, 120–21, *136/3*; death of, 153–54; *The Year of the Decision: 1846*, 121
De Wilde, Brandon, 127
dinosaurs, 276
Doig, Ivan, 2, 218, 273
Dolby, Al, *48/2*
"Driving Montana" (Hugo), 261

Ear Mountain, 230, 231, 249–50, 255, 290
Earth Day, 208–10
Eastern Montana College, 272
Easy Chair, The (DeVoto), 154
Edwards, Tom, 256–57
Egan, Richard, 157
Eide, Ingvard Henry, 180
Eisenhower, Dwight D., 117
Elephant Ear Mountain, 230, 231, 249–50, 255
Everitt, Helen, 120, 153

Fadiman, Clifton, 72
Fall, Victor H., 197, 198
Fetterman, William J., 244
Field, Mrs. Carl B., 5–6
Fisher, Dorothy Canfield, 101
Fisher, Vardis, 2
Fitzpatrick, Tom, 7
Flaptop Mountain, 152
Fleischer, Richard, 157
fly fishing, 15, 268–69
Fools Crow (Welch), 260, 263, 273
Ford, Richard, 218–19, 288
Ford, Thomas, 232–33, 235
Fort Bridger, 111
Fort Laramie, 244
Fort Phil Kearny, 244
Forty Years a Fur Trader on the Upper Missouri (Larpenteur), 73
Foss, Kendall, 83
Foster, Dianne, 129

Fox, Norman, 131, 149–50
From Here to Eternity (1953), 128
Frontier, The, 25, 255
Frost, Elinor, 92
Frost, Robert, 91–93, *136/1*, 152, 177

Gaede, Marc, 283–85
Gaede, Miles, *246/7*
Gannon, Fritz, *136/6*
Gannon, Shirley, *136/6*
Gibler, Ray, 256
Gill, Brendan, 116
Givens, Grace, 168, 172
Gleason, Alice, 173, 192, 257, 276, 288
Gleason, Ken, 257, 259, 276
Graetz, Rick, 290
Grapes of Wrath, The (Steinbeck), 265
Great Falls Tribune, 60, 67
Gries, Tom, 169
grizzly bears, 277–80
Guthrie, Alfred Bertram, Sr., *48/2*; death of, 141–42; health of, 71, 120; influences on Bud's writing, 66–68, 78–79; life after wife's death, 59–61, 65, 67–68; outdoor and fishing skills, 4–5, 15, *48/1*; ownership of *The Choteau Acantha*, 19–20; as principal of Teton County Free High School, 3, 4, 5, 162; reading habits of, 5, 6, 7–8, 71–72; storytelling by, 7–8; struggles to support family, 19, 20–21; temperament of, 8–9, 162; writing ambitions of, 22
Guthrie, Alfred Bertram "Bud," Jr.: alcohol consumption by, 50–51, 97, 134, 139–40, 142, 166, 173, 176, 179, 196, 220, 250–51; ambition for writing, 19, 21, 55–56; aversion to cities and crowds, 15–16, 21, 23; at Bread Loaf conferences, *136/1*, 151–52, 153; characteristics of, 1, 179, 182; childhood in Montana, 2–18; children of, 6, 40, *48/5*, 68, *136/4*; and coping with success, 100–101; correspondence with Carol, 181–83, 184, 185–87, 188–96; correspondence with Scoop Larson, 32, 34–38, 49–50, 52–53, 96–98; death of, 290; and dispute over Twin Lakes property, 226–31; divorce from Harriet, 167; education of, 21–26; environmental and conservationist views of, 16, 66–67, 130–31, 235–36, 291–92; family editing of writing, 203–4, 217–18, 271; and fishing the Pishkun Reservoir, 292–93;

Forest Service job, 27–28, *48/3*; friendship with Mary Lizzie Keating, 13, 35–36, 38, 52, 139, 167, 169; Front property and building project, 230–31, 237; grandchildren of, 289; on grizzlies in Montana, 277–80; health of, 70, 78, 95, 221, 255, 282–83, 285–86, 287–88; and Hollywood writing jobs, 123–29, 139–40, 155–57; honorary doctorates awarded to, 117; jobs in New York, 28–29, 31; lecture tour in Europe, 240–45; literary influences of, 24–26; and living with Janie, 172–88; marriage to Carol, 197–204; marriage to Harriet Larson, 38–39; marriage troubles with Harriet, 139, 140–41, 164; on mountain men, 78–79; move to Harvard, 81–82; move to Montana, 128–36, *136/2*; move to the Barn, 7, 237–38, *246/6*; newspaper job in Kentucky, 31, 32–48, 65–82, 94–99, 104; Nieman Fellowship awarded to, 80–82, 83–99; on nostalgic writings of lost West, 1, 2; outdoor and fishing skills of, 15, 17–18, *48/1*, 66–67; poems of, 177–78; printer's apprenticeship of, 19–20; public speaking abilities, 25–26, 56–57, 119; Pulitzer Prize awarded to, 117–18; recipes of favorite foods, 175–76, 231–32; on relationship with father, 8–9; on relationship with Harriet Larson, 23–24, 32, 34–38; religious fundamentalism influences of, 9-10; remembering his mother, 12–13; resignation from the *Leader*, 104; retracing Oregon Trail, *136/3*; siblings of, 4, 6, 7, 14, *246/1*; stay in Bismarck, 289–90; as stepfather to Carol's children, 198–99, 201–2, 247–48; teaching at university, 69, 104–5; and *These Thousand Hills* movie rights sold, 150–51; tour of Forest Service cutting regions, 238–40, *246/8*; trip to and work in Mexico, 26–27, *48/2*; Twin Lakes property of, 105–6, 123, *136/6*, 171–72, 178, 205, 226–31, *246/2*; on Western individualism, 132–33; writing process of, 25, 85–99, 108–9, 138, 217, 249–67
— Works: *Arfive*, 128, 159, 177, 182, 183, 187, 191, 195, 202–3, 205, 210–15, 216, 232; *The Big It and Other Stories*, 158, 160–61, 162, 211; *The Big Sky*, 1, 7, 51, 69, 75, 78–80, 85–99, *136/2*, 207, 234, 235, 262, 272; *Big Sky, Fair Land: The Environmental Essays of A. B. Guthrie, Jr.*, 282; *The Blue Hen's Chick*, 159, 169–70, 211, 282; children's stories, 183–84, 185;

— Works (*continued*)
"Days and Rainbows," 268–69; "Ebbie,"
8–9, 162; *Fair Land, Fair Land,* 7, 262, 263,
270, 271–72, 273, 277; "Faulkconer's Eagle,"
66–67; *A Field Guide to Writing Fiction,* 221,
286, 287; *The Genuine Article,* 251–53, 274;
"Here and Hereafter," 282; *The Last Valley,*
221, 232–37; "A Message to the Young"
(Earth Day essay), 208–10; "Montana," 207;
Murder in the Cotswolds, 251, 285; *Murders at
Moon Dance,* 56, 67–68, 73–74, 216, 221; *No
Second Wind,* 251, 271; *Once upon a Pond,* 211,
218, 221; "On Marrying a Younger Woman,"
273; "On the Death of an Eagle," 66–67;
"Our Lordly Mountains," 207, 256; *Playing
Catch-Up,* 251; "The Rockies," 207, 256;
"Settlement Trilogy," 232; *These Thousand
Hills,* 132–33, 137–52, 155, 211, 270; "Trail
Riding," 255; "Twin Lakes Hunter," 178;
"Twin Lakes Winter," 178; *The Way West,* 7,
10, 96, 107, 109–18, 270, 272; *Wild Pitch,* 216,
218, 221–24, 233, 251; "The Wreck," 162
Guthrie, Alfred Bertram, III (Bert), 6, *48/5,
136/2;* birth of, 40; education of, 78, 128; on
grizzly management in Montana, 277–80;
love of outdoors and animals, 40, 60, 61–62;
on parents' marriage troubles, 165; ranching
by, 78, 277–80; on relationship with father,
184, 247, 251; response to Bud's second
marriage, 200; teasing of little sister, 76–77;
travels with father, 110–11
Guthrie, Carol, *246/4, 246/8;* and "Barn" building project, 230–31, 237; on Bud's European
lecture tour, 240–45; children of, 181, 192,
195, *246/3;* health of, 289; and limiting Bud's
alcohol consumption, 219, 250–51; move to
the Barn, 237–38; parents' deaths, 229–30;
protective of Bud, 227, 240–44, 247, 255,
275; and spreading Bud's ashes, 290. *See also*
Luthin, Carol
Guthrie, Charles M. "Chick," *48/1, 48/6;* birth
of, 14; on Bud's Hollywood jobs, 139–40;
childhood in Montana, 18–19; correspondence with Bud, 141–42, 155–56; death of,
249; on father's temperament, 9; health of,
249; marriage of, 70; newspaper work of, 52,
60, 249; on Pulitzer Prize awarded to Bud,
117–18; on relationship with father, 6, 7, 9;

remembering his mother, 11–13; on rights to
Twin Lakes property, 228–29
Guthrie, Harriet "Scoop," *136/2, 136/6;* Bud's
divorce from, 167; correspondence with
Bud, 49–50, 52–53, 109–10; death of, 191–92;
health of, 49; marriage troubles with Bud,
139, 140–41, 164; move to Montana, 128–29;
summers in Montana, 49–50, 54–55, 60–61,
68, 93. *See also* Larson, Harriet "Scoop"
Guthrie, Helen, *48/4, 136/4;* antagonism toward
Carol, 226–30, 247, 251; on *Arfive,* 213; birth
of, 68–69; children of, 245–46; and dispute
over Twin Lakes property, 226–31; education
of, 77, 128; on father's quizzes and puzzles,
76; about mother, 77; on quarreling parents,
139, 140–41, 165; on relationship with father, 184–85, 226–31, 247; and remembering
grandfather Tom Larson, 134–36; response
to Bud's second marriage, 196, 200–201
Guthrie, Janie, *246/1;* on Bud's drinking, 166;
on Bud's gifts, 168; childhood in Montana,
7, 14; death of, 281; education of, 19, 52; and
living with Bud in Kentucky, 38; marriage to
Bob Haugen, 54; relationship with brother
Bud, 247–48; response to Bud's second
marriage, 196, 197, 200. *See also* Haugen,
Janie Guthrie
Guthrie, Jenny June Thomas, *48/2;* on conduct
and discipline, 12; cooking abilities, 12–13;
death of, 56; health of, 55–56; influences on
Bud's childhood, 10–11; pregnancies and
infant deaths, 14; views on housework, 11–12
Guthrie, John, 16
Guthrie, Mike, 31, 37

Hansen, Matt, *246/3*
Hanusa, Marguerite, 166
Hardwick, Elizabeth, 63
Harper's, 154, 170, 178
Hart, Sue, 272, 273
Harvard University, 63, 81–82
Haskell, Floyd K., 238
Haslam, Gerald, 126
Haugen, Bob, 54, 172
Haugen, Bobby, 120
Haugen, Janie Guthrie: children of, 120; divorce
of, 172. *See also* Guthrie, Janie
Hawks, Howard, 123
Hayes, Alfred, 157

Headon, James, 40
Heavy Runner, Chief, 283
Heflin, Van, 127
Helena Wilderness Ride, 256
Herald Leader, 68, 92, 94
Herald Tribune, 116
historical truth, 1
History of Montana (Leeson), 79
Hodge, Henry, 62; *The Kentucky Mountains*, 62–63
Holiday, 111, 117, 256
Hood, Charles E., biography of Guthrie, 10, 75, 113, 144–45, 162, 165–66
Horner, Jack, 248
Howard, Joseph Kinsey, *136/4*; on *The Big Sky*, 101; death of, 152–53, 208; friendship with Bud, 114–15, 120; on history of Montana, 2–3; inspiring Bud, 130–31, 132; *Montana: High, Wide, and Handsome*, 152–53, 208
Hughes, Paul J., 80
Hugo, Richard, *246/3, 246/6*; death of, 265–67, 268, 269, 273; "Driving Montana," 261; friendship with Bud, 177, 219–20, 257–60; marriage to Ripley Schemm, 219–20; as Montana writer and poet, 273, 288; "Pishkun Reservoir," 266–67; *The Triggering Town*, 258
Hugo, Ripley, *246/3*; friendship with Bud, 131–32, 219–20, 221, 257, 262, 288; marriage to Richard Hugo, 219–20, 258–59
Huntley, Chet, 201
Hutchinson, W. H., 162

If a Lion Could Talk (Walker), 131
Independence Rock, 111
Indians, 4, 99, 152, 260
internal monologue, 85
Iowa State University, 78

Jackson, George, *136/3*; on Bud's multitasking, 165–66; drinking habits of, 139; friendship with Bud, 9, 11–12, 26, 76, 107, 139, 150, 167, 173, 223–24
James, Jesse, 265
Jimps the dog, 9
Johnson, Dorothy, 162, 219, 220–21, 272, 274; "A Man Called Horse," 220; "The Man Who Shot Liberty Valance," 220

Johnson, Keen, 47
Johnson, Liver Eating, 7, 265
Jordan, Joe, 34, 42, 106, 167
Jovanovie, Harry, 31, 44

Keating, Mary Elizabeth, friendship with Bud, 33, 35–36, 38, 52, 139, 167, 169
Keedick, Lee, 119, 120
Kentuckian, The (1955), 128–29, 137, 157
Kentucky Mountains, The (Hodge), 62–63
Kesey, Ken, 273
Killing Custer (Welch), 260
Kirkus Reviews, 163, 272
Kittredge, William: on Bud's drinking, 176; friendship with Bud, 219, 260, 261, 288; introduction to *Murders at Moon Dance*, 74–75; refuting Western myth, 2
Kramer, Arthur, 150

Ladd, Alan, 127, *136/5*, 243
Lalley, J. M., 102
Lancaster, Burt, 129, 157
Larpenteur, Charles: *Forty Years a Fur Trader on the Upper Missouri*, 73
Larson, Alva, 106
Larson, Harriet "Scoop," *48/4*; childhood in Montana, 23, 26, 29–30; college education of, 30–31, 34; correspondence with Bud, 29–31, 32, 34–38, 49–50, 52–53, 96–98; engagements of, 34–35, 36; marriage to Bud, 38–39; relationship with Bud, 23–24, 38–39; teaching credentials of, 38. *See also* Guthrie, Harriet "Scoop"
Larson, Tom, *48/5*; conservative views of, 132–34; drinking habits of, 139; early life in Montana, 133–34; friendship with Bud, 39, 167; R5 cattle brand of, 191; ranch of, 39, 77, 78; as senator, 134
Lasker, Ed, 123
Lavender, David: *Bent's Fort*, 169
Lederer, Bill, 121, *136/3*; *The Ugly American*, 121
Lee Metcalf National Wildlife Refuge, 238
Leeson, M. A.: *History of Montana*, 79
Lewis, Meriwether, 283
Lewis and Clark expedition, 3, 121, 122, 163, 180
Lewis and Clark Journals, The, 6, 19
Lewis and Clark National Forest, 3
Lexington Leader, 31, 54, 62, 198. *See also Herald Leader*

Lexington Public Forum, 119, 120
Lexington Speakeasy Club, 57–59
Library Journal, 103, 163
Lindler, Bert, 67, 274–77, 278
Literary History of the American West, A
    (Chatterton), 104
Littleton Independent, 83
Logan, M. M., 47
Louisville Courier-Journal, 103–4
Lowell, Robert, 63
Luthin, Amy, *246/3*; on Bud as stepfather, 201,
    206–7, 210, 240, 247–48, 251, 288; on Bud's
    mystery writing, 216–17; childhood vacations
    in Montana, 192, 195; on Dorothy Johnson,
    220–21; education of, 248; marriage to Erik
    Sakarassin, 288; on Mildred Walker, 221;
    relationships with Bud's family, 248; work
    with Nature Conservancy, 276
Luthin, Bill, *246/3*; on Boone character, 263;
    on Bud as stepfather, 201, 206–7, 210, 237,
    247–48, 251, 259, 288; childhood vacations in
    Montana, 181, 192, 195; eulogy for Bud, 290;
    family reading of Bud's work, 271; on grizzly
    feud, 279; and quitting smoking with Bud,
    280–81; surveys for Shell Oil, 248; writing
    by, 259
Luthin, Carol: correspondence with Bud,
    181–83, 184, 185–87, 188–96; divorce from
    Herbert, 194–97; marriage to Bud, 197–204.
    See also Guthrie, Carol
Luthin, Herbert William, Jr., 180, 183
Luthin, Kay, 288
Lyman, Chalmer K., 154
Lynn, Dianna, 129
Lyons, Louis, 81, 84, 87, 89

MacDonald, Ted, 12
Maclean, Norman, 2, 273
Malmstrom Air Force Base, 284
Malone, Mike, 290
"Man Called Horse, A" (Johnson), 220
Manfred, Fredrick, 2
"Man Who Shot Liberty Valance, The"
    (Johnson), 220
Marias Massacre, 7, 262, 283–84
Marias River, 283–84
Marko, John, 168
Marshall, Margaret, 101
Masters, Edgar Lee, 71; *Spoon River Anthology*,
    71–72

Mathison, Richard, 249
Matthau, Walter, 129
McCaig, Robert, 131
McClanahan, Ed, 218, 273
McClark, Doug, 41
McGee, Gale W., 238
McIntire, John, 129
Menopause Marchers, 141
Merk, Frederick, 81, 84
Merkel, Una, 129
Merriam, H. G., 24, 25, 102
Metcalf, Lee, 238
Metis Indians, 152
Missoulian, 198
Missouri River, 110, 121
Mix, Tom, 264
Monroe, Frankie, 12
Montana: Bud and Harriet's move to, 128–36;
    forest clear-cutting practices in, 238–40; fur
    trade in, 3; Guthrie's childhood in, 2–16;
    mining in, 207; social and political condi-
    tions in, 129–30; writers living in, 130–32
Montana: High, Wide, and Handsome
    (Howard), 152–53, 208
Montana Historical Society, 273
Montana Magazine, 290
Montana Power Company, 132
Montana State University, 77
Montgomery, George, 106
Moore, Michael, 260
Morrison, Kay, 92, *136/1*
Morrison, Theodore, *136/1*; and advising on
    Bud's writing, 81, 84–86, 87–88, 89, 90, 93,
    138, 149; on Bud's autobiography, 159–60; as
    director of Bread Loaf conferences, 89–90,
    93, 151
Morrow, Edwin P., 43
Morton, Charles, 89
mountain men, 7, 78–79, 101–3, 161, 264, 265
Murray, Don, 157

Nation, 101
National Forest Management Act, 238, 239
National Observer, 236
Native Americans. *See* Indians
Nature Conservancy, 276, 280
New Statesman, 211
New Yorker, 72, 102, 116, 170
New York Herald Tribune, 101, 162

New York Times, 73, 163, 170, 272
New York Times Book Review, 101, 115, 149, 222, 237
Nieman Fellowship, 63, 80–82
"Nonny." See Guthrie, Alfred Bertram, III (Bert)

Observer, 212
Old South Pass, 111
open-range cattle ranching, 137
Oregon Trail, 7, 96, 113, 121–22
Oregon Trail (Parkman), 6, 7, 107
Osborn, Fairfield: Our Plundered Planet, 67
Our Plundered Planet (Osborn), 67
Owens, Patricia, 157
Ox-Bow Incident, The (Clark), 72, 74

Palance, Jack, 127, 244
Palmer, Joel, 109, 113
Parkman, Francis: Oregon Trail, 6, 7, 107
Pengelly, Les, 238–39
Perkin, Robert L., 170
Peterson, David, 282, 286
Phillips, John "Portuguese," 244
Pine Butte Guest Ranch, 276, 288
"Pishkun Reservoir" (Hugo), 266–67
Platte River, 110, 113
PM, 83
polio, 52
Price, Con, 144
Prohibition, 43–44, 57
Publisher's Weekly, 272
Pulitzer Prize, 117, 121

Remick, Lee, 157
Robertson, Nathan, 83
Robinson, E. A., 177, 269
Roethke, Theodore, 258
Rogers, Roy, 264
Rogers, Will, 134
Ronald, Ann, 126
Roosevelt, Franklin D., 46–47, 132
Rose, Jack, 12
Russell, Charles, 134, 144

Sakarassin, Alex, 289
Sakarassin, Emily, 289
Sakarassin, Erik, 288
Sampson, Flem D., 44

Sandoz, Mari, 2
San Francisco Chronicle, 162
Saturday Review, 101, 115, 163, 170, 222
Scannell, Vernon, 211–12
Schaefer, Jack: Shane, 124–27
Schemm, George, 131, 290
Schemm, Mildred Walker, 131–32, 136/4, 219, 220–21
Schemm, Ripley, 258
Schlesinger, Arthur, Sr., 81
Schultz, James, 6, 144
Sears, Paul B.: Deserts on the March, 67
"Sense of Place, A," 273
Service, Robert, 177–78
Sexton, George A., 136/4, 141, 223–24, 251, 257
Sexton, Helen, 141, 251, 257
Sexton, Mary, 223–24, 288
Shane (1953), 123, 136/5, 242, 244
Shane (Schaefer), 124–27
"Shooting of Dan McGrew, The" (Service), 178
Shore, Dinah, 106
Sloane, William, 90, 92, 94, 98, 99, 153
Smith, Annick, 288
Smith, Henry Nash, 162–63; The Virgin Land: The American West as Symbol and Myth, 163
Smith, Jedediah, 7
Sons of the Wild Jackass, 130
Southern Country Editor (Clark), 56
Speakeasy Club, 119, 160
Spoon River Anthology (Masters), 71–72
stagecoach, 4
Stahl, John G., 44
Stanley, Augustus, 43
Stegner, Wallace, 2, 158, 213–14; Wolf Willow, 158, 213
Steinbeck, John: The Grapes of Wrath, 265
Stevens, George, 123–24, 126, 127, 244
Stone, Arthur L., 22
Summit of the Years (Burroughs), 24
Sundance Kid, 265
Sunday Missoulian, 208
Sunday World-Herald Magazine, 222
Sun & Saddle Leather (Clark), 218
Swanberg, Helen, 68, 141, 165
Swanberg, Randall, 136/6; on Bud's writing, 111, 143, 146, 148; friendship with Guthrie, 111, 130, 143, 146, 164–65, 166, 201; political views of, 130

Tannenbaum, Fran, 276
Taradash, Daniel, 128
Ten Tough Trips: Montana Writers and the West (Bevis), 263–64
Teton County Free High School, 3–4
Teton River, fur trade on, 3
These Thousand Hills (1959), 157–58
Thomas, Jenny June, marriage to Alfred Bertram Guthrie, 10–11
Thompson, Lovell, 153
Thunkhouser, Professor, 40
Time, 83, 101, 116, 198
Triggering Town, The (Hugo), 258
Twain, Mark, 160
"Two Guthries Disagree Pointedly on Grizzly Management," 278–79

Ugly American, The (Lederer), 121
Ujifusa, Grant, 253, 254
United Nations, 48
University of Montana, 22–26, 238
University of Washington, 21–22
U.S. Forest Service, 153–54, 238–40, *246/8*

Van Cleve, Spike, 273
Veal, Dudley B., 41
Vinocur, Jake, 159
Virginia Quarterly Review, 233–34
Virgin Land: The American West as Symbol and Myth, The (Smith), 163

Wachs, Fred B., 94
Walker, Mildred, 131–32, *136/4*, 219, 220–21; *If a Lion Could Talk*, 131; *Winter Wheat*, 221
Wall Street Journal, 236
Waring, Houstoun, 83

Washington Post, 212
Waters, Frank, 2
Weeks, Edward, 115
Weisbart, David, 155, 156
Welch, James, *246/5*; education of, 259–60, 263; *Fools Crow*, 260, 263, 273; friendship with Bud, 257, 269, 288, 289; *Killing Custer*, 260; Montana landscapes in writing of, 219, 273; and refuting Western myth, 2, 283; *Winter in the Blood*, 261
Welch, Lois, 219, *246/3*, *246/5*, 257–58, 260, 288
West: "gun and gallop" stories of the, 2, 55; myth of the, 2, 137, 143–44, 163; nostalgic writings of, 2; open-range cattle ranching in the, 137
White Tail Ranch, 256
Whitman, Stuart, 157
"Who Owns the West" literary festival, 260
Widener Library, 84
Wilderness Riders, *136/6*
Williams, Joseph, 113–14
William Sloane Associates, 98, 163
Will Penny (1968), 169
Winter in the Blood (Welch), 261
Winter Wheat (Walker), 221
Wolfe, Thomas, 129
Wolf Willow (Stegner), 158, 213
World War II, 93

Yale Younger Poets Review, 261
Year of Decision: 1846, The (DeVoto), 121
Yellowstone, 73
York, Rosemary, 56
Youth's Companion, 6

Zesty Meat Balls, 175